International Review of Social History

PUBLISHED FOR THE INTERNATIONAAL INSTITUUT VOOR SOCIALE
GESCHIEDENIS, AMSTERDAM

Executive Editor

Marcel van der Linden, *Internationaal Instituut voor Sociale Geschiedenis, Cruquiusweg 31, 1019 AT Amsterdam, The Netherlands*

Editorial Committee

Bert Altena, Karel Davids, Lex Heerma van Voss, Angélique Janssens, Ulla Langkau-Alex, Jan Lucassen, Willem van Schendel, Erik Zürcher

Editorial Assistants

Aad Blok, Mona Hilfman

Corresponding Editors

Friedhelm Boll, *Friedrich Ebert Stiftung, Bonn* Eileen Boris, *Howard University, Washington DC* David De Vries, *Tel Aviv University* Nancy Green, *EHESS, Paris* Michael Hall, *Universidad Estadual de Campinas* David Howell, *University of York* Elina Katainen, *Helsinki* Amarjit Kaur, *University of New England, Armidale* Reinhart Kößler, *Bochum* Friedrich Lenger, *Friedrich-Alexander-Universität, Erlangen* Paolo Malanima, *Università degli Studi di Reggio Calabria* Siegfried Mattl, *Institut für Zeitgeschichte, Wien* Prabhu Mohapatra, *New Delhi* Irina Novičenko, *Center for Social History, Moscow* Lars Olsson, *University of Lund* Ricardo D. Salvatore, *Universidad Torcuato di Tella* Lucy Taksa, *University of New South Wales, Sydney*

Advisory Board

Shahid Amin, *University of Delhi* Jan Breman, *Universiteit van Amsterdam* Robin Cohen, *University of Warwick* Suraiya Faroqhi, *Universität München* Patrick Fridenson, *EHESS, Paris* David Montgomery, *Yale University* Richard Price, *University of Maryland* Wim Roobol, *Universiteit van Amsterdam* Jürgen Schlumbohm, *Max-Planck-Institut für Geschichte, Göttingen* Klaus Tenfelde, *Ruhr-Universität Bochum* Charles Tilly, *Columbia University in the City of New York*

Subscriptions

International Review of Social History (ISSN 0020–8590) is published in three parts in April, August and December plus one supplement in December. Three parts plus one supplement form a volume. The subscription price (excluding VAT) of volume 42 (1997) which includes postage and delivery by air where appropriate is £64 net (US$104 in the USA, Canada and Mexico) for institutions; £39 net (US$58 in the USA, Canada and Mexico) for individuals ordering direct from the publisher and certifying that the journal is for their own personal use. Single parts and the supplement are £18 (US$29 in the USA, Canada and Mexico) plus postage. EU subscribers (outside the UK) who are not registered for VAT should add VAT at their country's rate. VAT registered subscribers should provide their VAT registration number. Japanese prices for institutions are available from Kinokuniya Company Ltd, P.O. Box 55, Chitose, Tokyo 156, Japan.

Orders, which must be accompanied by payment, may be sent to a bookseller, subscription agent or direct to the publisher: Cambridge University Press, The Edinburgh Building, Shaftesbury Road, Cambridge CB2 2RU; or in the USA, Canada and Mexico: Cambridge University Press, 40 West 20th Street, New York, NY 10011–4211. Periodicals postage paid at New York, NY and at additional mailing offices. Postmaster: send address changes in USA, Canada and Mexico to *International Review of Social History*, Cambridge University Press, 110 Midland Avenue, Port Chester, New York, NY 10573–4930.

Information on *International Review of Social History* and all other Cambridge journals can be accessed via http://www.cup.cam.ac.uk/ and in North America via http://www.cup.org/.

International Review of Social History Supplement 5

The Rise and Decline of the Male Breadwinner Family?

Edited by
Angélique Janssens

CAMBRIDGE UNIVERSITY PRESS
Cambridge, New York, Melbourne, Madrid, Cape Town, Singapore, São Paulo

Cambridge University Press
The Edinburgh Building, Cambridge CB2 2RU, UK

www.cambridge.org
Information on this title: www.cambridge.org/9780521639668

© Internationaal Instituut voor Sociale Geschiedenis 1998

First published 1998

A catalogue record for this publication is available from the British Library

Library of Congress Cataloguing in Publication data

The rise and decline of the male breadwinner family? / edited by
Angélique Janssens.
    p. cm. — (International review of social history.
Supplement : 5
    Includes bibliographical references.
    ISBN 0–521–63966–2 (pb)
    1. Family—Economic aspects—History. 2. Working-class families—
History. 3. Heads of households—History. 4. Married people—
Employment—History. 5. Sexual division of labour—History.
I. Janssens. Angélique. II. Series.
HQ518.R55 1998
306.85′09—DC21   97–49574
                                               CIP

ISBN-13 978-0-521-63966-8 paperback
ISBN-10 0-521-63966-2 paperback

Transferred to digital printing 2005

CONTENTS

Angélique Janssens   The Rise and Decline of the Male
Breadwinner Family? An Overview of the Debate   1
Sarah Horrell and **Jane Humphries**   The Origins and
Expansion of the Male Breadwinner Family: The Case of
Nineteenth-Century Britain   25
Samita Sen   Gendered Exclusion: Domesticity and
Dependence in Bengal   65
Lina Gálvez-Muñoz   Breadwinning Patterns and Family
Exogenous Factors: Workers at the Tobacco Factory of
Seville during the Industrialization Process, 1887–1945   87
Michael Hanagan   Family, Work and Wages: The
Stéphanois Region of France, 1840–1914   129
Lena Sommestad   Welfare State Attitudes to the Male
Breadwinning System: The United States and Sweden in
Comparative Perspective   153
Christine von Oertzen and **Almut Rietzschel**
Comparing the Post-War Germanies: Breadwinner
Ideology and Women's Employment in the Divided
Nation, 1948–1970   175
Notes on Contributors   197

NOTES ON CONTRIBUTORS

Lina Gálvez-Muñoz, Istituto Universitario Europeo, via dei Roccettini 9, 50016 San Domenico di Fiesole (F1), Italy; e-mail: galvez@datacomm.iue.it

Michael Hanagan, Vassar College, Maildrop 369, 124 Raymond Avenue, Poughkeepsie, NY 12604-0369, USA; e-mail: mihanagan@vaxsar.VASSAR.edu

Sara Horrell, Faculty of Economics and Politics, University of Cambridge, Austin Robinson Building, Sidgwick Avenue, Cambridge CB3 9DD, United Kingdom

Jane Humphries, University of Cambridge, Faculty of Economics and Politics, Austin Robinson Building, Sidgwick Avenue, Cambridge CB3 9DD, United Kingdom; e-mail; jh100@econ.cam.ac.uk

Angélique Janssens, Vakgroep Geschiedenis, Katholieke Universiteit Nijmegen, P.O. Box 9103, 6500 HD Nijmegen, The Netherlands; e-mail: a.janssens@let.kun.nl

Christine von Oertzen, Vergleichende Gesellschaftsgeschichte, Freie Universität Berlin, Hechtgraben 6–8, 14195 Berlin, Germany

Almut Rietzschel, Zentrum für Zeithistorische Forschung, Am Kanal 4/4a, 14467 Potsdam, Germany

Samita Sen, Department of History, Calcutta University, 51/2 Hazra Road, Calcutta 700019, India

Lena Sommestad, Ekonomisk-historiska institutionen, Uppsala universitet, Box 513, 751 20 Uppsala, Sweden; e-mail: LenaSommestad@ekhist.uu.se

The Rise and Decline of the Male Breadwinner Family? An Overview of the Debate

ANGÉLIQUE JANSSENS

INTRODUCTION

In recent years feminist scholars have called for a complete rethinking and revision of the foundations of labour history as a necessary prerequisite for the integration of gender as a core concept into histories of labour and social class. In this attempt one of the most deeply rooted assumptions in male-oriented labour history needs to be identified and made subject to careful rethinking, namely the assumption that the public and the private sphere should be seen in terms of an essentially gendered opposition.[1] Undoubtedly, one of the most powerful images used not only to represent but also to justify the gendering of the public and the private sphere is the image of the male breadwinner family and the male household head as the sole provider for his dependent wife and children. For this reason, the articles in this volume are all firmly at the heart of what may currently be seen as the crucial intersections in the history of labour, gender and social class.

At the same time, the male breadwinner family is the focus of many pressing academic and policy concerns, receiving ample attention from historians and social scientists alike. In a recent review article, Colin Creighton summarized the ongoing historical and sociological debates on the male breadwinner family, calling for integration and synthesis.[2] It is tempting to relate this renewed interest in the male breadwinner family to its apparent demise in most parts of the Western world. Since roughly the 1960s or 1970s most Western countries have experienced a remarkable and substantial rise in female labour force participation. This is undeniably one of the major historical developments of the modern era. Partly in response to the current crisis of the welfare state, national governments have begun to implement social policies which are increasingly based on the principle of economically independent individuals rather than on the male breadwinner family.

In the history of male breadwinning, two important sets of questions stand out for investigation, and all the articles in this volume reflect on each of them. First of all, there is the issue of the precise development

---

[1] See Sonya Rose, "Gender and Labor History. The Nineteenth-Century Legacy", in Marcel van der Linden (ed.), *The End of Labour History?*, International Review of Social History, Supplement 1 (1993), pp. 145–162.
[2] Colin Creighton, "The Rise of the Male Breadwinner Family: A Reappraisal", *Comparative Studies in Society and History*, 38, 2 (1996), pp. 310–337.

International Review of Social History 42 (1997), Supplement, pp. 1–23

over time. In his recent review of the debate, Colin Creighton asserted that the outlines of the development of the male breadwinner family are now well established, implying that debates over this issue may be closed.[3] The contributions in this volume suggest that this may be an over-hasty conclusion, perhaps inspired by a heavy reliance upon British evidence to the neglect of other countries in Europe and certainly those in the non-Western world. This volume makes it clear that breadwinning practices varied greatly over time and space, from one neighbouring community to the next, between different parts of the world, and between different families in one and the same locality. I would like to link up with Horrell's and Humphries's conclusion in this volume where they stress that "systematic empirical investigation of the male breadwinner family has been lacking" and that "even the timescale of its appearance and development remains obscure".

The second important set of questions that needs to be addressed with regard to the male breadwinner family concern the factors responsible for its origin and expansion. Even a small excursion into this field will reveal that it abounds with controversy. Arguments range from economic explanations stressing the importance of rising male earnings to the contention that the male breadwinner family arose out of an unfortunate marriage between patriarchy and the industrial capitalist system. Recently, more complex explanations of the origins and the expansion of male breadwinning have been advanced, resulting in the identification of a wide range of factors relevant to the problem. Employers' strategies, seemingly gender-neutral labour market factors and processes of capital accumulation, concepts of masculinity and the complicated interactions between family strategies and the labour market, or indeed the role of institutional structures of power are some of the factors that have come to enrich the debate on male breadwinning. However, they have also left the debate to some extent in a state of confusion and fragmentation. The time has come for us to begin to tie up the various loose ends and to move beyond fragmented accounts towards the formulation of "theories of the middle range" which are both complex and sensitive to historical variation and context. One of the ways in which we can make progress in this direction is to develop detailed systematic comparisons. I hope that the articles in this volume will constitute important steps towards this goal. In this connection, I would like to stress that it is paramount to move away from an exclusively European focus and to include comparisons with non-Western histories of breadwinning. By including examples from the Western as well as the non-Western world, while ranging from the late eighteenth century to recent decades of the twentieth century, the articles in this volume offer new and encompassing histories of male breadwinning.

---

[3] *Ibid.*

Before entering into a discussion of each of the two sets of questions in relation to the articles in this volume, it will be useful to engage in a brief discussion of the definition of the concept of the male breadwinner family. The term "male breadwinner family" refers to a particular model of household organization in which the husband is the sole agent operating within the market sector, deploying his labour in order to secure the funds necessary to support a dependent wife and children. In exchange, the wife assumes responsibility for the unpaid labour required for the everyday reproduction of her husband's market work, such as cooking, cleaning and laundering. In addition, she provides for the intergenerational reproduction of labour: the bearing and raising of children. Through this parental division of labour, the children are exempted from productive activities until a given age and are provided with time for education and personal development. Or to put it differently, in the terminology employed by Lena Sommestad in this volume, male breadwinning may be seen as a particular way of organizing human reproduction. Although the ideology of male breadwinning precludes waged labour by either the wife or the couple's children, the employment of the latter, whether male or female, seems generally to have been viewed differently from the employment of the spouse. Male pride in being the family breadwinner seems to have been much more seriously undermined by the paid employment of wives than by that of children.[4] Finally, a concept of the male breadwinner family which focused exclusively on the issue of paid employment to the neglect of economic activities with less visible monetary links, such as self-provisioning, would unnecessarily limit the value of this concept as an analytical tool, in both historical and cross-cultural terms.

THE RISE AND FALL OF MALE BREADWINNING?

Returning to our two sets of questions, let us look first at the historical development of male breadwinning. Within the debate on the social and economic status of women in pre-industrial societies, some scholars argue that prior to the nineteenth century men and women engaged in egalitarian marriages in which both partners shared in productive work and what would now be seen as "domestic" work, and that (despite a clearly gendered division of labour) the contribution of women was looked upon as socially and economically valuable. A classic in this field is the study by Alice Clark on women's work in medieval and early modern England.[5]

---

[4] Wally Seccombe, "Patriarchy Stabilized: The Construction of the Male Breadwinner Wage Norm in Nineteenth-Century Britain", *Social History*, 11 (1986), pp. 53–76.
[5] Alice Clark, *Working Life of Women in the Seventeenth Century* (London, 1982; 1st ed. 1919). Others are: A. Oakley, *Housewife* (Harmondsworth, 1976); S. Lewenhak, *Women and Work* (Glasgow, 1980). For surveys of the debate see for instance: Olwen Hufton, "Women in History: Early Modern Europe", *Past and Present*, 101 (1983), pp. 124–141,

Clark argues that women lost their important economic role in the course of the seventeenth century, whilst their status as independent individuals became eroded as a result of the emergence of capitalist methods of production characterized by individual wage labour and the separation of home and workplace. Research into women's role in economic development in non-Western societies likewise indicates the important role of women in traditional agriculture. These authors argue that, although there has been a division of labour between men and women in most traditional rural societies, this division was (with the clear exception of the Arab world) horizontal and non-hierarchical.[6] In rural societies in Europe, female labour was similarly of vital importance to the family economy. Lena Sommestad points out in her contribution to this volume that Sweden, as a basically rural society, was heavily dependent on the labour of both unmarried and married women until well into the twentieth century. In agricultural production the role of married women was crucial, although limited to either economically inferior activities or activities which tied women exclusively to their homes. As a rule, agrarian women were engaged in heavy physical work in the fields, including piling hay, picking tomatoes, or even ploughing.

In the urban context, there is also evidence of women engaging in productive activities outside the home. In eighteenth-century England, women and girls may be found working as apprentices and craftswomen in a wide range of crafts, although it is unclear whether men and women were equally represented in crafts traditionally associated with men.[7] In a recent study of eighteenth-century Edinburgh, Elizabeth Sanderson demonstrates the extensive representation of women in the operation of various types of retail businesses, primarily in the clothing sector. Sanderson insists that these were skilled trades and that women were in no sense marginal to the Edinburgh business community.[8] Similarly, Jenneke Quast concludes that sixteenth-century Dutch urban women were economically active in the textile industry and the retail trade, both as independent masters and craftswomen and as wage workers. However, she also identifies various attempts to exclude women from independent occupations and to deny them access to guild organizations, which she assumes to be part of a very gradual process of the economic marginalization of women.[9] By contrast, in a study of the seventeenth-century Leiden textile industry, Els Kloek

---

or Harriet Bradley, *Men's Work, Women's Work. A Sociological History of the Sexual Division of Labour in Employment* (Oxford, 1989), pp. 33–42.

[6] Esther Boserup, *Women's Role in Economic Development* (New York, 1970).

[7] See Bradley, *Men's Work, Women's Work,* p. 37; K.D.M. Snell, *Annals of the Labouring Poor* (Cambridge, 1985), pp. 270–319.

[8] Elizabeth Sanderson, *Women and Work in Eighteenth-Century Edinburgh* (London and New York, 1996).

[9] Jenneke Quast, "Vrouwenarbeid omstreeks 1500 in enkele Nederlandse steden", in *Jaarboek voor Vrouwengeschiedenis,* vol. 1 (Nijmegen, 1980), pp. 46–64.

disputes the idea of gradual exclusion of women from independent craft production in the early modern period on the grounds that female labour appears always to have been marginal to the organization of the Leiden textile trade. Female textile workers did not have their own trades, but worked as assistants to their husbands or as day labourers with independent craftsmen (although as widows they might keep on their deceased husband's business).[10] Hettie Pott-Buter's conclusion in her study of female labour and family patterns is in line with this, in so far as that she states that male breadwinning was already firmly established as the dominant family ideal in seventeenth-century Dutch society, while high standards of living brought this family ideal within reach of large proportions of the population.[11]

It is important to note that not all critics in the opposing camp – for instance, historians such as Edward Shorter, Martine Segalen or Gay Gullickson – deny the important economic role played by women. Their criticism focuses more on women's assumed independent social and economic status, pointing out that women were confined to the home, that their economic activities were seen as inferior to those of males and that women's work was nearly everywhere strictly segregated from men's.[12] Although in the urban context women appear in all trades and occupations, the work they did was closely linked to their marital status and position in the life course. Women usually had access to work through their fathers or husbands, acting as their assistants or at best as co-workers.

In her assessment of women's economic position in pre-industrial societies, Harriet Bradley's primary conclusion is that work was sexually segregated, with women being restricted to carrying out tasks more firmly centred on the home, or at least to a much narrower range of occupations than men.[13] However, she also stresses both the variety of male and female work patterns and the flexibility that seems to be inherent in most pre-industrial gender divisions of labour. She rightly relates this flexibility in the labour system to the economic uncertainties of pre-industrial societies, in which families were forced to adopt flexible work patterns in order to survive. In addition, the system of family-based production forced households to juggle the labour capacity of all their members to fit changing economic conditions.

The argument that the economic precariousness of working-class life forced families to deploy the labour resources of all their members, includ-

---

[10] Els Kloek, *Wie hij zij, man of wijf. Vrouwengeschiedenis en de vroegmoderne tijd* (Hilversum, 1990), pp. 48–77.

[11] Hettie Pott-Buter, *Facts and Fairy Tales about Female Labor, Family and Fertility* (Amsterdam, 1993). See in particular pp. 319–321.

[12] E. Shorter, "Women's Work: What Difference did Capitalism Make?", *Theory and Society*, 3, 4 (1976), pp. 513–529; M. Segalen, *Love and Power in the Peasant Family* (Oxford, 1983); Gay L. Gullickson, *Spinners and Weavers of Auffay. Rural Industry and the Sexual Division of Labor in a French Village, 1750–1850* (Cambridge, 1986).

[13] See Bradley, *Men's Work, Women's Work*, pp. 38–39.

ing the labour of wives and children, is extended into the industrial era by Mike Hanagan in his contribution to this volume on family wage demands in France in the nineteenth century. Whilst stressing the wide variation in women's employment patterns in the industrial area of the Stéphanois, Hanagan argues that the families of miners, weavers and metalworkers could not afford to "narrow the scope of wage earning" by withdrawing their wives and children from the workforce. The only group of Stéphanois workers with wives not involved in waged work were the glass-workers of Rive-de-Gier, a well-paid elite whose high standard of living seems to have attracted ample interest in the contemporary imagination. It appears, therefore, that family employment patterns amongst the working classes in the Stéphanois were shaped much more by demand-side factors – in other words, by the availability of suitable employment for women and girls – than by socio-cultural constraints such as workers' aspirations for male breadwinner respectability or masculinity.

Much of the writing on male breadwinning has been heavily influenced by British authors, who contend that, even amongst the working classes, families had already become solely dependent on the earnings of the male head of household by the end of the nineteenth century. The assumption is that women's participation rates declined steadily from the early decades of that century, while compulsory schooling removed employment opportunities for children in the closing decades. In their paper in this volume, Sara Horrell and Jane Humphries even conclude that for "many families in a variety of economic circumstances the dependence on a male earner preceded industrialization"; in other words, they situate the development in the later decades of the eighteenth century. However, their data also indicate that sole male breadwinning existed primarily in the initial stages of the family life cycle. In the later stages, when family heads were aged forty or over, children began to be responsible for large proportions of the total family budget.[14] Horrell and Humphries also draw our attention to the fact that, given high levels of mortality and economic insecurity, most working people's lives included some time spent outside the male bread-winner family.

There are sufficient indications to argue that it is not possible to generalize from the British experience when discussing other countries in Europe, or elsewhere. For instance, around 1900 the majority of working-class families in Ghent were still heavily dependent on the contributions of

---

[14] In another paper by Sara Horrell, written together with Deborah Oxley, on the household budgets of British industrial workers around 1890, it becomes clear that even amongst the better-paid workers the family could not survive without their children's labour: see "Breadwinning, Poverty and Resource Allocation in Late Nineteenth-Century Britain", unpublished paper for session B17 of the forthcoming Twelfth International Economic History Congress, to be held in Seville in 1998.

wives and children to the family budget.[15] Wives contributed primarily in the earlier stages of the family life cycle, when the household head was still under thirty years of age; depending on the husband's occupation, wives were gainfully employed in between around 50 per cent and 85 per cent of the families. From that point onwards, children began to take over from their mothers as supplementary wage earners, so that by the time household heads reached the age of fifty about half of the family budget came from earnings by family members other than the household head. It is also true, however, that as soon as wage levels seemed sufficient, some of these Ghent families, notably those of artisans and metalworkers, were prepared to forgo the earnings of wives and mothers to procure the prestige and status of a "male breadwinner family".

Similarly, there is a growing body of evidence relating to late nineteenth- and early twentieth-century Spain revealing the inadequacy of the male breadwinner model for large groups of the working population. By taking in lodgers and providing them with meals and laundry services, miners' wives in the early twentieth-century Basque country were able to assume responsibility for large proportions of the total family budget, sometimes contributing more than their husbands.[16] Similarly, in fishing communities in Galicia during the same period it was impossible for families to forgo the paid employment of wives and mothers: here, the majority of married women worked for wages in the fishing and canning industries, even if in the older age category of forty and over.[17]

Another important writer on the issue of family forms and patterns of breadwinning, Wally Seccombe, has made strong statements concerning the history of the family in north-western Europe, claiming that the form of family organization by which men go out to earn the family's primary income while women stay at home to care for the family should be regarded both as a recent innovation and as historically exceptional.[18] Seccombe locates the gradual emergence of this exceptional family form amongst working-class households in the course of the nineteenth century and believes that it reached its heyday in the 1950s. We are urged to accept that the recent mass entry of women to the labour market represents

---

[15] Patricia Van den Eeckhout, "Family Income of Ghent Working-Class Families ca. 1900", *Journal of Family History*, 18, 2 (1993), pp. 87–110.

[16] Pilar Pérez-Fuentes, *Vivir y morir en las minas. Estrategias familiares y relaciones de género en la primera industrialización vizcaína: 1877–1913* (Bilbao, 1993). See in particular pp. 274–275.

[17] Luisa Muñoz, "The Family as a Work Group. Technological and Workplace Changes in Occupation in the Galician Fish-Canning Industry, an Empirical Case in Bueu, 1870–1930", paper presented at the Third Workshop on Family Economies and Strategies, Universitat Pompeu Fabra, Barcelona, March 1997.

[18] Wally Seccombe, *Weathering the Storm. Working-Class Families from the Industrial Revolution to the Fertility Decline* (London and New York, 1993). See in particular pp. 202–209.

a return to the historical norm, rather than a breakdown in traditional ways of family organization.

Finally, it should be borne in mind that the notion of the male bread-winner family is a concept originating in Western family ideology. In line with the statements made earlier regarding women's position in most non-Western societies, the study by Samita Sen in this volume highlights the productive role of women and children in agricultural and artisanal households in nineteenth- and twentieth-century India. Women worked on the family farm, reared cattle or processed grain, and engaged in (domestic) textile production or even in the production and trading of fuel; through these and other economic activities women sometimes contributed up to, or even more than, half the total family income. Nevertheless, women's earnings were still seen as "supplementary" to those from male sources. As Sen argues, even though the notion of a single male provider was not ubiquitous in Indian society before the 1950s, it was already insti-tutionalized in the family's property and labour arrangements, which sub-ordinated women and children. After the 1950s, however, the notion of male breadwinning and female domesticity also gained ground in India, particularly amongst the country's elite.

However, variation in married women's contributions to family income is not wholly absent from the non-Western world either. Indeed, it would seem that variation is even greater outside Europe than within it. For instance, in Latin America and the Hispanic Caribbean the cult of female domesticity and the emphasis on men as sole family providers was and is even stronger than in European family history. The roles of women and men were sharply divided through the basic distinction between the *casa* or home, the domain of women, and the *calle* or street, which was the domain of men. This division between a private and a public sphere ensured the economic dependency of women on men. However, even in Central and Latin America, the male breadwinner family model was not universal: it was certainly not the dominant family model amongst the black/mulatto or indigenous/mestizo working classes.[19] For example, in early nineteenth-century Mexico, women constituted one-third of the labour force, although it was largely poor women who worked and the majority of these women were either single or widowed. In all racial groups, single women and widows worked more often than married women. On the other hand, the Afro-Caribbean population never developed an ideology of female economic dependency upon men because black slave women had been dependent on their own labour to provide for themselves and their children. Furthermore, consensual unions, which were much more frequent amongst Afro-Americans than amongst other racial groups in the Caribbean, helped to weaken dependency on a male

---

[19] Helen I. Safa, *The Myth of the Male Breadwinner. Women and Industrialization in the Caribbean* (Boulder, CO, 1995), pp. 47–52.

breadwinner because the women concerned bore greater economic responsibility for their children than legally married women. It is not surprising, therefore, that between 1899 and 1920 Cuban labour force participation rates were three to five times higher amongst Afro-Cuban women than amongst white women. Obviously the lower income levels amongst the Afro-Americans are another explanatory factor. Nevertheless, Cuban female activity rates in urban areas were among the lowest in America;[20] even in 1953, the figure was only 24 per cent. By contrast, most Latin American countries in the 1940s and 1950s had activity rates for urban women that were amongst the highest in the world, ranging from 32 per cent in Argentina to as much as 73 per cent in Haiti.[21] Differences in urban female activity rates in the non-Western world in the middle of the twentieth century cannot be related exclusively to national levels of economic development, as might perhaps be assumed. A huge amount of variation existed; contrast, for instance, the Latin American figures quoted above with the participation rates for countries such as India, Pakistan and Egypt, which were as low as 3 to 14 per cent. The latter three countries might be characterized as exhibiting an "early marriage and female exclusion" model heavily influenced by Muslim attitutes towards women.[22] The early and universal pattern of marriage in most Islamic countries is connected with the prohibition on public activity on the part of women and the insistence that they should focus their attention exclusively on husband and children. Clearly, historical and cultural explanations concerning the relationships between family, gender and the economy must be deployed to account for global differences in breadwinning patterns.

In summarizing this brief overview, we may first of all state that the sole male breadwinner has been a powerful ideal in most Western societies. However, to what extent the male breadwinner family has been predominant in empirical reality is still open to dispute. Seen within a long-term and global perspective, the male breadwinner family may appear as a historical exception, confined to specific countries or regions in the Western world or to certain limited periods in the historical development of these areas. Nevertheless, there is no doubt that, while breadwinning patterns have varied enormously from one period, region or industry to another, as well as at different points in the family life cycle, sexually segregated systems of labour division have everywhere determined men's and women's work activities in a more or less rigid way. It is clear that the debate on the male breadwinner family has suffered from the often

---

[20] See Safa, *The Myth of the Male Breadwinner*, p. 50.

[21] Andrew Collver and Eleanor Langlois, "The Female Labor Force in Metropolitan Areas: An International Comparison", *Economic Development and Cultural Change*, 10, 4 (July 1962), pp. 367–385.

[22] See *ibid.*, p. 375. A note of caution seems appropriate here. The official statistics obviously do not cover all the economic activities that poor women may undertake in the home, varying from domestic production to self-provisioning activities.

diffuse, indirect and scattered nature of the historical evidence that has been brought to bear. Decisive conclusions concerning breadwinning practices can evidently only be based on direct evidence such as is contained in family budgets, as opposed to indirect or impressionistic evidence stating or denying the important contributions of women and children to the family economy. For this reason, the time has come to launch a systematic cross-country comparison of breadwinning patterns based on family budgets in conjunction with other related evidence. It is time for a systematic "Reconstruction of the Male Breadwinner as the Historical Norm".

BETWEEN SWEEPING THEORETICAL STATEMENTS AND COMPLEX HISTORICAL EXPLANATIONS?

How can we explain patterns of breadwinning or, to be more precise, identify the factors responsible for the rise and expansion of male breadwinning? In recent years the debate on how to explain women's economically subordinate position has shifted from more schematic accounts with universalistic pretensions to studies that are more sensitive to historical variation and complexity. Within the debate on male breadwinning, a number of different approaches may be distinguished and the articles in this volume all touch upon several of the key issues.[23] I shall briefly discuss the main outlines of the debate, again without pretending to provide a complete overview, and situate the contributions in this volume within it. As a collection, these papers help to meet the need for more complex, historically sensitive and integrated approaches to the attempt to explain the male breadwinner family.

Economists and economic historians tend to explain female labour force participation and patterns of breadwinning by reference to standard models of labour supply. The supply of female labour, as seen in neoclassical economic theory, is determined by typical supply-side variables such as a woman's age and marital status, the total family income, and her husband's and her own earning power.[24] In most twentieth-century Western economies, there is evidence of the so-called "income effect" which means that the more husbands earn, the less wives will work, irrespective of their theoretical earning power. However, the substantial rise in female labour force participation in more recent decades, and thereby the demise

---

[23] Some parts of the following account are based on the excellent review article by Creighton, "The Rise of the Male Breadwinner Family".

[24] Additional supply-side variables for female labour force participation are numbers and ages of children present in the household. Whereas in more recent times the presence of very young children has had negative effects on labour force participation by married women, this effect is not generally found in more historic populations. See the article by Humphries and Horrell in this volume, or T.J. Hatton and R.E. Bailey, "Female Labour Force Participation in Interwar Britain", *Oxford Economic Papers*, 40 (1988), pp. 695–718.

of the male breadwinner family, can only be explained by assuming a more dominant positive effect of the woman's own wage rate in the market, known in economists' jargon as "the substitution effect". Thus, in families where husbands' incomes are similar, the more the wife is capable of earning in the market, the more she will work.[25] Examples of a neoclassical economic approach may be found in the discussions of workers' living standards in England during the Industrial Revolution by Peter Lindert and Jeffrey Williamson, or in Hatton's and Bailey's analysis of female labour force participation in England in the 1930s. Supply-side factors also figure prominently in recent explanations of the consistently low labour market participation by married women in the Netherlands. In her comparison of nineteenth-century Dutch and German female labour force participation, Plantenga argues that Dutch families were able to achieve a closer match between family reality and the ideology of male breadwinning and female domesticity because of higher (male) labour productivity and higher standards of living in the Netherlands.[26] Similarly, Hettie Pott-Buter in her seven-country comparison of female labour and family patterns explains the strong male breadwinner character of Dutch society in part by reference to high standards of living. However, apart from economic factors, she also recognizes the decisive importance of the distinctive social structure of Dutch society, as a result of which the bourgeois family came to be the predominant family ideal as early as the seventeenth century. High levels of labour productivity and the pillarization of Dutch society along primarily religious lines ensured the achievement and perpetuation of this family ideal for large parts of the population until well into the 1970s.[27]

Although these economic models may generally speaking perform relatively well in quantitative analyses of female labour force participation in Western economies, even economists admit that an approach limited to supply-side variables alone is not adequate when faced with the considerable historical and geographical variation in female labour force participation.[28] Differences in occupational and industrial structures, as well as in attitudes and industrial traditions are identified as relevant factors to be taken into account.[29] Moreover, supply-side explanations of female labour

[25] See *International Encyclopedia of the Social Sciences*, vol. 8 (1968), pp. 478–481, entry: "Labour force: participation, women".

[26] Janneke Plantenga, *Een afwijkend patroon. Honderd jaar vrouwenarbeid in Nederland en (West-)Duitsland* (Amsterdam, 1993). See p. 189.

[27] Pott-Buter, *Facts and Fairy Tales*, see in particular pp. 319–321.

[28] See Hatton and Bailey, "Female Labour Force Participation in Interwar Britain", pp. 695–718.

[29] Historical evidence shows that working wives were not necessarily married to the poorest workers. Two examples, both relating to industrial textile towns, Preston in England and Enschede in the Netherlands, suggest that the organization of the local labour market based on informal labour recruitment systems may help explain the labour force participation of these wives. See M. Savage, *The Dynamics of Working-Class Politics: The Labour*

force participation ignore the gendered positions of men and women in both the family and the labour market, which gave the male household head his customary prerogative as the family's primary breadwinner and made housekeeping and childcare the primary responsibilities of the wife. A perspective which views married women as "added workers" who are "driven" into the labour market in response to changing family needs and/ or changing economic family fortunes argues within the very concept that needs to be clarified.

For this reason, feminist researchers have developed different perspectives which focus on the societal and ideological structures underpinning the male breadwinner family. One of the main approaches in this field, known as the dual systems theory, argues that the male breadwinner family should be seen as the result of contingent historical developments by which a capitalist system was constructed on the basis of pre-existing patriarchal structures and gender practices.[30] Whilst capitalist modes of production, based on individualized wage labour and the separation of home and work, eroded women's traditional economic roles, patriarchal institutional and ideological structures ensured the continuation of women's subordinate position, for instance through exclusionary strategies and gender differentials in the wage system. The dual systems approach rejects the earlier claim of much Marxist-inspired writing that the capitalist mode of production necessarily required a male breadwinner type of household organization.

Dual systems theory therefore begs the question which groups should be held responsible for the emergence of the male breadwinner family and, consequently, which groups benefited most. At this point, agency enters the historical accounts of the rise of male breadwinning, causing different authors to produce different answers to the question posed. As an important early representative of this approach, Michele Barrett, for instance, argues that the conversion of women into full-time housewives served the interests of the bourgeoisie. Her argument is based on the fact that this particular type of household organization became an important organizing principle of the capitalist relations of production.[31] To what extent other groups, such as the working-class family or married women themselves, have had an active interest in the male breadwinner family will be discussed later.

Movement in Preston, 1880–1940 (Cambridge, 1987), pp. 74–79; W.H. Posthumus-Van der Goot, *Onderzoek naar den arbeid der gehuwde vrouw in Nederland* (Leiden, 1938), pp. 21–22.

[30] Dual systems theory continues to inform research in the field of women's subordination in the home, at work and at the level of the state. See, for instance, Safa, *The Myth of the Male Breadwinner*, pp. 37–41.

[31] M. Barrett, *Women's Oppression Today: Problems in Marxist Feminist Analysis* (London, 1980), p. 211.

Another point of contention within the dual systems approach is the question of the status of patriarchy. To what extent should patriarchy be seen as something transcending a set of coherent ideological beliefs and convictions? Some writers argue that patriarchy should be seen rather as an autonomous system with its own political, socio-economic and ideological relations and structures.[32] It is only then that we can begin to explain why capitalists were prepared to relinquish cheap female labour, thereby subordinating short-term interests in maximizing profits to the longer-run political advantages accruing from a household organization based on male breadwinning.

This argument also provides an initial explanation of why working-class families were prepared to forgo certain short-term financial benefits which their wives' and daughters' labour might bring in exchange for other, non-material signs of value and status. In her article on Indian patterns of breadwinning, Samita Sen presents an example which is illuminating in this connection. She poses the question why families in the Bengal jute and cotton mills did not use their informal, but highly effective, recruitment system to channel their wives, mothers and daughters into the better-paid jobs such as weaving and spinning. The "nepotism" of male textile workers was extended exclusively to male relatives or fellow villagers, whilst wives and daughters were given the lower-paid jobs in preparing and finishing. This enabled the better-paid males to afford to keep their wives at home, an important symbol of higher social status.

For this reason, authors such as Sylvia Walby and Heidi Hartmann argue that the debate on the male breadwinner family should focus more strongly on the interests of men as men. Working-class men are identified as the central actors in establishing women's subordination within the home. It is suggested that working-class men either drive women out of the labour market entirely or marginalize them into segregated positions at the lower end of the job ladder. In this way they are able to "rescue" their domestic privileges and authority from the threat posed by the spread of individualized wage work.[33] Protective legislation and job segregation are seen as the principal mechanisms by which working-class men achieve

[32] See, for instance, H. Hartmann, "Capitalism, Patriarchy and Job Segregation by Sex", in Z.R. Eisenstein (ed.), *Capitalist Patriarchy and the Case for Socialist Feminism* (New York, 1979); idem, "The Unhappy Marriage of Marxism and Feminism: Towards a More Progressive Union", in L. Sargent (ed.), *Women and Revolution: The Unhappy Marriage of Marxism and Feminism* (London, 1981); S. Walby, *Patriarchy at Work* (Cambridge, 1986); idem, *Theorizing Patriarchy* (Oxford, 1990). Other authors also recognize the dynamic dimension of the patriarchal system, which may make it differ historically or cross-culturally. See, for example, Safa, *The Myth of the Male Breadwinner*, p. 38.
[33] Hartmann, "Capitalism, Patriarchy and Job Segregation by Sex"; idem, "The Unhappy Marriage of Marxism and Feminism"; Walby, *Patriarchy at Work*; idem, *Theorizing Patriarchy*.

their goals.[34] In recent years, an important modification has been advanced to the way in which dual systems theory identifies male interests as the link between class and gender antagonisms. This approach, which has been developed by Sonya Rose, defines male interests as the wider issue of the preservation of masculine identity rather than as the narrower definition of male domination over women.[35] Rose argues that masculine identity was rooted in the possession of skill, independence and the ability to organize the family's labour supply. When work was transferred to the factories, men sought to marginalize or exclude women in an attempt to find a new basis for masculine identity. Retaining the skilled and supervisory positions in industry as well as claiming breadwinner's prerogatives in the labour market came to be the key concepts of masculine identity under conditions of industrial capitalism.

In a recent attempt to integrate both "capitalist constraints and proletarian choice" within a setting of patriarchal ideologies, Wally Seccombe distinguishes between different phases of capitalist development.[36] His main perspective, however, is the analysis of household strategies. In the early stages of industrial capitalism, households relied on a multi-earner strategy in response to capital's "rapacious consumption of labour-power".[37] Under these circumstances "wages funded merely the daily replacement costs of labour-power, not the full generational reproduction costs".[38] As capital accumulation proceeded, however, "the vitality, stamina and skills of the [. . .] urban labour force were not keeping pace with the development of industry".[39] The second Industrial Revolution necessitated a new production regime based on an intensive mode of labour power consumption, a reduced working week and greater investments in the intergenerational reproduction of labour. Couples responded to these shifts by designating husbands as primary breadwinners and wives as full-time homemakers, a choice which was facilitated by patriarchal ideologies con-

---

[34] These claims are difficult to substantiate. Protective legislation did not always lead to falling participation rates for women; and countries with different legislative measures had similar gender divisions of labour. But judgements differ. See, for instance, C. Goldin, *Understanding the Gender Gap. An Economic History of American Women* (Oxford, 1990), p. 198; P. Hudson and W. Lee, "Women's Work and the Family Economy in Historical Perspective", in P. Hudson and W. Lee (eds), *Women's Work and the Family Economy in Historical Perspective* (Manchester, 1990).

[35] See Sonya O. Rose, "Gender at Work: Sex, Class and Industrial Capitalism", *History Workshop*, 21 (Spring 1986), pp. 113–131; idem, "Gender Segregation in the Transition to the Factory: The English Hosiery Industry, 1850–1910", *Feminist Studies*, 13, 1 (1987), pp. 163–184; idem, "Gender Antagonism and Class Conflict: Exclusionary Strategies of Male Trade Unionists in Nineteenth-Century Britain", *Social History*, 13, 2 (1988), pp. 191–208; idem, *Limited Livelihoods. Gender and Class in Nineteenth-Century England* (London, 1992).

[36] Seccombe, *Weathering the Storm*, pp. 71–80.

[37] *Ibid.*, p. 79.

[38] *Ibid.*, p. 74.

[39] *Ibid.*, p. 79.

cerning a woman's proper place.[40] However, like all other models based on different versions of the dual systems theory, Seccombe's is unable to account for the considerable regional and sectoral variations in the extent of married women's employment.[41]

In this volume, Sara Horrell and Jane Humphries argue that explanations of the male breadwinner family based on simple and exclusive references to industrial capitalism and/or a universal patriarchal system are untenable in the light of the considerable historical variation that has existed in breadwinning practices, even in England. This conclusion is based on evidence from an extremely interesting dataset of 1,350 British household budgets, covering the period between 1787 and 1865. They demonstrate that the male breadwinner family is the result both of the influence of rising male wages and positive income effects on women and children, and of the disappearance of suitable employment opportunities for women and children. Married women's and children's earnings decreased as industrialization advanced, while at the same time self-provisioning activities (which had previously represented important economic contributions to the family budget by married women) were curtailed. However, as Humphries and Horrell point out, this overall trend was complicated by considerable variations by region, trade and industry. Factory workers' families, for instance, did not respond to high earnings and labour legislation by adopting a male breadwinner household organization, as did most mining families. Local norms and ample employment opportunities in industrial areas enabled factory workers' wives and daughters to continue their paid employment, further boosting their families' relatively high material living standards.

Other criticisms have been raised against explanations of male breadwinning based on male interests. One of the points made is that current explanations completely ignore the family as an arena for potential class and gender conflicts.[42] This omission is surprising given the fact that men's desire to preserve domestic privileges is seen as a key factor, and that great importance is attached to an analysis of the labour market in terms of the interaction of both class and gender struggles. Thus, the important question of whether working men and women may not have shared a number of common class-based interests in the male breadwinner family

---

[40] *Ibid.*, pp. 82–83. In a forthcoming article on Spain, however, Enriqueta Camps has shown that in the Catalan textile industry the second Industrial Revolution actually led to an increase in married women's participation in paid labour, as a substitute for children's work. A reduction in skill qualifications and declining fertility rates together with compulsory schooling for children and a relative improvement of female wages are considered to be key factors. See Enriqueta Camps, "Transitions in Women's and Children's Work Patterns. Implications for the Study of the Family Income and the Household Structure, a Case Study from the Catalan Textile Sector (1850–1925)", *The History of the Family. An International Quarterly* (forthcoming, 1997).
[41] Seccombe, *Weathering the Storm*, p. 114.
[42] Creighton, "The Rise of the Male Breadwinner Family", p. 322.

model is completely ruled out, as is the possibility that the male bread-winner family model represents the result of a "cooperative conflict" between male dominance and collective class interests.[43]

A clear example of such a cooperative conflict is presented in Von Oertzen and Rietzschel's article on breadwinning ideologies in the two Germanies between 1945 and 1970. When it was proposed as part of the 1958 West German tax reform to introduce an income tax system based on the principle of equal rights for men and women, thereby denying men a privileged tax status and corresponding financial benefits as the sole family breadwinner, male indignation was such as to abort implementation of the new system. Within the family sphere, the wives gave in to their husbands' protests, as Von Oertzen and Rietzschel indicate, in recognition of the shared family interest in the social respectability associated with the male breadwinner family.

The question of the extent to which men and women shared an interest in the male breadwinner family has been central to studies focusing on working-class demands for a family wage. In his article on the construc-tion of the male breadwinner wage norm, Wally Seccombe argues that the demand for a family wage, whether or not accompanied by demands for outright female exclusion, was related to struggles between families rather than within them.[44] Similarly, authors such as Humphries have stressed in earlier articles the proposition that the withdrawal of women from the workforce served to maintain working-class living standards through redu-cing competition in the labour market while providing family members with valuable but unwaged personal care and support.[45] The accompanying working-class demand for a family wage sought to protect the family, in the interests of both its male and female members, from the undermining pressures of the advancing capitalist system.[46] In their present paper in this volume, Horrell and Humphries also recognize the potentially benefi-cial effects of male breadwinning on the working-class family in terms of

---

[43] This concept is derived from Amartya Sen (*Resources, Values and Development* (Oxford, 1984), pp. 374–376) and denotes a family bargaining model in which all members cooperate to achieve certain outcomes beneficial to all compared with non-cooperation, whilst all parties at the same time have conflicting interests in the choice of effective cooperative outcomes.

[44] Seccombe, "Patriarchy Stabilized".

[45] J. Humphries, "Class Struggle and the Persistence of the Working-Class Family", *Cambridge Journal of Economics*, 1, 3 (1977), pp. 241–258.

[46] The argument that the male breadwinner family served the interests of the working-class family as a whole may also be found in Brenner and Ramas. However, their perspective is different. Brenner and Ramas argue that the gendered division of labour within the working-class family arose out of the conflicting demands between childcare and work outside the home under the conditions of capitalist production. Families opted for the male breadwinner system in order to ensure their family's biological survival. See J. Brenner and M. Ramas, "Rethinking Women's Oppression", *New Left Review*, 144 (1984), pp. 33–71.

welfare enhancement, *provided* male breadwinning was accompanied by increases in male wages.

In the ensuing scholarly debate, demands for a family wage came to be equated with demands for the exclusion of married women (and sometimes girls) from the labour market.[47] One of the best-known examples is Hall Benenson's critique of Jane Humphries on the basis of a study of Lancashire cotton workers between 1890 and 1914. This shows that well-organized female workers resisted male attempts to introduce a marriage bar.[48] Benenson argues that male and female workers had conflicting interests in the labour market and that demands for a family wage served the exclusive interests of male – as opposed to female – workers.

In his contribution to this volume, Mike Hanagan seeks to redress the balance in the debate on the family wage, arguing that it is far from clear that in all cases demands for a family wage also involved demands for the exclusion of married women from waged work. His case study of Sté-phanois working-class life indicates the dangers of attempts to generalize from the British nineteenth-century experience. In France, women's participation in the industrial labour force was taken for granted and demands for women's exclusion were therefore rare. However, this did not prevent male workers from using the family wage demand in the face of imminent wage cuts, a demand therefore aimed at ensuring their families' survival. At the same time, however, the survival of the working-class family required the continuation of "multi-stranded relationships" to wage work. The resulting patterns of labour allocation and household organization in the Stéphanois, Hanagan argues, may be explained by reference to the complex interaction between family strategies, labour markets and changing labour relations in the main Stéphanois industries, as well as gendered conceptions of work and ideals of domesticity.

The notion of a male provider responsible for a dependent wife and children is quite clearly a concept originating in Western family ideology. In her paper on patterns of breadwinning in India, Samita Sen demonstrates that the phenomenon of a male breadwinner hardly existed in India before the 1950s. Women's and children's work, based on a strictly gendered division of tasks and carried out under the authority of male relatives, had been an essential economic component in the functioning of the rural household. However, the introduction of the factory system took men away to the city, to earn the major part of the family's cash needs as migrant workers, leaving women to make a living on the family farm. The fact that women operated at a remove from the emerging modern economic sectors and the urban labour market ultimately made their economic

---

[47] Judy Lown, "Not so Much a Factory, More a Form of Patriarchy: Gender and Class during Industrialisation", in Eva Gamarnikow *et al.*, *Gender, Class and Work* (London, 1983), pp. 11–27; Rose, *Limited Livelihoods*.

[48] H. Benenson, "The 'Family Wage' and Working Women's Consciousness in Britain, 1880–1914", *Politics and Society*, 19, 1 (1991), pp. 71–108.

contributions to the family "invisible" and stripped their labour of any recognized (monetary) economic value. The patriarchal family system, by which husbands and fathers owned the labour of their wives and children, provided the crucial underpinning for this process.[49] Female labour was manipulated for the benefit of the changing needs of the men in the family, rather than in response to changing demands from employers. In the context of this process the notion of the male breadwinner emerged, originating in elite groups who had adopted Western symbols of social status.

The contribution by Sen also considers the importance of seemingly gender-neutral processes such as capital accumulation and the concomitant rise of large markets. Women's craft activities in India were organized as low-skilled, capital-extensive production processes, and were hence also characterized by low productivity levels. With the development of large capital-intensive, mechanized and highly productive networks of production and trade, women's craft activities became eroded. Limited as they were both by family obligations, and by a lack of skills and capital, women had no access to these newly emerging networks of production and trade. Parallels with the British case as outlined by Horrell and Humphries inevitably come to mind when Sen proceeds to argue that commercialization and pressures on land restricted women's access to woods and common lands, thereby curtailing female trading and self-provisioning.

In his reappraisal of the male breadwinner debate, Colin Creighton stresses the importance of taking into account successive phases in the accumulation of capital and employers' strategies. This may, for instance, help to explain the concentration of women in certain industries in the Western world at times when they were almost absent elsewhere. The inherent danger, however, is a return to "a non-gendered account of the labour market" which overlooks the fact that capital accumulation affected women differently from men because the workforce was already sexually differentiated. Creighton's distinction between these processes and conscious attempts by male employers or male workers to restrict women's employment opportunities is to some extent cosmetic.[50] The fact that male employers and/or male workers abstained from voicing objections regarding the effects of capital accumulation on a gendered workforce cannot possibly be proof of any conscious, let alone unconscious, motivation they may have had concerning women's economic role.

Capital accumulation and employers' strategies were in a variety of ways "preconditioned by, and built upon, aspects of gender and household economy that originated outside the immediate sphere of industrial

---

[49] Compare for a similar argument on Central and Latin America, Safa, *The Myth of the Male Breadwinner*, pp. 46–58.
[50] See Creighton, "The Rise of the Male Breadwinner Family", p. 329.

production and the labor market".[51] This citation is taken from a study by Don Kalb in which he demonstrates, amongst other things, the relationships between gender, class formation, processes of industrialization and managerial practices in the Philips company in Eindhoven around the turn of the century. In the successful introduction and consolidation of mass production in the electrical plants, Kalb argues, the Philips management exploited the existence of multi-earner households and the family as a unit of labour recruitment in the low wage area of Eindhoven. These managerial policies secured a steady and massive supply of young, cheap and acquiescent female labour. The Philips example demonstrates how women were brought in almost immediately to fill the highly mechanized jobs in the newer electrical industries, jobs which were labelled "feminine" from the start because they were repetitive, monotonous and required dexterity.[52] The massive deployment of female labour in the Philips factories did not, however, effect any changes in terms of married women's employment in industry. In the event of their marriage, the "Philips girls" – as they were called – left the factory, so long as company interests permitted it: that is so long as an adequate supply of unmarried female labour was available.[53] Thus, employers' strategies were to a large extent informed by established cultural notions of appropriate (industrial) work for men and women.

The article by Lina Gálvez in this volume on the Seville tobacco industry presents another informative example of the way in which employers' strategies and the conditions imposed by different phases of capital accumulation influenced the gendering of the workforce. To some extent in the same way as in the case of the Philips company, gender formed a crucial factor in the transition to industrial production. Based on the exploitation of the flexible workforce of skilled female tobacco workers and their household economies, the company's management was able to implement a gradual process of mechanization while maintaining the match between supply and demand. As Gálvez indicates, this transition would have been impossible with a male workforce, since male workers usually operated on a fixed time system. The mechanization of the Seville tobacco industry transformed the company's workforce in fundamental ways: the primarily female skilled workforce composed of family breadwinners and marked by a culture of time flexibility and absenteeism was gradually replaced by a workforce which consisted primarily of male workers on fixed pay and employed on a fixed time schedule in technical, supervisory and maintenance positions, plus a smaller group of young

---

[51] Don Kalb, "Expanding Class: Power and Everyday Politics in Industrial Communities, North Brabant Illustrations, ca. 1850–1950" (unpublished Ph.D. thesis, University of Utrecht, 1995), p. 13.

[52] Bradley, *Men's Work, Women's Work*, pp. 166–171.

[53] Annemieke van Drenth, *De zorg om het Philipsmeisje. Fabrieksmeisjes in de elektrotechnische industrie in Eindhoven (1900–1960)* (Zutphen, 1991), p. 89.

female workers, the daughters of the old *cigarreras*, who operated the new tobacco machines to fixed time schedules. The labour allocation policy of the *cigarreras'* household economy responded to the change by switching over to promoting male labour with the company management. The article by Gálvez is an instructive example of the way in which gender, the family economy and its dynamic labour allocation mechanisms interacted with the wider labour market and employers' labour policies in the subsequent phases of capital accumulation.[54] However, as Gálvez concludes, for a correct understanding of the outcomes of the interplay between these historical actors, we need to remain aware of their differential and fundamentally gendered positions. The breadwinning *cigarreras* remained first and foremost associated with family and household responsibilities, and this determined the way they were incorporated into subsequent phases of capital accumulation.

Evidently, if we wish properly to understand the rise of male breadwinning, and in particular the variations that may be found in these patterns, we cannot neglect the influence of the institutional structures of power, as they have become embedded in the modern welfare state. As Lena Sommestad contends in her contribution to this volume, there is no industrialized society in which male breadwinning has been capable of sustaining an adequate national reproductive process without public support. Similarly, Hanagan concludes that it was only with the gradual establishment of a welfare state based on male wage earning in the period after 1914 that French families could begin to contemplate a household organization based on male breadwinning. Moreover, studies indicate that employers and state policies have considerable effect on the different ways in which men and women share productive tasks.[55] Welfare state formation did not everywhere identify men exclusively as earners and women as carers.

Sommestad's paper designates economic and demographic factors, which combine to form particular reproductive conditions, as key elements in shaping welfare state attitudes towards breadwinning. In this approach Sommestad has constructed two interesting tools for research on the gendering of welfare state formation, by distinguishing between a country's "capacity for reproductive investments" and its "reproductive chal-

---

[54] It is tempting to associate this case of female breadwinners with manual production, which allows for greater flexibility in work schedules than mechanized production. That female breadwinning and a fully mechanized production system are not mutually exclusive is demonstrated, however, by Joyce Parr's study of two Ontario towns in the first half of the twentieth century. In Paris, one of these two towns, female breadwinning throughout the family life cycle was made possible in the local textile industry through adaptations by employers, family members, the community and working mothers: see Joyce Parr, *The Gender of Breadwinners. Women, Men, and Change in Two Industrial Towns, 1880–1950* (Toronto, 1990).

[55] See, for instance, Susan Pederson, *Family, Dependence, and the Origins of the Welfare State, Britain and France, 1914–1945* (Cambridge, 1993); and Diane Sainsbury, *Gender, Equality and the Welfare States* (Cambridge, 1996).

lenges". Sweden's particular position within this constellation at the beginning of this century paved the way for a "weak male breadwinner state" which was prepared to intervene in the private sphere of the family on the basis of universalistic citizen-based and largely gender-neutral social provisions. Sommestad's model is thrown into relief by a comparison with the construction of the "strong male breadwinner state' in the United States. By developing these gender-relevant dimensions in the genesis of the welfare state, Sommestad also contributes to the mainstream debate on possible welfare state variation.[56]

Ultimately, however, as Von Oertzen and Rietzschel underline in their contribution to this volume, breadwinning practices are the result of struggles and claims fought over in the private sphere of the family, between the spouses. In their comparative case study on the history of the male breadwinner ideology in West and East Germany between 1945 and 1970, they suggest that – despite huge differences in the rates of women's labour force participation – the underlying ideological differences were considerably smaller. As the crucial factor, Von Oertzen and Rietzschel point to the lack of East German policies aimed at reforming the deeply gendered system of labour division within the family to match the reform of gender divisions within the labour market. The mere fact of East Germany's massive female labour force participation was not sufficient decisively to alter breadwinning ideologies so long as the institutional structures of power continued to define women as earners/carers while men were seen exclusively in their role as earners. This conclusion dovetails neatly with the importance that is attached in this volume by Lena Sommestad to the intervention in the private sphere of the family by the institutional structures of power.[57]

CONCLUSIONS

It is clear that the debate on the male breadwinner family abounds with disagreements. There is disagreement concerning the precise historical development of breadwinning patterns, and disagreement concerning the complex of factors explaining the assumed rise and expansion of the male breadwinner family. Disagreement concerning the actual historical and regional development of breadwinning patterns arises out of a lack of direct and systematic evidence on the breadwinning activities of men and

---

[56] On this debate see, for instance, *ibid.*, pp. 40–44.

[57] For a comparable position see Pedersen, *Family, Dependence, and the Origins of the Welfare State*. Pedersen argues that the weak French male breadwinner system was supported by employers' policies, which were later incorporated into state policies, providing family benefits for both male and female workers with children. This undercut male workers' claim for a family wage. Pedersen contrasts the French case with the British system, which directed state efforts more towards protecting the integrity and superiority of male wages, thereby institutionalizing relations of dependence within the family.

women. This collection of articles first of all identifies the need for an intensification of research effort by historians and social scientists aimed at a systematic and comparative reconstruction of historical breadwinning practices based on family budgets. This reconstruction would have to cover strategically chosen periods and geographical areas, as well as carefully targeted economic sectors and social groups. For this future research agenda to be successful, it is essential that we move away from the heavy focus on north-western Europe. There is every reason to believe that north-western Europe does not represent the historical norm. Southern Europe, but above all Eastern European countries, also need to be included. Indeed, it is paramount that we move away from an exclusively European focus and include comparisons with non-Western histories of breadwinning. Any "European Historical Norm" – or "Asian Historical Norm", for that matter – can by definition only be established through cross-cultural comparison. The present volume therefore calls upon historians and social scientists alike to undertake creative, imaginative and painstaking empirical research in order to determine historical and regional patterns of breadwinning with greater precision.

Second, this volume also makes clear that monocausal theories, with or without explicit claims of universal validity, have lost their explanatory power. Evidently explanations of breadwinning patterns cannot be based solely on exclusive references to patriarchy or to industrial capitalism. Neither can a purely economic model offer sufficient explanation of patterns of breadwinning. Historical and regional variation is too wide for monocausal explanations to suffice. The debate so far had already suggested additional, often interrelated, factors as relevant variables for the study of breadwinning patterns. These range from institutional constraints and local gender norms and attitudes to household strategies, economic differentiation, capital accumulation, the development of large commercial networks, the patriarchal interests of men and the changing structure of local labour markets. However, it is wholly unfruitful to study any of these factors in isolation from the others. The time has now come to move beyond these fragmented accounts towards the formulation of "theories of the middle range" which are both complex and sensitive to historical variation and context. Together, the articles in this volume provide insights into the type of complex realities and connections yielded by this approach. One of the ways to progress in this direction is to develop detailed systematic comparisons in which the various factors which have so far been identified as relevant to historical outcomes are studied in their mutual interrelationships.

Third, the articles in this volume all indicate that the family acted as a central mediator for the construction and preservation of gendered patterns of breadwinning. For this reason, within the research agenda articulated above, particular attention needs to be paid to the way in which family decision-making on labour division interrelated with external factors such as institutional constraints, the labour market and economic change. What labour allocation choices did families make, given a particular external constellation, and under what conditions did they opt for dual or perhaps even sole female breadwinning? And if they did not do so, why was this? Counterfactual analysis might be enormously illuminating in this respect, but is unfortunately difficult to implement given the nature of the problem. We need, therefore, to trace the structures that enabled families to pursue alternative routes in order to get a clearer view of determining factors and of the different options available to various social groups. In this connection, ample attention should be paid to conflicting or converging interests within the family and in particular to the interests of women. Their voices are less often heard in this debate, which is surprising given the far-reaching consequences breadwinning patterns had for gender relations, both within the family and outside it. We need therefore to examine the precise options and limitations faced by women at any given period, and the motives that led them to make the choices they did.

Calling for the family to become the key focus of future research on breadwinning patterns should not be seen as a circumspect way of introducing a new monocausal explanatory perspective. Rather, taking the perspective of the family in relation to and in interaction with the external factors listed above is the only way we can ever hope to arrive at the type of complex and historically specific explanations that we have set ourselves to achieve without losing sight of the fundamentally gendered positions of men and women in society. It is within the family that gendered external opportunities and constraints converge with equally gendered family patterns and attitudes. This is the framework within which breadwinning patterns are worked out. It is towards this goal that the articles in this volume will, I hope, constitute important advances and in this area that they will provide pointers for future research.

The Origins and Expansion of the Male Breadwinner Family: The Case of Nineteenth-Century Britain

SARA HORRELL AND JANE HUMPHRIES

INTRODUCTION

The transition from a family economy in which incomes were democratically secured through the best efforts of all family members to one in which men supported dependent wives and children appears as a watershed in many otherwise very different histories of the family. It looms large in both orthodox economic analyses of historical trends in female participation rates and feminist depictions of a symbiotic structural relationship between inherited patriarchal relationships and nascent industrial capitalism.[1] Both camps agree, as Creighton has recently put it, about "the outlines of [the] development" of the male breadwinner family. Where they disagree is in "the factors responsible for its origins and expansion".[2] Why did families move away from an asserted "golden age" of egalitarian sourcing of incomes, which involved husbands, wives and children, to dependence on a male breadwinner who aspired to a family wage? Neoclassical economic historians emphasize the supply conditions, concentrating on income effects from men's earnings, family structure variables and alternatives to women's employment in terms of productive activities in the home. In contrast, dual systems theorists emphasize demand conditions in terms of institutional constraints on women's and children's employment exemplified by the exclusionary strategies of chauvinist trade unions, labour legislation which limited the opportunities of women and children, and the legitimation of men's wage demands by references to their need for a family wage.[3] Our view is that systematic empirical investigation of the male breadwinner family has been lacking,[4] even the timescale of its

---

[1] Peter H. Lindert and Jeffrey G. Williamson, "English Workers' Living Standards During the Industrial Revolution: A New Look", *Economic History Review*, XXVI (1983), pp. 1–25, exemplifies the neoclassical approach. Michele Barrett and Mary McIntosh, "The 'Family Wage': Some Problems for Socialists and Feminists", *Capital and Class*, 11 (1980) locates the emergence of the male breadwinner family within capitalist patriarchy, as does Jane Humphries, "Class Struggle and the Persistence of the Working Class Family", *Cambridge Journal of Economics*, 1 (1977), pp. 241–258, but these authors draw different conclusions. For an excellent recent reappraisal of the debated rise of the male breadwinner family, see Colin Creighton, "The Rise of the Male Breadwinner Family: A Reappraisal", *Comparative Studies in Society and History*, 38 (1996), pp. 310–337.
[2] Creighton, "The Rise of the Male Breadwinner Family", p. 310.
[3] For a survey of the literature on the different routes to dependency see Katrina Honeyman and Jordan Goodman, "Women's Work, Gender Conflict, and Labour Markets in Europe, 1500–1900", *Economic History Review*, XLIV (1991), pp. 608–628.
[4] This is surprising in that the English empirical tradition has been strongly evident in the historiography of women's work and the golden age controversy has been informed by a number of empirical studies based on British evidence. As in the evaluation of industrializa-

International Review of Social History 42 (1997), Supplement, pp. 25–64

appearance and development remains obscure.[5] Unless we fill in the out-lines with more empirical detail we will never discover the reasons for its origins and expansion.[6]

This paper uses empirical evidence on the composition and adequacy of family incomes and men's wages to investigate the extent and growth of the male breadwinner family system during industrialization. The evidence is provided by an innovative dataset of British household budgets which detail household structure, income and expenditure for the years 1787 to 1865. These budgets are used to investigate the extent to which families' incomes were compiled from the efforts of all members and to trace patterns across time, occupations and regions in the dependence on men and male earnings.

The results are surprising. For many families in a variety of economic circumstances the dependence on a male earner preceded industrialization. None the less, women, and more importantly children, continued to make significant contributions in some types of families and in many families at certain stages of the family life cycle. Close inspection of the empirical evidence suggests that there was no single set of circumstances which generated the male breadwinner family and that the nature of dependence on men and male wages was conditional on its specific origins. There seem to have been two routes to the male breadwinner family: a beneficent route through rising male wages, positive income effects and increased leisure for women and children, and a darker sequence involving the disappearance of locally available work for women and a descent into dependence and poverty. Legal, political and ideological institutions influenced women's and children's participation, particularly by the middle of the nineteenth century, and augmented the economic pressures promoting dependence on men and male wages. To emphasize the beneficent route to the male breadwinner family, with its corollary of a "preferred" and welfare enhancing dependence, and to neglect the appearance of a demand deficient dependence or institutional constraints on women's and children's work, with their less rosy implications for welfare, is to misrepresent the historical origins of a family form which remains a powerful ideological image even today.

Following a description of the family budgets, we use the data for husband-wife households to document the composition of family income for different occupations over the course of the Industrial Revolution. Then we investigate in more detail the importance of women's and children's

---

tion more generally, the British experience (for all its possible idiosyncrasies) poses as the archetype.

[5] The issue of timing is discussed in Jane Humphries, "Women and Paid Work", in June Purvis (ed.), *Women's History: Britain, 1850–1945* (London, 1996), pp. 85–106.

[6] This paper takes up the injunction in Creighton's survey to develop an account of the development of the male breadwinner family which is sensitive to variations by region, trade and industry.

earnings in supporting the family through certain phases of the life cycle, shading the male breadwinner story with longitudinal considerations. We note the importance of self-provisioning of goods and services and the need to include other sources of income as well as earnings. Next we explore the effect of industrialization on women's and children's labour force participation. Finally we provide a contrast to our husband-wife households by looking at families which lacked a male breadwinner. Absences of husbands and fathers, either temporary or permanent, left families dependent on the earnings of women and children. Yet men's absences were commonplace in the high mortality and economically inse- cure early industrial economy. Thus for all its growing dominance numeri- cally, and even more important ideologically, most working people's life- time experiences included some years lived outside the male breadwinner family.

THE DATA

We use a dataset of household budgets that detail household composition, sources of income (in kind or in cash), and the earnings of different family members as well as expenditures for the years 1787 to 1865. The dataset has been compiled from 59 sources that include contemporary social com- mentators, Parliamentary Papers, local archives, provincial record offices and village autobiographies.[7] Some of the sources are well known and widely quoted, others unpublished and unused. Neither type has been sys- tematically analysed to reveal patterns in the composition of household income across sectors and over time during industrialization. These house- hold accounts facilitate the investigation of the emergence of the male breadwinner household.

Where we focused on the composition of family income we selected only households containing a man and wife. This gave us a sample of 1,350 households distributed over time, place and occupation. The house- holds varied in composition and in number of workers, both of which affected the level and structure of family incomes. We checked that the sample's household composition over time and across occupations was not grossly unrepresentative and so likely to distort conclusions about the evolution of incomes and changes in their sourcing. Our sample's average household size varied little over time, though it was larger than the 4.5 to 4.75 persons quoted as typical of the population as a whole, because of

---

[7] For full details of the sources, the information they contain, and the geographical, occupa- tional and temporal distribution of the budgets see Sara Horrell and Jane Humphries, "Old Questions, New Data, and Alternative Perspectives: Families' Living Standards in the Industrial Revolution", *Journal of Economic History*, 52 (1992), pp. 849–880, appendix 1.

our initial exclusion of single-person households.[8] Aside from the two adults, most family members were children. Family composition varied by occupation broadly in line with expectations. Outworker, mining and factory families were larger than artisan, agricultural and casual labouring families.

There was no reason to expect the budgets that we had managed to collect to be a representative sample of the population. A preliminary investigation of the data confirmed the a priori expectation that families' economic experiences over the course of industrialization varied according to the occupation of the husband/father which proxied for a variety of local labour market conditions, and perhaps for cultural influences on family labour supply. But the occupational distribution of household heads in the sample was neither stable nor representative of the population as a whole. Our strategy was first to identify and describe the individual occupational experiences which could be checked against other occupationally-specific evidence, both quantitative and qualitative. Region also influenced income and earnings. Again, the sample of surviving records was not representative of the relevant population. Although the occupational categories in part captured this distinction, the a priori difference in the experience of agricultural labourers justified a further subdivision into high-wage and low-wage counties.[9] The budget estimates of nominal male earnings exhibited reassuring similarities with existing wage series and earnings taken from detailed accounts of specific industries.[10] A compar-

[8] Peter Laslett and Richard Wall (eds), *Household and Family in Past Time* (Cambridge, 1972); Peter Laslett, *Family Life and Illicit Love in Earlier Generations: Essays in Historical Sociology* (Cambridge, 1977); and Michael Anderson, *Approaches to the History of the Western Family, 1500–1914* (London, 1980). For a full discussion of the comparison of household size from the budgets with other sources see Sara Horrell and Jane Humphries, " 'The Exploitation of Little Children': Child Labor and the Family Economy in the Industrial Revolution", *Explorations in Economic History*, 32 (1995), pp. 485–516.

[9] The broad occupational breakdown for heads of household is as follows: agriculture subdivided into high- and low-wage counties according to E.H. Hunt, "Industrialization and Regional Inequality: Wages in Britain 1860–1914", *Journal of Economic History*, 46 (1986), pp. 935–966; mining and metalworkers; textile factory workers; outworkers (including handloom weavers, glove and stocking makers, silk weavers, framework knitters, winders, sewers, combers, shoemakers, tailors and nailers); trades (compositors, cutlers, carpenters, glaziers, masons, blacksmiths, millers, sawyers, coopers, carters, ostlers, spectacle framers, clerks and teachers); and casual and labouring jobs (railroad and road builders, dockyard workers and travellers).

[10] The full details of the comparisons made are discussed in Horrell and Humphries, "Old Questions", pp. 854–858 and are extensively documented in "Male Earnings Estimates from Household Accounts", available from the authors on request. For example, comparisons of occupational earnings were made with wage series taken from A.L. Bowley, "The Statistics of Wages in the United Kingdom During the Last Hundred Years: I. Agricultural Wages", *Journal of the Royal Statistical Society*, 61 (1898), pp. 702–722; M.W. Flinn, *The History of the British Coal Industry. Vol. 2, 1700–1830* (Oxford, 1984); John Lyons, "Family Response to Economic Decline: Handloom Weavers in Early Nineteenth Century Lancashire", *Research in Economic History*, 12 (1989), pp. 45–91; G.H. Wood, "The

ison of our occupational earnings with estimates constructed from wage data, and internal checks to ensure that the broad occupational categories were not biased by changes in intra-category skill levels or geographical locations, reinforced our confidence in the dataset and in the evidence on incomes from which the male earnings were extracted.

Subsequently the occupationally specific stories were recombined, using representative weights, to identify the average picture.[11] Aggregated male earnings were compared with indices of nominal wages developed by other researchers. Overall growth rates appear similar.[12] This confirmed that the weighting used to combine the occupational series into one representative of the working class was appropriate. That our men's wages moved in line with trends identified elsewhere further reassured us that the sample of household budgets was suitable for the investigation of family incomes and would produce reliable estimates of average trends.

THE COMPOSITION OF FAMILY INCOMES

Consider the proportion of family income contributed by the man in households which had both a husband and wife present and where the husband was in work, though perhaps not full work (Table 1).[13] Men already contributed a high proportion of family income in many occupations on the eve of the Industrial Revolution. At this point democratic sourcing of income was largely a feature of factory and outworking families. Reduced contributions from the man can be observed in many occupations in the early 1800s, probably a consequence of war-related trade dislocation which entailed more reliance on other family members' earnings. But thereafter this tendency was reversed. From the 1830s onwards the dominance of male earnings was reasserted in families which had drifted towards more democratic earnings structures, such as those headed by

Statistics of Wages in the United Kingdom During the Nineteenth Century: XVI. The Cotton Industry Section II", *Journal of the Royal Statistical Society* (1910), pp. 128–163.
[11] For the employment weights used to construct the aggregate figures see Horrell and Humphries, "Old Questions", n. 40. The main sources used to calculate the national proportions of males in each occupation were Phyllis Deane and W.A. Cole, *British Economic Growth 1688–1959* (Cambridge, 1962), p. 143; Brian Mitchell and Phyllis Deane, *Abstract of British Historical Statistics* (Cambridge, 1962), p. 60, and Peter H. Lindert, "English Occupations 1670–1811", *Journal of Economic History*, 40 (1980), pp. 702–704.
[12] Comparisons were made with Deane and Cole, *British Economic Growth*, p. 23; G.H. Wood, "The Course of Average Wages between 1790 and 1860", *Economic Journal* (1899), p. 59; and Lindert and Williamson, "English Workers' Living Standards", p. 7. For full details of these comparisons see Horrell and Humphries, "Old Questions", pp. 865–869.
[13] Continuous, annual data were not available and some years have only one or two observations, so we averaged over several years to mitigate this problem.

men in low-wage agriculture, and began to mark occupational groups which had appeared initially less dependent on men and men's earnings, such as outworkers. In general a picture of increasing dependence on the adult male earner emerges, with the occupational attachment of the male head conditioning the pace and evenness of this trend. By the middle of the nineteenth century, on average, some four-fifths of family income was contributed by the husband/father. Families headed by men with factory jobs appear anomalous, retaining the shared responsibility for family income displayed in the late eighteenth century through industrialization.

The economy-wide trend may still have been away from a male bread-winner family form if more household heads were in occupational categories in which male earnings were relatively unimportant within their families. Although the economic restructuring associated with industrialization may have initially increased the relative weight of families headed by factory workers and outworkers, the declining importance of domestic industry by the second quarter of the nineteenth century, alongside the increased importance of artisan and mining families in which husbands'/fathers' earnings were always dominant, implies that in aggregate the trend was away from more equal contributions to family income. The use of employment weights to aggregate the occupational trends confirms a deepening dependence on men and their earnings.

What do these untidy and occupationally specific patterns tell us about the origins of dependence? Was increased dependence on men a result of higher male earnings allowing women and children to withdraw from the labour market? Certainly the average picture seems to correlate closely with movements in real male earnings within the period. As earnings declined, the man's relative contribution fell suggesting the necessity of getting other household members into the labour force. As they rose from the 1830s, the trend reversed and the man's contribution increased. But such a clear picture is not discernible within and between occupations. The relationship is inverted for factory and mining families, suggesting a positive correlation between high wages and robust earning opportunities for family members. Moreover, relatively poorly-paid agricultural labourers contributed much higher percentages of their families' incomes than did men with better-paid jobs in mining and factories. The emergence of the male breadwinner family form seems to have been related to the availability of opportunities for other family members to earn as well as to the level of male earnings.[14] In fact, in so far as high male earnings were positively correlated with plentiful employment opportunities for

---

[14] Other empirical evidence suggests that working wives were not necessarily married to the poorest workers and that local labour market conditions could override predictions made solely from considering the family economy. For example, Savage has shown that, in Preston in 1881, the largest percentage of working wives were married to cotton and metalworkers and not to the least well-paid men: see M. Savage, *The Dynamics of Working-Class Politics: The Labour Movement in Preston, 1880–1940* (Cambridge, 1987).

Table 1. *Real male earnings and male earnings as % family income*

	High-wage agriculture	Low-wage agriculture	Mining	Factory	Outwork	Trades	Casual	All[a]
Male earnings as % family income								
1787–1790	86	74	-	53	-	-	-	-
1791–1795	89	77	70	58	47	77	82	73
1796–1800	84	70	-	-	60	64	-	68
1806–1810	-	-	-	77	57	-	-	-
1811–1815	-	-	85	73	54	-	-	-
1816–1820	69	-	62	71	55	73	69	66
1821–1825	-	-	100	-	42	-	-	-
1826–1830	-	79	-	-	66	-	-	-
1831–1835	59	57	100	43	39	49	37	55
1836–1840	88	64	61	55	50	80	58	64
1841–1845	89	70	69	63	56	95	98	73
1846–1850	-	100	90	52	-	100	-	83
1851–1855	-	-	-	-	-	68	-	-
1860–1865	82	74	-	-	69	-	-	81
Real male earnings[b]								
1787–1790	25.34	22.59	-	39.31	-	-	-	-
1791–1795	31.33	26.21	34.88	32.15	20.64	41.25	40.75	30.59
1796–1800	28.72	18.06	-	-	24.50	36.11	-	26.53
1806–1810	-	-	-	71.32	29.98	-	-	-
1811–1815	-	-	42.57	46.57	27.15	-	-	-
1816–1820	24.03	-	29.36	38.35	19.83	29.08	12.87	24.33
1821–1825	-	-	52.31	-	24.23	-	-	-
1826–1830	-	31.87	-	-	25.90	-	-	-
1831–1835	35.12	19.49	38.24	40.81	18.76	21.30	12.00	27.08
1836–1840	29.12	20.91	66.44	43.47	24.76	41.97	18.06	35.92
1841–1845	32.65	23.16	45.07	52.11	18.35	41.14	24.68	34.49
1846–1850	-	23.45	70.75	48.98	-	61.87	-	42.15
1851–1855	-	-	-	-	-	54.61	-	-
1860–1865	33.47	26.83	-	-	28.26	-	-	40.70
(Sample)	(176)	(325)	(98)	(78)	(412)	(84)	(17)	(1190)

Notes:
[a] Weighted average using male employment weights, see n. 11. The average is only calculated for those years where there is sufficient information on the individual occupations to make this possible.
[b] Using cost of living index from Charles H. Feinstein, "Changes in Nominal Wages, the Cost of Living and Real Wages in the United Kingdom over Two Centuries, 1780–1990", in Peter Scholliers and Vera Zamagni (eds), *Labour's Reward: Real Wages and Economic Change in 19th- and 20th-Century Europe* (Aldershot, 1995), pp. 3–36; 1820–1824=100.

women and children, the relationship between male earnings and men's contribution to family incomes may have been the opposite of that predicted by the standard income-effect.[15]

Figure 1 further subdivides family income into its component parts.[16] With the exception of factory families, women and children do not appear to have increased their relative contributions to family incomes in most of the occupational groups. If anything there was a decline in their contributions, with increasing dependence on male earnings as its mirror image. Moreover male earnings appear to have increased in relative importance more than other family members' earnings contracted, as other income such as self-provisioning and poor relief declined from the modest levels seen in late eighteenth-century budgets. In so far as there was a heyday for the democratic sourcing of family incomes it appears to have been in the years after the Napoleonic wars and before 1835, though perhaps later for outworkers.

In general, it is clear that children's contributions exceeded those of their mothers. Only in low-wage agriculture in the middle of industrialization did wives and mothers match the contributions of their children. In agricultural families the relatively high participation rates of wives and mothers generated at most 5 per cent of family incomes in high-wage and 12 per cent in low-wage counties: clearly conveying the seasonal and discontinuous nature of the work undertaken. In mining families, married women's contributions were most important early on but even then constituted only around 8 per cent of income. Women who were married to men employed in factories also appear to have made small relative contributions except in certain exceptional families. Outworkers' wives added over 11 per cent during "the hungry forties" but their help was halved by mid-century. Artisans' wives were dependent on husbands' and other family members' earnings throughout the period. Only perhaps in low-wage agriculture and outworking families in certain periods did wives' and mothers' earnings make up over a tenth of families' incomes and even then children's earnings were as or more important.

---

[15] E.H. Hunt argues that the participation rates of women and children were positively correlated with men's earnings because high male earnings meant robust demand for labour which spilled over into women's and children's employment opportunities and pay rates: see E.H. Hunt, *Regional Wage Variations in Britain, 1850–1914* (Oxford, 1973).

[16] The remaining components of household income were poor relief and income-in-kind, for instance gleaning and coal provided by the employer. Figure 1 demonstrates the relative unimportance of this other income beyond 1815 and outside the agricultural sector. Families were heavily dependent on earnings. Poor relief formed much the largest part of other income, but this was unimportant for factory, mining and outwork families and it is only found in 1821–1840 for our broadly defined trades families, constituting 7 per cent of total income. The main recipients were agricultural families, but it was less than 1 per cent of total income on average and was virtually non-existent by the final period. The exception was low-wage agriculture in 1821–1840 when 8 per cent of family income was from poor relief.

Wives' earnings did not boost those of their husbands to generate significant increases in disposable income. From a rather uniform picture at the end of the eighteenth century, with wives contributing 3 to 10 per cent of family income across occupations, untidy and occupationally specific patterns developed: a fairly steady decline in high-wage agriculture and mining; growth and then decline in low-wage agriculture and outwork; perhaps some increase in families whose heads were employed in factories though the lack of observations in the later periods make this little more than guesswork; and stability in the archetypal male-breadwinner families of artisans. In almost all the groups married women's contributions were fading by mid-century and had anyway never been a mainstay of family incomes.

Was industrialization increasing children's earning opportunities and enabling them to contribute more to the family budget as industrialization proceeded (see Figure 1)? Children's contributions varied both by father's occupation and over time. In early industrialization, children in non-agricultural families did contribute more to household income than those in agricultural families, but the children of factory workers were not exceptional, if anything contributing less than their counterparts in other non-agricultural families. Children's contributions were largest in out-working families, corroborating the view that domestic industry witnessed the cusp of child employment. But children's earnings in these families represented only a third of total income. In general, the importance of children's earnings to the family economy declined, particularly after 1840, but the gradient and pattern depended on the father's occupation. There was a rapid and monotonic decline in children's contributions in agricultural, mining, outworking and trades families, whereas their contributions to the families of factory workers were more sustained, but even here children contributed less in the final period.

The household budget evidence suggests that there was a large variation in the extent and development of dependence on men in the course of industrialization. Moreover, the variation in women's and children's contributions over time and across occupations was not consistently related to family income levels. Low-wage agricultural families at the beginning and the end of the period were among the poorest, yet wives' and children's percentage contributions were small relative to much better-off families whose fathers were employed in factories, for example, which suggests demand-side constraints: an interpretation reinforced by the evidence that as family real incomes in this sector struggled upwards after 1835, wives and children contributed proportionally more not less. On the other hand, for miners' families the evidence is consistent with a story where increasing family incomes, driven by higher male earnings, purchased a relaxation of the efforts of wives and children. Symmetrically, stagnant male earnings perhaps enforced the persistently high contributions from other family members in outworking families. Artisans seem

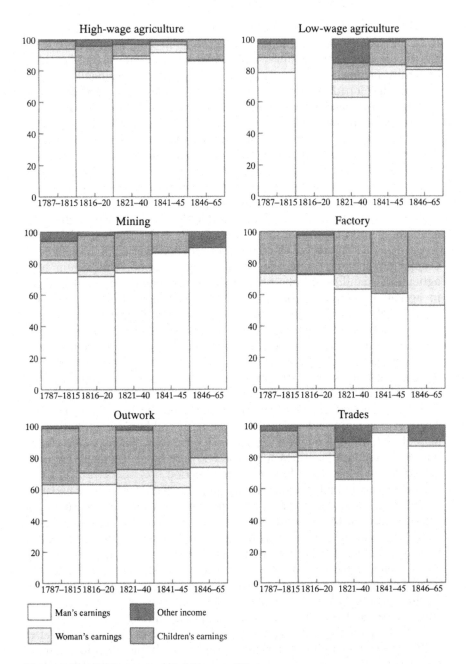

Figure 1. Contributions to household income (%)
Notes: Other income is the residual after men's, women's and children's earnings are taken from total income. Women's and children's contributions are separated using the information on women's contributions, leaving children's as a residual. There is no information on the split of women's and children's earnings in the trades occupations in 1841–1845; the diagram shows the whole amount attributed to children.
Source: Sara Horrell and Jane Humphries, "Women's Labour Force Participation and the Transition to the Male-Breadwinner Family, 1790–1865", *Economic History Review*, XLVIII (1995).

to have made an early transition to a family structure in which women's and children's earnings were relatively unimportant though they were not the highest earners and real male earnings did not increase until 1835.

These trends leave room for occupationally-specific, demand-based, institutional and ideological explanations. In particular, it appears likely that in the agricultural sector women and children were demand constrained in their attempts to contribute to family income. In mining protective labour legislation probably contributed to the withdrawal of women's and children's labour, a trend which simultaneously was underpinned by increasing male earnings, but there is little evidence that the early Factory Acts reduced children's economic contribution in families headed by men employed in factories. The experience of artisans suggests that a man's occupational status could carry with it ideas about appropriate employment patterns within families that were relatively independent of his earnings.

These preliminary findings have several implications. First, stories about women's and children's contributions to family incomes must be conditional on their occupational and regional identities, which limits "grand theorizations" of the origins and expansion of the male breadwinner family. Second, our analysis has also implicated institutions such as the law and cultural representations of fit work for women in the patchy development of dependence on men, themes pursued below. Third, within this heterogeneity of experience, one feature of husband-wife families stands out: while few families were entirely dependent on husbands and fathers, for most families male earnings were of crucial importance at the end of the eighteenth century and remained dominant through the Industrial Revolution. But this does not mean that women's and children's contributions were unimportant. First, the proportional contributions of women and children must be seen in the context of their relative earnings. At a time when a woman could earn perhaps one-third to one-half of a man's daily wage, an adolescent child perhaps the same, and a young child somewhat less, the levels of contribution recorded here suggest that, even before addressing issues like self-provisioning in which women and children probably specialized, women's and children's relative contributions in time exceeded their relative contributions in money. Second, although small on average relative to men's earnings, the contributions of women and children may have been crucial to most families during certain stages in the family life cycle, and to many families facing occasional but not uncommon critical life situations. The life cycle issue is addressed first.

THE ADEQUACY OF MALE EARNINGS FOR FAMILY SUPPORT OVER THE LIFE CYCLE

Is our picture of dependence on husbands and fathers a result of capturing families at certain stages of the life cycle when, for example, men's earnings were maximized in order to support small children and a childbearing wife? More generally, were men able to win most of the bread for growing numbers of children over the family life cycle? Did their earnings expand to accommodate increasing demands from a growing family? Or did women's and children's contributions play a key role in certain phases of a family's life? It is possible to investigate this issue using a sample of 296 budgets for 1816/1817 taken from two surveys conducted in Lanca-shire and Cheshire which systematically recorded the ages of husbands/fathers and other family members.[17]

Although women's and children's earnings were on average small rela-tive to men's for most occupations they were crucial in supporting the family through certain stages in its life cycle (Figure 2). Men's relative earnings declined in importance in the middle stages of the life cycle when children's earnings made up about one-third of income. Children's earnings were particularly important at this stage in mining, factory and outworking families. Women did not contribute much through earnings and there is evidence of a decrease in their relative contribution as children began to substitute for them in the labour market, an aspect discussed below. Women's earnings were particularly important in outworking fam-ilies, where they were engaged in paid work and also supplemented income by taking in lodgers. In this sub-sample there were 26 lodgers, 24 of whom resided with outworking families, particularly families at younger stages in the life cycle and where family size was relatively large. Other income became more important as the household head aged.[18] The occupational variation in life cycle patterns of dependence shades the occupationally-specific stories sketched above. The dependence in agricul-tural and trades families on the male earner is now seen to characterize the whole life cycle and the greater dependence on children's earnings in mining, outwork and factory families can be seen to reflect the importance of children's contributions even when the household head was elderly, which reflects a combination of both higher earnings and higher retention of children in families with these occupational ties.

The importance of children's earnings in life cycle patterns of income is highlighted when income is compared with the claims upon it (Figure 3). There is a close correlation between income and the number of adult

[17] The surveys were taken from two unpublished sources: *A Census of the Poor of Ashton and Haydock, 1816*, Warrington Library, Cheshire County Council and *Tottington, Lanca-shire, A Survey of the Poor 1817*, Manchester Public Library. The sample sizes for each occupation are: agriculture 30, mining 51, factory 15, outwork 174, trades 26. They were combined to give an average picture using the male employment weights stated in Sara Horrell, "Home Demand and British Industrialization", *Journal of Economic History*, 56 (1996), pp. 561–604, n. 38.

[18] The exception is one factory family which had a lot of investment income in the 40–49 age group.

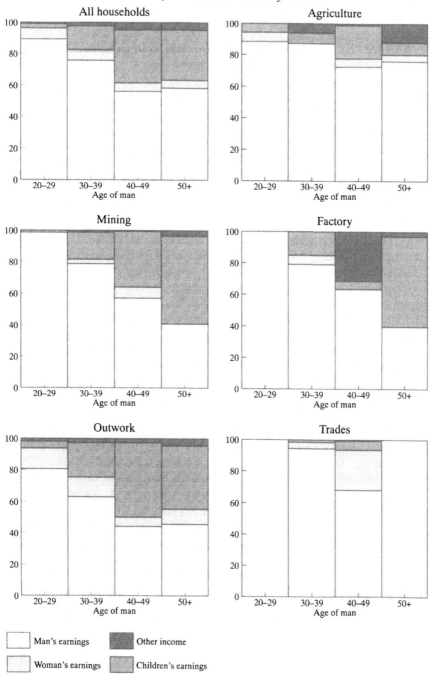

Figure 2. Life cycle composition of family income (% total income)

equivalents in the household.[19] Income rose and fell in line with family demands on it, but not because the man's earnings rose with age and experience. Earnings increased initially with the husband's/father's age but soon plateaued out and fell from about age 45. Adult male factory workers were exceptional in showing a more sustained rise of earnings with age. But apart from factory workers, in the early nineteenth century, men were not able to earn a family wage in the sense of being able to increase their earnings in line with the demands of a growing family. Instead it was women's and children's earnings which augmented incomes in the face of additional needs as family size and the ages of children rose. Thus after an initial slight fall in the very first stages of the family life cycle when adult equivalents rose faster than incomes (husbands/fathers aged 20 to 30), adult equivalent incomes stabilized through the middle age of the male head. But it was the earnings of other family members which ensured this stability, with total family incomes drawing away from the flat age-earnings profiles of the husbands/fathers, as older siblings contributed to the support of their younger brothers and sisters.

There is some variation in the life cycle pattern of contributions by occupation. Outworking, agricultural and trades families follow the standard pattern with family size and total incomes increasing *pari passu* until the father reached 45–50 years of age by which time children started to leave home. The size of outworking families seems to have increased earlier and more rapidly than families headed by men in other jobs which accords with earlier marriage and consequent increased family size, but income per adult equivalent was stabilized by a slight increase in men's earnings accompanied by contributions from other family members. Thus the proto-industrial marriage pattern seems to have been underpinned by children's ability to contribute to family incomes earlier in outworking occupations. Total income and adult equivalent trajectories for factory and mining households have steeper gradients, household size and family incomes increase until the head was aged about 50 and then show a sharp drop. The children in families headed by men in these occupations left home later and had high earnings. In general, then, without the earnings of children, families in most occupational groups would have faced declining adult equivalent incomes in the middle years of the life cycle, declines which would have put pressure on the structure and functioning of the family. In this sense children's earnings played a key role in the evolution of the family as an institution by enabling it to continue to exist in a semi-nuclear form at least through the difficult years of the life cycle.

Our finding that children's earnings were important to the family's survival in the middle stages of its life cycle is consistent with the views of

---

[19] Adult equivalents were calculated as man 1, wife 0.9, child aged 11–14 0.9, child 7–10 0.75, child 4–6 0.4, child 0–3 0.15. These values were suggested in a US study for the late nineteenth century as given in Henry Higgs, "Workmen's Budgets", *Journal of the Royal Statistical Society*, 56 (1893), pp. 255–285.

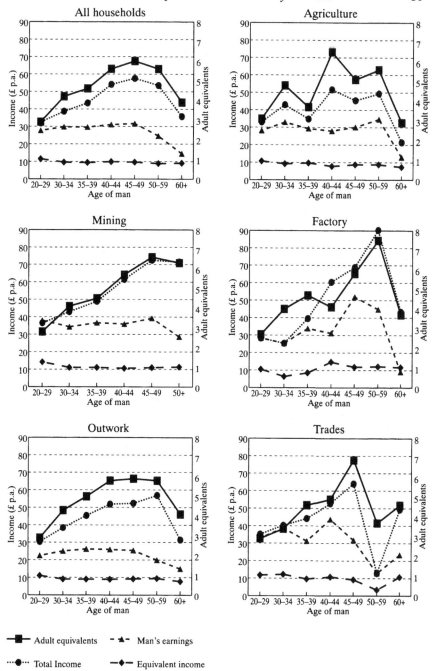

Figure 3. Family size and income over the life cycle

nineteenth-century social commentators expressed in the context of the debate about child labour legislation. Anthony Austin, for example, in his survey of children's employment in various unregulated industries in Warrington in 1841, concluded that working children came from poorer families, ones where husbands were absent or ill, or where there was a large number of dependent siblings.[20] Even in industries where men earned relatively high wages and a male breadwinner family was well developed, such as coalmining by the 1840s, a large family still required older children to contribute. John Robertson, the pragmatic manager of a Scottish colliery in 1842, was well aware of the origins of pressures for children to work. He told the Royal Commission investigating children's employment in mines that he did not allow children under 12 years of age to be employed below ground "even if they are forward, unless it be necessary for the subsistence of some widowed mother or very large family".[21] Those few working people themselves whose voices have been recorded on this topic cited the needs of large families and many small children in seeking to explain parental complicity in the employment of young children. As Isobel Wilson put it to the same Royal Commission, "when women have children thick (fast) they are compelled to take them down early".[22] Parliamentary evidence suggests that parents were often desperately unhappy about the employment which their children undertook but felt that in the economic circumstances it was the best that could be done.[23]

Did the adequacy of male earnings to support families change over industrialization? Table 2 summarizes real adult equivalent male earnings from the budgets for each occupation over time. Real male earnings were low and declining relative to the number of adult equivalents in households for men in agriculture and trades until 1850 and for men with casual work throughout the whole period of industrialization. Factory workers' earnings were relatively high initially but in adult equivalent terms they too faced decline. The pattern in mining is strikingly different, male earnings were high and increasing throughout even when deflated by adult equivalents and were therefore capable of sustaining male breadwinner aspirations for these households. Adult equivalent real male earnings also improved for outworking families until the 1830s, with cyclical interruptions, evidence of their "golden age"; but thereafter relative deterioration set in. The budgets provide little evidence that male earnings were rising relative to the demands upon them, and so increasingly able to support a family over time. The emergence of the male breadwinner family was not

[20] Parliamentary Papers (hereafter PP), 1843, vol. XV.

[21] PP, 1842, vol. XV, p. 19.

[22] PP, 1842, vol. XVI, p. 461.

[23] For a summary of relevant evidence, see Linda A. Pollock, *Forgotten Children: Parent-Child Relations from 1500 to 1900* (London, 1983), pp. 62–63 and Jane Humphries, "Protective Legislation, the Capitalist State and Working-Class Men: The Case of the 1842 Mines Regulation Act", *Feminist Review*, 7 (1981), pp. 1–33.

Table 2. *Real adult equivalent male earnings (1791–1795=100)*[a]

	High-wage agriculture	Low-wage agriculture	Mining	Factory	Outwork	Trades	Casual
1787–1790	82.3	94.9	-	-	-	-	-
1791–1795	100.0	100.0	100.0	100.0	100.0	100.0	100.0
1796–1800	89.	149.9	-	-	108.5	80.6	100.0
1806–1810	-	-	-	107.4	142.8	-	-
1811–1815	-	-	160.4	70.1	129.8	-	-
1816–1820	76.0	-	88.4	56.2	88.6	73.1	34.4
1821–1825	-	-	200.2	-	115.3	-	-
1826–1830	-	166.6	-	-	159.3	-	-
1831–1835	118.5	85.0	98.2	37.8	78.5	46.0	31.5
1836–1840	96.4	86.3	153.4	86.9	128.9	104.1	45.1
1841–1845	93.7	86.6	176.2	61.8	92.6	74.1	61.1
1846–1850	-	130.2	230.6	-	-	250.1	-
1851–1855	-	-	-	-	-	156.0	-
1860–1865	133.3	108.9	-	-	150.2	-	-

Real adult equivalent male earnings (£ p.a.)

1791–1795	8.43	7.09	8.29	17.95	5.68	10.67	12.74
(Sample)	(175)	(324)	(94)	(61)	(411)	(54)	(17)

Notes:
[a] Real earnings calculated using cost-of-living index from Feinstein, "Nominal Wages", p. 26. Adult equivalence scale uses 1.7 for man and wife and 0.5 for each other household member.

always or even usually accompanied by the payment of a family wage, so dependence on male earnings meant static standards if not hardship for members of many families.

This conclusion is further supported by analysis of expenditure for a sub-sample of households for which evidence was available (Table 3).[24] The proportion of men's earnings spent on necessities (food and housing) was not decreasing over time, a pattern confirmed even when we control for increasing rents and changing family composition over time by considering adult equivalent expenditure on food as a proportion of the man's earnings.[25] There was some improvement for some groups, but this was short-lived and for other occupations, such as outworking and agriculture, necessities were taking an increasing proportion of the man's earnings.

[24] For a detailed examination of the expenditure data from these household budgets see Horrell, "Home Demand".
[25] Necessity expenditure is taken to be expenditure on bread, flour, potatoes, other grains, meat, lard, fish, eggs, cheese, milk, butter, tea, coffee, sugar, treacle and rent. Expenditure on fuel, clothing and other food was excluded to compensate for some element of discretionary, rather than subsistence, expenditure on food and housing. Adult equivalents were calculated as man 1, wife 0.7, other household members 0.5 as the ages of all members of the household were not always recorded in the surveys.

Table 3. *Expenditure on necessities from men's earnings (%)*

	High-wage agriculture	Low-wage agriculture	Mining	Factory	Outwork	Trades
Expenditure on food and housing as % man's earnings						
1787–1796	98.2	113.7	114.5	120.8	136.2	123.6
1810–1817	-	-	98.3	-	70.4	78.3
1824–1825	-	-	110.7	54.2	-	-
1830–1840	155.9	74.6	-	72.2	128.4	81.1
1841–1854	100.2	107.2	85.2	97.8	177.3	82.1
Adult equivalent expenditure on food as % man's earnings						
1787–1796	26.6	31.1	25.9	53.6	34.6	30.3
1810–1817	-	-	30.7	-	20.7	29.0
1824–1825	-	-	34.6	16.9	-	-
1830–1840	30.6	21.2	-	23.1	34.1	19.3
1841–1854	23.9	31.7	25.5	31.2	50.2	24.4
(Sample)	(45)	(93)	(29)	(37)	(37)	(13)

For groups experiencing improvement, such as trades and mining families, the transition to a male breadwinner household may have been eased, or even caused, by higher male earnings. In others, such as outworking and factory households where there had been an increasing reliance on the earnings of other family members, a decline in family work opportunities and increased dependence on the man alone must have been a painful transition. In only a few occupations were men earning enough to buy their families' sustenance and to provide the roof over their heads; for most households the earnings of women and children were essential and not becoming noticeably less so over time.

SELF-PROVISIONING

The eighteenth-century household had considerable opportunity to augment earnings through self-provisioning activities such as gleaning, growing potatoes, keeping a pig or cow, or collecting firewood; activities traditionally undertaken by women and children.[26] Recently historians have rekindled interest in these activities, suggesting that they were important to the family economies of the poor and implying that they probably disappeared in the course of industrialization. Peter King, for example, has shown how through the period 1750 to 1850, gleaning, a form of customary right that was almost exclusively the preserve of women, made a very

---

[26] R.W. Malcolmson, "Ways of Getting a Living in Eighteenth-Century England", in R.E. Pahl (ed.), *On Work: Historical, Comparative and Theoretical Approaches* (Oxford, 1988), pp. 48–60.

considerable contribution to the annual income of labouring families.[27] Jane Humphries has looked more broadly to suggest that the value of many gathering and self-provisioning activities undertaken by women and children has been underestimated by economic historians.[28] Several authors have suggested that the ability of women and children to contribute directly to household resources probably declined alongside their earning power as access to common resources and the scope for self-provisioning was curtailed by the enclosure movement, in particular, and the privatization of rural resources more generally.[29] If this was the case then the broad social and economic movements which obliterated these activities and contributions also contributed to the emergence of the male breadwinner family. Variation in these movements across regions and economies may then help to explain the uneven development of dependence on men and its incompleteness even today in some areas and counties. Do the household budgets cast light on the hypothesized decline in self-provisioning and its contribution to dependence on men and men's earnings?

The household accounts often noted self-provisioned produce, although a monetary value was not always imputed to it. The proportions of households for which some self-provisioning was reported are shown in Table 4.[30] These proportions declined from the 1820s onwards. Self-provisioning was important in the primary sector occupations and also to outworking families throughout the Industrial Revolution, but was rarely mentioned by families headed by men working in factories after 1800. Most households only undertook one form of self-provisioning. Reporting more than one form of self-provisioning was more common before than after 1830.

The form that self-provisioning took varied by occupation and over time. Not surprisingly gleaning largely occurred in low-wage agricultural counties, the arable south-east, but even here it was not common. Most

[27] Peter King, "Customary Rights and Women's Earnings: The Importance of Gleaning to the Rural Labouring Poor, 1750–1850", *Economic History Review*, XLIV (1991), pp. 461–476.

[28] Jane Humphries, "Enclosures, Common Rights and Women: The Proletarianization of Families in Late Eighteenth and Early Nineteenth Century Britain", *Journal of Economic History*, 50 (1990), pp. 17–42.

[29] King argues that access to gleaning was reasonably constant from 1750 to 1850 but Humphries suggests that although gleaning was not strictly linked to common rights, it was more difficult to glean over enclosed fields than over open ones and of course the right to glean meant nothing if land was converted to pasture, so it too was threatened by enclosure. There is considerable evidence documenting the late eighteenth-century/early nineteenth-century curtailment of the poor's access to resources to self-provision: see Humphries, "Enclosures"; and J.M. Neeson, *Commoners: Common Rights, Enclosure and Social Change in England, 1700–1820* (Cambridge, 1993).

[30] Only budgets taken from sources where some self-provisioning was mentioned were used for this analysis to avoid non-random bias in the collection of this information by commentators. 250 households engaged in some form of self-provisioning.

Sara Horrell and Jane Humphries

Table 4. *Self-provisioning activities*

	High-wage agriculture	Low-wage agriculture	Mining	Factory	Outwork	Trades
% households reporting self-provisioning activities						
1787–1800	45	31	25	50	14	13
1806–1820	21	-	15	7	23	4
1821–1830	-	100	100	-	-	-
1831–1840	41	14	-	9	33	20
1841–1850	25	71	64	0	19	0
1851–1865	28	16	-	-	0	67
(Sample)	(190)	(320)	(93)	(30)	(221)	(45)
Types of self-provisioning reported						
1787–1800	fuel/ale	fuel/pig/glean	fuel	fuel	fuel/pig/pot	fuel
1806–1820	pot	-	pot/cow	pot	pot	pot
1821–1830	-	pig/pot	fuel	-	-	-
1831–1840	pig/pot/cow	glean	-	cow	pot	glean
1841–1850	pig/pot	pig/pot/cow	fuel/pig/pot/cow	-	pot	-
1851–1865	pig/pot/cow	pig/pot	-	-	-	pig/pot
Value of self-provisioning as % men's earnings in self-provisioning households						
1787–1800	7	13	3	3	53	3
1806–1820	6	-	15	3	4	4
1821–1830	-	14	2	-	-	-
1831–1840	16	8	-	23	6	3
1841–1850	29	31	10	-	9	-
1851–1865	19	11	-	-	-	9

households collected fuel in the late eighteenth century but only miners did so by the nineteenth century. Increased urbanization, the enclosure of commons and wastelands and disappearance of estover and turbary, and cheaper coal which made collecting firewood or turfs less worthwhile, probably all contributed to the decline in self-provisioning of fuel. On the other hand, agricultural, mining and outworking households apparently turned with greater enthusiasm to growing potatoes. Factory and trades families' failure to cultivate potatoes clearly signals the lack of access to land in urban areas. Keeping a pig was a common activity in agricultural areas, but keeping a cow was confined to the higher paying rural occupations, high-wage agriculture and mining. Thus the extent of self-provisioning declined with industrialization. Many households lost access to opportunities for engaging in these activities with increased urbanization and the static numbers employed in agriculture. With the exception of miners, occupations in which families could engage in lucrative rearing of livestock were in decline. Overall, industrialization reduced households' supplementation of income by the efforts of women and children in non-market forms of work.[31] But how important had this contribution been? Did the loss of these activities hit working families hard?

The valuation of self-provisioning is difficult.[32] Our budgets contain forty-two cases where values were ascribed to different types of self-provisioning in different years. These accounts were used to impute values to the products of all self-provisioning, including those which were not valued in the sources. The value of self-provisioned goods in the sample ranged from £0.59 to £8.30 per annum. There is some evidence that self-provisioning took on higher values over time in agricultural and mining households and lower values for secondary sector occupations.[33] A useful comparison is with the male earnings in the households where self-provisioning was undertaken.[34] The increased importance of self-provisioning to these households over time is apparent. The value reached nearly one-third of men's earnings in agricultural families in the 1840s and in most cases was greater than the contribution of women's earnings to the family. Self-provisioning was clearly an important way in which women and children augmented the household's resources. But, although self-provisioned produce represented a significant resource to those households which continued to enjoy it, self-provisioning's importance to households generally was declining over time as fewer households were involved in foraging, growing crops, keeping animals, gleaning and gathering. Averaged across all households, including those with no self-provisioning, something less than 6 per cent of the man's wage, more often 2 per cent, was provided through self-provisioning in non-agricultural families, and although more important in agricultural families, particularly in low-wage agricultural areas, the decline in this form of contribution is visible from mid-nineteenth century onwards. The budget evidence cannot discriminate between the argument that families ceased to self-provision because it became inefficient as more productive employments became available, and the argument that families ceased to self-provision because their access to resources was curtailed. The maintained and perhaps even enhanced value of subsistence production to those families which continued to self-provision follows in either case. But independent historical evidence on the paucity of opportunities for women and children to earn in the Victorian countryside, supports the second inter-

[31] See Horrell, "Home Demand", for a discussion of how increased urbanization and a reduced proportion of the population engaged in primary sector occupations reduced self-provisioning and increased expenditure on basic necessities.

[32] See Humphries, "Enclosures", for a discussion of the issues and presentation of imputed values for self-provisioned produce.

[33] The number of occurrences of any type of self-provisioning are multiplied by the value ascribed, then all types of self-provisioning were summed and divided by the number of households recording at least one of these activities. This avoids inaccurately representing those households which record more than one form of self-provisioning.

[34] No obvious differences were observed in the incomes or male earnings of households according to whether they engaged in self-provisioning or not.

pretation. Self-provisioning was probably not replaced by alternative more productive uses of time in southern agricultural districts characterized by under- and unemployment for women and children. Thus the likelihood is that the decline of self-provisioning left women and children increasingly dependent on earnings, and that meant on men.

INDUSTRIALIZATION AND THE EMPLOYMENT OF WOMEN AND CHILDREN

Women's labour force participation, defined as having either earnings and/ or occupation recorded in the budget source, shows occupationally, and, for agriculture, regionally, specific trends (Table 5).[35] In all occupations the effects of the post-war depression in 1816–1820 on women's work opportunities is evident. While some of the decline may have been a consequence of the regional concentration of these observations some is undoubtedly real. Other authors have noted the severity of this downturn and the male earnings estimates from the budgets are comparable to alternative occupational series based on wider regional dispersions.[36] The post-war dislocation had a common impact on women's work experience. Subsequently trends diverged.

The participation rates of women married to miners or casual workers appear to have declined during industrialization. The story is more ambiguous for agricultural labourers' wives. In high-wage agricultural areas women's participation declined then increased around mid-century, developments which are consistent with Ivy Pinchbeck's argument that allowances in aid of wages, made under the Old Poor Law, enabled agricultural labourers to maintain their wives and children despite their miserable earnings whereas the elimination of these subsidies by the New Poor Law forced wives in these families to seek employment. In low-wage counties, women's participation remained high but showed some tendency

---

[35] For a full discussion of the use of this definition of participation see Sara Horrell and Jane Humphries, "Women's Labour Force Participation and the Transition to the Male-Breadwinner Family, 1790–1865", *Economic History Review*, XLVIII (1995), pp. 89–117. Here we use a subset of the husband-wife sample where the husband's earnings are positive and can be identified separately from those of women and children and where the male is employed in a known occupation (1,161 cases). We subdivide the years into five uneven sub-periods. This is a compromise between the conventional perception of a watershed in 1815 and our own interest in separating periods of economic recession, 1816–1820 and 1841–1845, from periods of relatively full employment. The occupation of the male head of household is still used as the organizing criterion as it is taken to be the best summary indicator of local economic conditions and specifically of the job opportunities and types of work available to other family members.

[36] Lindert and Williamson, "English Workers' Living Standards", p. 15, shows the severity of the post-war slump. For comparisons of male earnings from different sources, see Horrell and Humphries, "Old Questions", p. 854, table 6 and n. 25.

Table 5. *Married women's participation rates and earnings (earnings or occupation recorded)*

	High-wage agriculture	Low-wage agriculture	Mining	Factory	Outwork	Trades	Casual	All
Participation rates (%)								
1787–1815	55	85	40	37	46	63	100	66
1816–1820	34	n.a.	28	4	42	30	67	49
1821–1840	22	85	33	86	54	63	67	62
1841–1845	40	56	9	100	73	100	0	58
1846–1865	48	63	0	100	69	43	-	45
(Sample)	(176)	(325)	(98)	(78)	(413)	(54)	(17)	(1161)
Women's earnings as % family income, where woman works only								
1787–1815	9	11	41	23	15	5		
1816–1820	17	n.a.	14	18	21	18		
1821–1840	14	16	9	16	25	n.a.		
1841–1845	13	10	9	n.a.	19	n.a.		
1846–1865	13	13	n.a.	24	18	8		
(Sample)	(37)	(153)	(20)	(16)	(141)	(12)		

to decline after 1840.[37] In contrast the participation rates of outworkers' wives increased after the 1816–1820 slump. Perhaps their contributions became increasingly necessary as male earnings were squeezed by falling piece-rates and competition from machine methods.[38] Women in factory areas also showed steadily increasing participation after the post-war decline. The consequences of industrialization for women's work varied and any overall picture must depend on the weights attached to these individual experiences.[39] The last column in Table 5 summarizes the occupationally weighted, aggregate participation series. This shows the sharp decline in participation in the post-war slump, the increase in the 1830s and further loss of jobs in the "hungry forties", a trend which continued after mid-century.

[37] Declining opportunities for women in agricultural areas after Waterloo are found elsewhere: see Robert C. Allen, *Enclosure and the Yeoman* (Oxford, 1991); K.D.M. Snell, *Annals of the Labouring Poor: Social Change and Agrarian England, 1660–1900* (Cambridge, 1985).

[38] This would be consistent with the evidence of John Lyons, "Family Response to Economic Decline: Handloom Weavers in Early Nineteenth-Century Lancashire", *Research in Economic History*, 12 (1989), pp. 45–91.

[39] For a qualitative survey of women's work in several occupations largely supportive of our results, see Duncan Bythell, "Women in the Workforce", in Patrick K. O'Brien and Roland Quinault (eds), *The Industrial Revolution and British Society* (Cambridge, 1993), pp. 31–53.

Overall, then, there is a suggested decline in participation. But these data do not, as yet, tell us anything about causation. Were women leaving the labour force voluntarily as husbands' incomes rose, or were they being driven out by discrimination or structural changes that reduced women's jobs? Certainly there was a decline in women's relative contribution to family income (see Figure 1). But was this decline simply the result of decreasing participation or was it the case that even considering only women who worked, their relative earnings were not maintained? A look at those working married women for whom earnings are separately identified suggests that while falling participation was one factor in the decline of women's relative contributions, the latter also fell (as in the case of mining), or rose and then fell (as in all other groups but factory workers) in the all-worker sample (see Table 5).[40] Except for the wives of factory workers, married women who earned in 1816–1840 added larger percentage shares to incomes than those who worked after 1840. Women's earnings relative to men's earnings followed the same occupationally specific trends.

The variation in relative earnings power over time and across occupations might help to explain the patterns in participation. While for some occupations women's earnings increased relatively in the second quarter of the nineteenth century, for all occupations they grew less than men's (or children's) earnings after 1840. Perhaps it was married women's inability to hold their relative earnings positions even if they did work that fed the declining participation rates and not an exogenous decline in participation rates that drove their falling contributions to family incomes.

Neoclassical economic theory models the decision whether or not to work as the outcome of a rational weighing of alternatives with the goal being to maximize utility or satisfaction.[41] Individuals, including married women, decide whether or not to participate in waged work by comparing the value of their time in the market (indexed by the wage rate) to the value of their time in the home ("the reservation wage").[42] The probability of participating is reduced to a function of own real wage, other real income, including husband's earnings (which affect the reservation wage) and a vector of variables to allow for constraints on the participation

---

[40] The particularly small samples for factory workers' wives for 1816–1820 and 1846–1865 make it hard to comment on their experience.

[41] See Gary S. Becker, "A Theory of the Allocation of Time", *Economic Journal*, 80 (1965), pp. 493–517, and Jacob Mincer, "Labour Force Participation of Married Women: A Study of Labour Supply", in Alice Amsden (ed.), *Women and Work* (Harmondsworth, 1980), pp. 41–52.

[42] Major early empirical work on this topic includes: G.C. Cain, *Married Women in the Labor Force* (Chicago, 1966), and W.G. Bowen and T.A. Finnegan, *The Economics of Labor Force Participation* (Princeton, 1969). Reuben Gronau and James Heckman have contributed to the development of relevant statistical techniques: see, for example, the collection of papers in J.P. Smith (ed.), *Female Labour Supply: Theory and Estimation* (Princeton, 1980).

Table 6. *Probit regression of female participation*[a]

Constant	−1.873	(−5.10)[*]
Predicted female real earnings	1.670	(15.31)[*]
Male real earnings	−0.049	(−5.10)[*]
Real income from parish	−0.071	(−2.16)[*]
Other family members' real income	−0.031	(−4.42)[*]
Child under 2	0.666	(4.33)[*]
Number of children	−0.040	(−1.34)
Time	0.065	(2.16)[x]
Time^2	−0.0034	(−3.59)[*]
Time^3	0.000023	(3.16)[*]
Mining	−1.842	(−7.18)[*]
Factory	−5.203	(−11.34)[*]
Outwork	−3.713	(−13.19)[*]
Trades	−1.406	(−5.01)[*]
Casual	−1.017	(−2.37)[x]
Chi-squared	555.6	
Predicted correctly	86.2%	
Sample size	930	

Notes:
[a] Participation defined as earnings recorded; t-ratios in parentheses.
[*] Indicates significance at 1 per cent level.
[x] Indicates significance at 5 per cent level.

decision and for heterogeneous tastes. Examples of the former include local employment opportunities, and of the latter, the number and ages of children and husband's work status conventionally assumed to imply "a taste" for home production. These variables should then be able to explain all the occupational and temporal differences in women's participation rates, with no role remaining for the influence of ideological and institutional factors. We use regression analysis to see how well these variables can explain the labour force participation of married women during industrialization and also include a time trend which is intended to capture other possible influences (Table 6).[43]

Perhaps surprisingly the conventional neoclassical model appears to fit the behaviour of our early industrial wives and mothers. Specifically women had a positive response to their own real earnings, whereas increased income from other sources reduced the probability of participation. Children had a negative effect on participation but having a child of under two years of age increased the probability of the woman working. The positive relationship between the presence of a baby and the probability of participating, so surprising in the context of contemporary studies, documents the historically important life cycle variation in women's work. Women worked during the early years of family formation but dropped

---

[43] The full explanation of the technique used can be found in Horrell and Humphries, "Women's Labour Force Participation".

out when children matured enough to take their place in the labour market.[44] Finally the cubic time trend is significant in all three terms.[45] Calculation of turning-points showed a maximum in 1797 and a minimum beyond our period in 1871. Controlling for real earnings and income effects, the first half of the nineteenth century was associated with a rapid decline in the labour force participation of married women.

The significance of the time trend suggests that economic variables (wages and incomes) and household characteristics (numbers and ages of children) do not constitute a complete explanation of trends in women's participation rates. Omitted variables (changing institutional and ideological factors), operated to adversely affect women's participation. The trend follows the predominantly downward path indicated by aggregate participation in Table 5 and confirms the importance of exogenous factors in the overall picture of women's work during industrialization. But the patterns for individual occupations are not always the same as those for the whole sample, occupational specificity once more suggesting that any search for institutional and ideological obstacles to women's participation be conducted at the disaggregated level. Indeed disparate patterns would be expected from the timing of changes that occurred. Fears of replacement by cheap, female labour, evident in cotton spinning as early as 1818, have been argued to be significant in the exclusion of women from well-paid, expanding occupations as industrialization progressed and was institutionalized through legislation. In 1842 the Mines Regulation Act restricted the employment of women and children underground and the Ten Hour Act of 1847 limited their hours of work in factories; however, work in unregulated areas of employment continued until curtailment started with the 1867 Workshop Act.[46] The chronology of the emergence of a male breadwinner ideology is more difficult to map. There was opposition to the assumption of dependency on a father's wage in the 1834 Poor Law Amendment Act, but by the later nineteenth century female

---

[44] This effect is found in other historical studies: see Claudia Goldin, "Household and Market Production of Families in a Late Nineteenth Century American Town", *Explorations in Economic History*, 16 (1979), pp. 111–131; Elyce J. Rotella, "Women's Labor Force Participation and the Decline of the Family Economy in the United States", *Explorations in Economic History*, 17 (1980), pp. 95–117; A. Meyering, "La Petite Ouvrière Surmenée: Family Structure, Family Income and Women's Work in Nineteenth Century France", in Pat Hudson and W.R. Lee (eds), *Women's Work in the Family Economy in Historical Perspective* (Manchester, 1990), pp. 76–103. Modern studies would be more likely to interpret the negative relationship between the presence of children and participation in terms of the effects on the shadow price of time in the home.

[45] The time trend is in three terms to allow for the possibility of changes in the effect of ideological and institutional influences over time.

[46] See Sonya O. Rose, "Gender Antagonism and Class Conflict: Exclusionary Strategies of Male Unionists in Nineteenth-Century Britain", *Social History*, XIII (1988), pp. 191–208 for a detailed account of the exclusion of women from certain jobs, and Katrina Honeyman and Jordan Goodman, "Women's Work, Gender Conflict and Labour Markets in Europe 1500–1900", *Economic History Review*, XLIV (1991), pp. 608–628 for a general overview.

domesticity and a male breadwinner became not only an accepted image but also a symbol of working-class respectability.[47]

What happened to children's work during the Industrial Revolution has also been fiercely debated. Economic historians appear to agree that the Industrial Revolution involved an increase in child labour, but the timing, nature, causes and consequences of this increase are not well established.[48] Again systematic empirical investigation, hampered by the fragmentary nature of the data available, has not been undertaken. Some authors associate the increase in child labour with the spread of domestic industry.[49] Other authors see factory production as promoting child labour.

Alongside the issue of the growth of child labour there is also the question of the age at which children started work. Part of the outrage over child employment in factories concerned the tender years at which children were employed. It was charged that children were starting work in factories much younger than they had customarily begun employment in agriculture or traditional manufacturing, and parents were accused of complicity in this infant exploitation. For instance, Sadler's Report of 1832 suggested that many children were supporting parents in idleness.[50] But children in domestic industry also had been put "to work as soon as they were able to earn a few pence". Daniel Defoe, for example, mentions four-year-old children at work weaving wool.[51] Perhaps the early nineteenth-century outrage about child labour did not occur because child labour was a new phenomenon, but because it was more visible, "more readily observable in the factory than in the obscurity of the cottage, the conditions and consequences of employment in the mills [...] were increasingly made a matter for concern".[52]

Even if debate remains over whether or not children's participation in the labour market increased in total during the first three decades of the nineteenth century there is general agreement that by the 1840s it appeared

[47] W. Seccombe, "Patriarchy Stabilized: The Construction of the Male Breadwinner Wage Norm in Nineteenth-Century Britain", *Social History*, XI (1986), pp. 53–76 gives an account of the transition, but argues that a male breadwinner ethos was only found in skilled trades prior to 1850. Sonya Rose, "Gender Antagonism", also discusses the emergence of the breadwinner ideology.

[48] See, for example, J.L. Hammond and Barbara Hammond, *The Town Labourer* (London, 1932), p. 143; E.P. Thompson, *The Making of the English Working Class* (London, 1963), p. 331; Phyllis Deane and W.A. Cole, *British Economic Growth, 1688–1959* (Cambridge, 1962), p. 294; Neil McKendrick, "Home Demand and Economic Growth: A New View of the Role of Women and Children in the Industrial Revolution", in Neil McKendrick (ed.), *Historical Perspectives: Studies in English Thought and Society in Honour of J.H. Plumb* (London, 1974), p. 185; Clark Nardinelli, *Child Labor in the Industrial Revolution* (Indiana, 1990), p. 740; Pat Hudson, *The Industrial Revolution* (London, 1992), p. 124.

[49] For example, Ivy Pinchbeck and Margaret Hewitt, *Children in English Society. Vol. 2. From the Eighteenth Century to the Children Act 1948* (London, 1973).

[50] See Nardinelli, *Child Labor*, for a full discussion of this Parliamentary report.

[51] Pinchbeck and Hewitt, *Children in English Society*, p. 390; Defoe is cited in Louise A. Tilly and Joan W. Scott, *Women, Work and Family* (New York, 1978), p. 32.

[52] Pinchbeck and Hewitt, *Children in English Society*, p. 406.

to have been in decline. Levine sees families in outwork as by then dependent on a male breadwinner who contributed around two-thirds of total income.[53] The declining numbers of children employed in factories have been explained by both demand- and supply-side shifts associated with: the Factory Acts of 1833 and 1844; increased male real wages (in part a result of the exclusion of cheaper labour); and changes in technology which reduced demand for tasks performed by children.[54] However, it is not known whether children displaced from factories found work elsewhere or remained unemployed, or whether their withdrawal from the labour force more generally was voluntary.

If industrialization did increase child labour through intensified participation and long hours worked in factories and mines and at outworking occupations, children's contributions to family income should have increased, muting tendencies towards dependence on men. Similarly the withdrawal of child labour from the 1840s should have heralded increased dependence on a male breadwinner. We have already seen that trends in children's contributions to household income support this general interpretation. However, a closer look at the evolving patterns of children's work not only provides greater detail but begins to cut through to explanations of the trends observed.[55]

Table 7 summarizes the evidence from the budgets on children's participation rates.[56] What happened appears to have been conditional on father's occupation, as a proxy for local job opportunities and family attitudes, which helps to explain the diverse, and sometimes inconsistent, views about the effects of industrialization found in the literature.

In 1787–1816 the children of men with agricultural occupations, whether in high- or low-wage counties, had similar relatively low participation rates. Thereafter their experiences diverged. In low-wage counties, children's participation rates fell precipitously, while in high-wage counties, they increased and then declined: both patterns are consistent with trends in contributions, and with independent evidence of deteriorating employment opportunities for children in the agricultural sector.[57] The participation rates of the children of miners and metalworkers declined in line with their contributions. The children of factory workers began with the highest participation rates and increased them from first to last. Con-

[53] David Levine, "Industrialization and the Proletarian Family in England", *Past and Present*, 107 (1985), pp. 935–966.

[54] Clark Nardinelli, "Child Labor and the Factory Acts", *Journal of Economic History*, 40 (1980), pp. 739–755, and *Child Labor*.

[55] Here the sample is reduced to 903 households as we are only concerned with those that have at least one child resident. These households contain 3,841 children.

[56] Participation is defined as either having an occupation coded or earnings recorded. A number of children did not have earnings recorded separately from those of older brothers or sisters or, in some cases, parents, so an earnings definition alone would understate the numbers working.

[57] See Allen, *Enclosure and the Yeoman*.

Table 7. Children's participatin in the labour market

	High-wage agriculture	Low-wage agriculture	Mining	Factory	Outwork	Trades	Casual	All Households	All Children
Participation rates of children by father's occupation (%)									
1787–1816	17	16	32	47	37	32	11	25	>24
1817–1839	33	12	30	55	26	14	17	26	>30
1840–1872	4	6	23	70	29	35	0	24	>24
(Sample)	(425)	(756)	(406)	(295)	(1756)	(168)	(35)	(3,841)	
Children's contribution to household income (%)									
1787–1816	8	9	29	28	33	30	0		
1817–1839	20	5	24	28	28	6	11		
1840–1872	4	4	13	23	21	0	0		
Age of first participation									
1787–1816	13.8	11.4	12.8	9.9	11.4	12.5			
1817–1839	10.3	11.0	11.3	8.3	10.4	12.0			
1840–1872	15.0	15.4	13.3	8.3	11.4	11.2			

temporaries who believed that industrialization was increasing child labour probably had factory work in mind, although it was not representative. From initially high levels the participation rates of outworkers' children declined only to increase again slightly from 1817–1839 to 1840–1872, perhaps in response to the deterioration in their parents' relative (and in many cases) absolute status. The divergent trends in children's participation rates and contributions to family income in factory and outworking families after 1840 suggests that children's work was becoming less regular and/or less well paid. Perhaps it reflects shorter hours in factory employment as children were worked in relays to accommodate the Factory Acts. The relatively high participation of tradesmen's children in the final period should qualify the dramatic decline in contributions to family incomes recorded for this group in the sample where children's earnings can be separately identified. It is likely that children's contributions were larger for tradesmen than estimated, albeit in decline.

Table 7 provides estimates of participation rates for all children living in families based on the weighted averages of our occupationally-specific findings.[58] The striking feature is the remarkable stability of the participation rate of children within families: one-quarter of whom worked through industrialization.[59] The decline in participation rates for the children of fathers in most occupational groups was offset by the shift of the adult population towards jobs associated with higher child activity rates. Although the absolute number of children working increased, along with population, this left the participation of children, at least of those in families, stable over time. How does this square with contemporary belief that children were working at younger ages which would appear inconsistent with the steady participation rates of children in households?

The budget data allows us to consider age-specific participation rates and to compute the age of first participation.[60] For all occupational groups the age at which children first became employed declined between the first and second time periods. Children were being sent to work at younger ages after the Napoleonic wars and the shift of the adult population towards occupations in which children's age at first participation was lower than average, for instance factory work, must have exaggerated the occupationally-specific trends.

---

[58] The aggregate figures are obtained by estimating the proportion of males that would be heads of households with children, using male employment weights calculated for different years to weight the average experience, and using the average number of children in these households to obtain a national picture. For full details of this computation see Horrell and Humphries, "The Exploitation of Little Children", n. 16.

[59] Here we are only concerned with the numbers who do some work, not the amount of work performed. A stable participation rate is not necessarily an indicator of stable labour input from children.

[60] The full working for this computation can be found in Horrell and Humphries, "The Exploitation of Little Children", pp. 496–499.

But if children were working at younger ages, why is this not reflected in the proportion of children in households who were working? Younger working might be expected to mean a higher proportion of children working. Examination of the ages of children in the sample households indicates that older children were leaving home earlier in the first four decades of industrialization. More under 20 year olds were living apart from families. By making the reasonable assumption that all children and adolescents who had left home were in the labour force, we calculated the participation rates of all children, that is those living in families and those living independently (Table 7).[61] While the actual numbers are subject to wide margins of error, the evidence suggests that in aggregate, including both children who lived with their families and those who had left home, participation rates rose between 1787–1816 and 1817–1839. The mechanism for the increase is supported by contemporary observation. For instance, Disraeli commented on the new fashion for children to leave home, move into lodgings and neglect their parents.[62]

Industrialization did involve more children working. But neither the mechanisms by which this change occurred nor its transience have been fully understood and for these reasons the links between children's employment and the rise of the breadwinner family system have been obscured. Industrialization did not significantly increase the relative number of children in families who were employed, although the absolute number rose dramatically given the increase in the relevant population. However, the larger proportion of under-19 year olds living apart from families in 1817–1839 boosted the participation rate of the child population. The younger age at leaving home meant that the stable proportion of working children in families was only achieved by younger children working. The larger proportion of teenagers living apart from families had knock-on effects on the age at which their younger brothers and sisters began employment. In this way increased child labour was not only the result of increased demand during the first phase of industrialization but also the product of a change in family structure in terms of larger numbers of older children living apart from their families.[63] Older and younger children were substitutes in the labour market in families in some occupa-

---

[61] Here we looked at the age structure of children in households compared with the population aged 0–19 in England and Wales to try to infer something about the age of leaving home. We find that the number of children estimated as living in households overstates child population 1787–1816, understates it 1817–1839 and overstates it again around mid-century, implying that more children were to be found outside homes in this middle period. For full details of these comparisons, see Horrell and Humphries, "The Exploitation of Little Children". The estimates of children working are very rough as they only look at the shortfall of the population under 20 missing from our households and assume these people are working outside the home.

[62] Benjamin Disraeli, *Sybil* (London, 1845).

[63] Although of course increased demand for juvenile labour underpinned the increased independence manifest in larger proportions of older children living apart from families.

tions. The ability of younger children to work may have released older children from their familial obligations and allowed earlier independence. Alternatively, increasing real earnings for 15–19 year olds may have facilitated their independence and put pressure on young children to work if a certain proportion of child labourers was needed for family support. Whatever the underlying mechanism, pessimists who have seen industrialization forcing more children into the labour market and at younger ages carry the day. But this bulge in children's participation did not inhibit the developing dependence on men, for the participation rates within households were only maintained by younger children's employment and these childish workers could not replace the earnings of those older siblings who had sought independence. So, ironically, increased child labour coincided in the British case with men's earnings increasing in importance within family incomes.

Moreover, the increase in the aggregate participation rate was not maintained. The nexus of related variables, the proportion of children living outside families, the age at starting work and aggregate participation rates all moved in the opposite direction after 1840. If there was a revolution in the relative incidence of child labour, it characterized only the crucible of industrialization from 1817–1839 and did not extend into the second half of the nineteenth century. Thereafter families retained older children, but lower participation rates even of children in families meant children's contributions continued to slide leaving families ever more dependent on men.

What threw the participation rates of children in reverse, reduced the independence of adolescents and raised the age at which children in families were sent to work? As we have seen in the context of married women's participation, economic theory posits that changes in wages are crucial in explaining participation decisions. But industrialization witnessed changing employment opportunities, the introduction of protective labour legislation, and changing attitudes to children's employment; all factors which may have independently affected the demand for and supply of child labourers.

Nardinelli explained the decline in children's participation in factory work after 1840 not by legislative changes but by rising male real earnings which allowed fathers to purchase leisure time for their children.[64] Our weighted averages of participation rates of children in families do not decline despite increases in average adult male real earnings from the mid-1830s onwards, cautioning against an overemphasis on income effects as explanations of patterns in children's participation rates. Nor do the occupational experiences offer unambiguous support for Nardinelli's position. True, in mining and outworking families, increases in male real

[64] Nardinelli, *Child Labor*, p. 154.

wages were accompanied by declining child participation between the first and second time periods, and many occupations experienced increasing male real earnings from the 1840s onwards when the participation of younger children in particular declined. Moreover, the increased participation of children with fathers in outwork from 1817–1839 to 1840–1872 was accompanied by declining male earnings. However, children with fathers in factory work and trades exhibited increased participation alongside increased male earnings, indicating the importance of other explanatory factors. Indeed, participation of factory workers' children increased in all time periods, as did their earnings, whereas in low-wage agricultural families male earnings decreased until the 1840s along with their children's participation. These exceptions point to the importance of the availability of jobs in determining the incidence of child labour, and suggest that children's work was the norm, performed if opportunities were available.

However, economic theory allows the possibility that children may not have left the labour market even if their fathers' earnings increased if their own wages were increasing faster. There is evidence in the budgets that children's earnings rose faster than male earnings initially but lost ground subsequently. Low-wage agriculture is the only exception. Thus children's participation could fit a relative earnings explanation. Children, or their parents, may have been choosing work over leisure in response to the increasing opportunity cost of leisure time. We estimate a model of children's labour supply to test this and related hypotheses.[65]

In modelling the decision to participate, the standard explanatory variables include the real earnings of other family members and non-wage income (expected to have negative effects), and the wage (or earnings) which the child could obtain in the labour market (expected to have a positive effect). The child's age is included to represent availability for work. But the individual child's labour force participation will also be part of a household's allocation decision and will reflect the relative preference for home production and for earned income, and each family member's comparative advantage in the labour market. To capture this effect the numbers of older and younger siblings and of other persons in the household are included. The presence of older children can be expected to decrease the probability of a child's participation at any given age as the income needs of the family were more likely to be met from the earnings of older siblings. More little brothers and sisters, and the presence of other people, for instance lodgers, can be expected to increase the productivity of any child in home production (child minding, cooking and so on). A

---

[65] Full details of the technique used is given in Horrell and Humphries, "The Exploitation of Little Children". Gender differences in the relationship of children's participation to the family economy are also discussed.

dummy variable for the mother working is included to capture any substitution between mothers and children in market work.[66] In addition, dummy variables for fathers' occupations and occupationally-specific time trends are incorporated to capture variations in employment opportunities for children. Finally, composite variables which interact age with time and number of older children with time are included to pick up changes over time in the age of participation and the effect of older children on participation.

Various alternative specifications were tried and the final regression is reported in Table 8. For all children, some variables do have the expected effects. Father's earnings have a negative effect on participation and own earnings a positive effect. However, other family income, which should have a negative effect, has a positive and significant coefficient. This reflects the positive correlations across regions and over time between the employment opportunities facing any one child and those facing other family members. The probability of participation increases with age.

Household composition effects suggest that there was some substitution between older and younger children. The more older children there were in the family, the less likely was any one child to work as (presumably) income needs were satisfied by the participation of the older brothers or sisters. But the combined variable of number of older children and time suggests that this relationship was weakening. Earlier we noted that some families seem increasingly to have harboured older, non-working children. Perhaps this signifies gender overriding age as the main determinant of the order in which children worked. Significantly, there appear to have been few opportunities for children to be involved profitably in home production. The larger the number of younger children in the family the higher the probability of any individual child working in the market. Income needs dominated any useful role that could be played in child minding or home production more generally: a point also illustrated by the insignificant effect that the presence of others in the household had on participation, and by the apparent lack of substitution between children's and mother's waged work.

The time trend shows an increase in the probability of children working until 1807 and then a decrease, although the trend turns down earlier in agriculture (1798). The pattern is reversed for the children of factory workers who were more likely to work than other children throughout the whole period, but for whom the trend in participation declined until 1828 and then increased. These two occupationally-specific stories are readily explained. The early loss of children's employment in agriculture has been

---

[66] We do not expect this to be important. Consideration of mother's earnings relative to children's earnings shows mothers to be earning less once the children are over 10 years of age in all occupations. As children have an advantage over mothers in the labour market we would not expect to see children substituting for mothers in the home.

Table 8. *Probit equations of individual children's participation*

	All children	
Constant	−1.542	(−8.86)*
Real earnings of father	−0.008	(−2.11)³
Real other income	0.032	(8.13)*
Predicted own real earnings	0.073	(2.03)⁴
Number of younger children	0.176	(7.69)*
Number of older children	−0.533	(−8.23)*
Other non-family household members	−0.181	(−1.57)
Mother works	−0.090	(−1.31)
Age of child	0.060	(4.06)*
Time	0.013	(1.73)⁸
Time²	−0.00031	(−3.55)*
Factory dummy	2.986	(2.74)*
Factory x time	−0.131	(−2.18)³
Factory x time²	0.0017	(2.15)³
Agriculture x time	−0.0055	(−2.07)⁴
Number of older children x time	0.0037	(2.39)⁴
X²	1,653.4*	
Predicted correctly	86.6%	
Sample	3,336	

Notes:
* Indicates significance at 1 per cent level.
³ Indicates significance level below 1 per cent and above 10 per cent; t-ratios in parentheses.
The sample excludes children whose earnings were given only as a family total or with the earnings of the mother or other children.

widely noted. Parents may have resisted their children working in factories in the era of pauper apprentices and rural locations, but this resistance was overcome when employment became available in towns.[67] The overall trend captures patterns in mining, outwork and trades. It suggests a general decline in employment opportunities for children *ceteris paribus*. Possible explanations include the decline in the apprenticeship system; the earlier transition to male breadwinner families in, say, trades and mining; and handloom weavers' aspiration to the lifestyle of the artisan when incomes rose but discovery that earnings opportunities for children were no longer there when adult earnings came down. The significance of these time trends is that explanations of the labour force participation of children during industrialization must go beyond wage and income effects.

[67] See Pinchbeck and Hewitt, *Children in English Society*; Nardinelli, "Child Labor and the Factory Acts".

FAMILIES WITHOUT MALE BREADWINNERS

The overarching significance of men's earnings within family incomes indicates another enduring feature of the economic timescape: families which were without an adult male and/or his earning power were in grievous circumstances.[68] In an earlier paper Humphries analysed a small sample of female-headed households and an even smaller sample of families whose male head was sick and not working.[69] These families were poorer than families headed by men in almost all occupational groups with the possible exception of low-wage agriculture. Unfortunately this small sample is not spread evenly through the period of industrialization and we have complete evidence for only one family in each of the latter two sub-periods. But there is no evidence that these families improved their position relative to husband-wife households, a conclusion which is consistent with other independent evidence (see Table 9 compared with Tables 1 and 2).[70] The inability of women and children in these families to sustain relative standards is further evidence that disappearing job opportunities for women and children, sluggish relative pay and institutional constraints on employment were characteristic of the period. This early feminization of poverty has the same economic and ideological roots as the darker path to dependence on men in families where they were present.

The participation rates of women in the sample of female-headed households were higher than those of wives of men in most occupational groups and held up over the course of industrialization (Tables 9 and 5). The participation rates of women married to men who were ill and not working were lower than those of wives of men in some occupational groups and lower than those of all wives. These women were older on average than the wives of working men, which might have contributed to this differential. Perhaps these families lived in areas of high unemployment or perhaps morbidity ran in families so unhealthy men were more likely to be married to unhealthy women, both explanations offered for the relatively low participation rates of the wives of unemployed men observed in modern data.[71] Children in families headed by women and in families headed by men who were not able to work had higher participation rates than those in families with fathers present (Tables 9 and 7). The age structure of parti-

---

[68] A sample of families headed by women (widows, unmarried mothers and deserted wives) is studied in Jane Humphries, "Female-Headed Households in Early Industrial Britain: The Vanguard of the Proletariat", *Labour History Review* (forthcoming, 1998). Results from this paper will be cited where relevant.

[69] *Ibid.*

[70] See *ibid.* and sources cited therein.

[71] See Richard B. Davies, Peter Elias and Roger Penn, "The Relationship Between a Husband's Unemployment and His Wife's Participation in the Labour Force", *Oxford Bulletin of Economics and Statistics*, 54 (1992), pp. 145–171.

Table 9. *Income and participation in female-headed households*

	1787–1815	1816–1820	1821–1840	1841–1845	1846–1865
Family income (£ p.a.)	40.1	30.8	26.9	19.0	40.3
Real family income (£ p.a.)[a]	37.87	22.84	31.72	20.04	40.10
Real adult-equivalent family income (£ p.a.)[b]	9.00	7.25	9.01	7.62	13.37
Contribution from (%)					
woman	30.9	38.5	44.0	69.4	49.9
children	50.3	45.3	38.2	25.0	43.3
other sources	18.7	15.2	17.8	5.6	6.8
of which self-provisioning	5.3	1.7	0.0	0.0	1.8
Participation rates:					
woman[c]	94.7	76.3	80.0	75.0	100.0
children	43.2	46.2	42.4	44.4	33.3
(Sample)	(19)	(59)	(25)	(4)	(4)

Notes:
[a] Deflated using cost-of-living index from Feinstein, "Nominal Wages", p. 26; 1820–1824=100.
[b] Adult equivalents calculated as 1 for woman, 0.5 all other household members.
[c] Participation defined as earnings or occupation recorded.

cipation rates suggested that fatherless children or those with invalid or unemployed fathers began work at younger ages. More intensive working and working at younger ages was an economic exigency forced on families by inadequate or non-existent male earnings.

Female-headed households, on average, had higher non-earnings components of family incomes (Table 9). That poor relief was often important to such families is not surprising, but it is interesting that they made less use of self-provisioning than families with husbands present. Perhaps informal but vigilant means-testing of relief provision made female-headed households even more reluctant than husband-wife households to reveal income in kind; perhaps the urban bias of the sample disguises the self-provisioning undertaken by female-headed households in the countryside; perhaps these families faced a hierarchy of needs in which the demands for money income were pre-eminent, hence the high labour market participation rates which crowded out the use of time in self-provisioning. The contribution which other sources of income made to families headed by sick or unemployed men was also distinctive. A high proportion of these families had access to other sources of income but self-provisioning was relatively unimportant.[72] These families were able to tap forms of assistance which were unavailable to the female-headed households in similarly miserable circumstances, most notably sick clubs and friendly societies. They also sold and pawned possessions. The picture is one of families in disequilibrium; the other sources of income represent short-run responses to life crises, not long-run sustainable strategies for survival. Significantly even in these grim conditions their main lifelines continued to be the remnants of their husband/fathers' breadwinning: the subsidies from sick clubs and doles. In the prolonged absence of male earnings, of course, the situation had to be different. Either families went under, ceased to exist as independent entities, or women in particular increased their participation and with the help of their children struggled to some new miserable equilibrium, becoming in essence like the female-headed households in the sample. The welfare costs of the labour expended by the women and children in these families at this level of poverty were considerable.[73]

The experience of families without men's earnings and without men throws into relief an important historical conclusion: the presence of men in families, men's superior earnings power and even dependence on men had its benefits as well as its costs. The death or desertion of a father, as several working-class autobiographies of the period illustrate, threatened not only the material well-being of family members but the very existence of the family.[74] But the experience of families headed or effectively headed by women uncovers another context in which women and children were the mainstays of family life: at times and in circumstances when men could or would not be breadwinners. The important point is that these times and circumstances were not unusual. Death or incapacity of the male household-head was commonplace given the mortality and morbidity of early industrial Britain. Desertion was probably also increasing at the end of the eighteenth century when the growing cities and expanding empire offered dissatisfied men a refuge and recruitment into the army or navy an escape route.[75] Less dramatic, but probably just as disruptive, were the ordinary absences of men moved around in search of work.[76] If we include such temporary separations, as well as cases where men were unable to

---

[72] This was also true of the female-headed households.

[73] See Sara Horrell, Jane Humphries and Hans-Joachim Voth, "Stature and Relative Deprivation: Fatherless Children in Early Industrial Britain", *Continuity and Change* (forthcoming, 1998).

[74] See David Vincent, *Bread, Knowledge and Freedom: A Study of Nineteenth-Century Working Class Autobiography* (London, 1981), ch. 4.

[75] David A. Kent, " 'Gone for a Soldier': Family Breakdown and the Demography of Desertion in a London Parish, 1750–91", *Local Population Studies*, 45 (1990), pp. 27–42.

[76] Humphrey Southall, "The Tramping Artisan Revisited: Labour Mobility and Economic Distress in Early Victorian England", *Economic History Review*, XLIV (1991), pp. 272–296.

work because of chronic illness or who were long-term unemployed, and not forgetting men in the army and navy and in prison, Humphries estimates that about 20 per cent of families in early industrial Britain, were headed by women.[77] Thus a large minority of people at any one point in time, and an even larger minority at some stage in their lifetimes, experienced family life without a breadwinner male. Despite a welfare system and an economy which operated by and large as though all households had such a prop, many of these families survived and lived to see a better day. It was a heroic achievement by the women and children involved.

CONCLUSION

Women's independence was eroded over the course of industrialization as families became increasingly dependent on men's earnings. The faltering of married women's own earned contributions to family income was only one part of this story. Economic and social changes weakened women's control over resources through several other channels. Opportunities to contribute substantially to the household through self-provisioning activities were curtailed and the earnings of children, which had previously been important in supporting the children themselves and might have been seen as the preserve of the mother, were also diminished. With these changes women, and children, became dependent on men instead of providing non-market, but tangible, resources for the household economy. The alterations seen in women's access to the means to contribute towards their families' well-being were felt most acutely by those households without male breadwinners, the female-headed households, whose relative status deteriorated. Although clearly showing the relative importance of men's earnings in family incomes, our study emphasizes how few households could rely entirely on a male breadwinner for their security. The prevalence of female-headed households and the inadequacy of male earnings to cover family needs in certain key stages of the life cycle show that for most families the participation of women and children in some circumstances or at some stages was essential for survival.

Our story has been one of a patchy, incomplete and sometimes miserable dependence on men and male earnings, with its origins clearly in the period before the Industrial Revolution and its genesis markedly different in families with different occupational identities and economic bases. Some families, such as miners, followed the beneficent route where legislation and high male earnings combined to create dependency. Others, like the families of outworkers and agricultural labourers, were forced along the darker route of low earnings and few opportunities for work. Yet others, for instance factory workers, eschewed the male breadwinner family form despite labour legislation and high earnings. Their family

---

[77] Humphries, "Female-Headed Households".

structure was more influenced by employment opportunities, local norms and the relatively high material living standards which women's and children's contributions afforded. The evidence does not support those grand theorizations which depict either capitalism or industrialization as inaugurating an era of dependence and degradation for women, nor does it show a universality of patriarchal subservience. Instead it offers support to newer themes emerging in family and gender history.

First, it suggests that historians of the family might be well advised to question periodization adopted from mainstream narratives and think instead of the continuities and discontinuities evident in their own imperfectly reconstructed worlds. Although our analysis implicates economic changes in the origins and expansion of the male breadwinner family, it does so in an occupationally and regionally differentiated way and on a timescale not transparently linked to "the Industrial Revolution" as conventionally dated. Second, our evidence is consistent with a more general rejection of attempts to produce all-encompassing frameworks for and explanations of social phenomena, represented here both by the economistic modelling of labour supply and the feminist emphasis on intentional exclusion. Grand theorizations of the rise of the male breadwinner family provide falsely homogenizing accounts which are obsessed with monocausality, outcomes and finished worlds. We cannot read backwards from those circumstances which promote the male breadwinner family today to its origins. Finally, it supports the rejection of any claim that there can be a specific cause of transition to male breadwinning and highlights the pluralistic and multifaceted nature of the family in the past.

Gendered Exclusion: Domesticity and Dependence in Bengal[*]

SAMITA SEN

In Western Europe, industrialization brought far-reaching changes in the family-household system by separating the household from the workplace. Factories, especially, took work away from home and eroded the integrity of the household. The spatial separation between the household and the workplace became the foundation for a conceptual separation between the community and the market. Families were separated from trades, consumption from production, women's activities from men's. These separations, often expressed in the generalized formula of a "private-public" divide, have underscored a thoroughgoing gender division of labour far beyond the original divisions supposed to be rooted in biological reproduction. In industrialized Europe, the working-class household's needs could not be met from the combined economic activities of its members: men, women and children. Rather, the daily bread was to be "won" by individual wage earners and clearly the breadwinners were to be men. In contrast, the home became the site of women's reproductive activities devoid of assignable exchange value. Wives' and daughters' unpaid work was increasingly underwritten by family ideology and was eventually to be covered by the "family wage" paid to husbands and fathers.

In South Asia this type of household arrangement did not take effect among the working classes in the early phase of industrialization and is still not yet widespread. No clear separation of the household and production was effected: the household's own productive functions proved tenacious and in poor households, especially, women combined consumption, wage earning and reproduction, often simultaneously. The notion of a male wage earner as the single source of the household's sustenance – the single male breadwinner – was not a ubiquitous one and the inception of the modern factory system was not critical in this regard. Factory industry was introduced in India in the mid-nineteenth century. Yet the demand for a family wage was not heard until the 1920s and then only at the instigation of British labour reformers and activists. The notion of a "fair wage" based on a family of five to be paid to individual male factory workers became concretized in industrial bargaining and state policies only in the 1940s and 1950s. Even then, the workers of the "organized" sector to whom these arrangements exclusively applied, were a bare 20

[*] This paper draws on my doctoral research: Samita Sen, "Women Workers in the Bengal Jute Industry, 1890–1940: Migration, Motherhood and Militancy" (Ph.D. thesis, Cambridge University, 1992).

International Review of Social History 42 (1997), Supplement, pp. 65–86

per cent of the total manufacturing employment in 1951.[1] Obviously, a large number of workers earned wages from a wide variety of production and service activities. For many of these workers a broad notion of a male provider grew in significance. Such a notion was already institutionalized in the family – in property and labour arrangements which subordinated women and children.

This paper attempts to trace the increasing importance of the notion of a male provider in Bengal in eastern India from the nineteenth to the twentieth century. In Bengal, and arguably in South Asia, the phenomenon and the ideologies associated with a male provider did not follow from a separation of production from the household. Rather, I will argue, it was a progressive differentiation of men's and women's work which led to a devaluation of women's work and to an ideology of female dependence. The paper is organized in three sections. The first section examines the importance of the family in the deployment of women's labour and its significance in India's capitalist development. Women's access to their traditional sources of independent earnings was reduced by the establishment of mills and factories which in their turn progressively excluded women. The second section focuses on how women were marginalized in industrial work. On the whole, women became dependent on male wages or on family-based economic activities as in the case of small peasant farms. Moreover, as the third section attempts to show, a growing commitment to an ideology of domesticity tended to divest women's activities of economic value and promoted female dependence on male earnings.

WOMEN'S WORK AT THE TURN OF THE CENTURY

In recent years, researchers have pointed out that South Asian capitalist development, under the aegis of the colonial state, depended particularly on the state's ability to harness the non-capitalist relations of production. The state's long-term revenue and economic policies were premised on the continuation of small peasant agriculture which, in the case of Bengal, helped rather than hindered market penetration.

Small peasant farmers relied upon unpaid family labour. From roughly the 1860s two significant processes transformed the functioning of the rural household: the increase in the unpaid component of women's and children's labour and the decline in its paid component.[2] The imbalance within the household economy was exacerbated – control of capital and

---

[1] J.N. Sinha, *The Indian Working Force: (Its Growth and Changing Composition)*, Census of India, 1, Monograph 11 (1961).
[2] Sugata Bose, *Peasant Labour and Colonial Capital. Rural Bengal Since 1770*, New Cambridge History of India, III-2 (Cambridge, 1993), pp. 66–111.

capital-intensive labour concentrated in the hands of men while women undertook labour-intensive tasks of low status and poor reward.[3]

In the 1890s G.A. Grierson, a British revenue officer, attempted to quantify women's contribution to the household budget. According to his estimates, artisans in Gaya derived 44 per cent of their earnings from "supplementary" activities, of which women contributed at least 30 per cent. Women worked on the family farm, for hire in transplanting seasons and reared cattle.[4] In the household of the agricultural labourer, the "supplemental" income, amounting to 40 per cent of total earnings, derived primarily from women's miscellaneous activities. In small cultivating families, women not only worked on the family farm but provided about 20 per cent of the supplementary income by cattle rearing and grain processing.[5] We do not know how Grierson collected his data, so one cannot assume that his quantitative assessment is absolutely precise. But his figures do indicate the importance of women's labour in the maintenance of the household in Bihar at the close of the nineteenth century.

In the early part of the nineteenth century, another British observer, F.H. Buchanan, had found that though women were paid very poorly for grain processing, their principal sustained work throughout the year, they made up for it by weeding. Among agricultural labourers, women's total earnings exceeded that of men.[6] By the early twentieth century, in Muzaffarpur, more than half the "supplementary" income of the agricultural labourer, crucial in the lean periods of March and October, was provided by women.[7] In Saran, for instance, women predominated in many occupations.[8] Even in Bengal, women were associated with a wide range of non-agrarian activities.[9] An accelerated agrarian crisis after World War I increased the small and marginal cultivator's dependence on women's "supplementary" income.[10]

Even if women contributed almost half the household income, or even more, Grierson accepted the income from male resource (land, craft or

---

[3] Nirmala Banerjee, "Working Women in Colonial Bengal: Modernization and Marginalization", in Kumkum Sangari and Sudesh Vaid (eds), *Recasting Women: Essays in Colonial History* (New Delhi, 1989), pp. 283–288. Also see Amartya Sen, "Family and Food: Sex Bias in Poverty", in idem, *Resources, Values and Development* (Oxford, 1984).

[4] G.A. Grierson, *Notes on the District of Gaya* (Calcutta, 1893), p. 121.

[5] *Ibid.*, p. 112.

[6] F.H. Buchanan, *An Account of the District of Purneah in 1809–10* (Patna, 1928), p. 444.

[7] C.J. Stevenson-Moore, *Report on the Material Condition of Small Agriculturists and Labourers in Gaya* (Calcutta, 1898) [hereafter *Stevenson-Moore Report*], p. 364.

[8] *Bihar and Orissa District Gazetteer* [hereafter *BODG*], Saran (Patna, 1930), pp. 85–86.

[9] In 1901, there were 1.4 million women in agriculture, 462,000 in grain processing and 200,000 in making and selling forest products: *Census of India* (1901), VI, 1, p. 197.

[10] Lord Dufferin, Report Submitted to the Viceroy; P. Nolan, *Report on the Condition of the Lower Classes of Population in Bengal* (Calcutta, 1888) [hereafter *Dufferin Report*], Main Report, pp. 7–9; *Stevenson-Moore Report*, pp. 23–24.

labour) as the "main" earnings. The rest, including women's varied activities, was labelled supplementary. It was not the source or the proportion of the income as much the sex of the earner that provided a consistent basis for this categorization. Women's work, if not their earnings, was marginalized.

Women's work was associated with poor returns, and was casual and intermittent. In Bengal and Bihar a very large number of women traded in fuel.[11] Women collected cowdung and litter, and made cowdung cakes with them and carried them to the market to sell. It was a labour-intensive and poorly rewarded occupation. Thus women collected and sold firewood, grass and fodder, made baskets, ginned cotton, cleaned and sold farm or cottage products. Grierson remarked that women usually made up the household's deficits "by odds and ends, supplemental sources of income, such as cutting of fuel in the *jangal* and the like".[12]

Some skills were widely disseminated and often handed down through generations of women. Spinning, for example, was compatible with domesticity and seclusion, undertaken at home and in intervals from housework. Thus spinning formed the employment of the largest number of women in Bengal. At the beginning of the nineteenth century Buchanan presumed that in Bihar all adult women spun because "all castes are permitted to spin [. . .] and this is an employment suited well to the jealousy of the men [sic]."[13] But, he added, women were suffering from a declining demand for yarn.[14]

Hand-spinning was hard hit by competition from cotton mills and women were able to earn only one *anna* a day. Yet, as A.C. Chatterjee, a government labour surveyor pointed out, hand-spinning would continue so long as "it provided a small income for purdah women and widows who were not prepared to leave their village to enter factories".[15] Despite its declining fortune, cotton spinning and weaving remained in popular memory as a most suitable occupation for women. In 1931, it was "carried on in the household with the help of women".[16] A woman wrote in a popular journal,

Dependent women are not always welcome [. . .] earlier they would weave or spin [. . .] "*Charka* is my husband and son, *charka* is my grandson, it is due to *charka* that there is an elephant tied to my door" [. . .] whether, as in the old

[11] *Census of India* (1911), VI, 1, p. 549.

[12] Grierson, *Notes on the District of Gaya*, pp. 111–112.

[13] F.H. Buchanan, *An Account of the District of Bhagalpur in 1810–11* (Patna, 1939), pp. 607–611.

[14] Buchanan, *An Account of the Districts of Bihar and Patna, 1811–12* (Patna, 1928), p. 647.

[15] A.C. Chatterjee, "Notes on the Industries of the United Provinces", 1907, quoted in G.M. Broughton, *Labour in Indian Industries* (London, 1924), p. 59.

[16] R.K. Das, "Women Labour in India', *International Labour Review* (October–November 1931), p. 383.

saying, one could actually have an elephant tied to one's door, I do not know. But [spinning] certainly provided a means of earning money within seclusion [...][17]

Spinning, however, like other superior crafts for extended markets where women worked in the household unit as helpers, did not always give direct access to markets. Many women spun thread for the male members of the family to weave.[18]

There were some tasks which women generally performed for their own families but occasionally extended for sale in the market. These included animal husbandry, making and selling of dairy products, preparing vegetable oil and producing and selling forest products. Much the largest employment in this category was in grain and food processing. In textile industries men were still three times as numerous as women but in food processing women, chiefly employed as rice pounders, huskers and flour grinders, outnumbered men by six to one. The processing of grain was usually a part of most women's domestic routine, often undertaken also for sale. Thus, "husking and boiling rice [...] is done entirely by women".[19] In the early nineteenth century Buchanan noted that all grain processors were women and a few of them were able to purchase, process and retail grain in shops.[20] The *dhenki* was used for cleaning and husking rice which was part of the daily routine of housework, though sometimes women would sell cleaned rice.[21]

Quite frequently, women assisted the men in the household by selling the products of the business. Among the Agraharis in Bihar, "the women are not secluded as among the Agrawalas, but take part in business of their husbands by selling rice, flour".[22] Among the Mallahs, the fishermen and boatmen caste, "their women work in the village and sell fish".[23] In Hooghly, half the fish-sellers were women.[24] Among the Gauras of Cut-

---

[17] Manorama Ghose, "Banganarir Kaaj" [Bengali women's work], *Mashik Basumati*, 1 (1922), p. 33.

[18] *Report of the Census of the Town and Suburbs of Calcutta* (1881), p. 144. To every 1,000 men, there were 19,737 women spinners but only 207 female weavers, 442 cotton cleaners, pressers, and ginners, 498 yarn and thread sellers, and 624 dyers: *Census of India* (1901), VI, 1, p. 497.

[19] Major Ralph Smyth, *Statistical and Geographical Report of the 24 Pergunnahs District* (Calcutta, 1857), p. 27. The "domestic" industries of rice – pounding and husking and the parching of grain – "naturally fall to the women's lot": to every man in Bengal there were 27 women and in Bihar and Orissa there were 16: *Census of India* (1911), VI, 1, pp. 548–549.

[20] *Ibid.* Also see p. 402.

[21] The decline in household grain processing is traced in Mukul Mukherjee, "Impact of Modernisation of Women's Occupations: A Case Study of Rice Husking Industry in Bengal", in J. Krishnamurty (ed.), *Women in Colonial India: Essays on Survival, Work and the State* (New Delhi, 1989).

[22] *Bengal District Gazetteer* [hereafter *BDG*], Monghyr (Calcutta, 1909), p. 134.

[23] *Ibid.*

[24] *BDG*, Hooghly (1912), p. 176.

tack, the women sold milk and dairy products but they eschewed field labour of all kinds.[25] In Saran, "[Ahir] women, who are very hardworking, add to the family earnings by making and selling cowdung cakes, milk, ghi, and curd".[26] In fact, "it is regarded as a woman's job to dispose of the articles that her husband makes, grows, or catches, such as pots and household utensils, milk, ghee and fish".[27] In some caste-specific artisan (handloom and pottery) and service (laundry and sweeping) occupations, women usually had no independent role but had to work as part of the household team.

A few independent professions were followed by women without reference to their male relatives. But such activities were strictly limited and the largest such occupation for women – midwifery – was devalued by ritual pollution. Only low-caste women could practise as midwives. In most districts of Bihar, midwives were chamar women. In Bengal proper, women from Hari, Muchi, Dom and other castes could practice midwifery.[28]

Among the low castes, men and women often worked together at basket weaving, tea gardens, coalmining, field labour, *jhum* cultivation, etc. While women did not usually work on the cotton loom, they wove jute, which was much heavier work. In Bengal, apart from prostitution and midwifery, women were registered as actually outnumbering men in three occupations. "Two of these are domestic industries to which women are well-suited": silkworm rearing and the making of twine or string.[29]

Many of these traditional occupations declined in the twentieth century. The characteristic features which had made them more accessible to women also made them vulnerable to "modernization". Many of women's crafts were basically for daily use and, therefore, had potentially large markets. Competition had already substantially eroded the textile handloom industry and some other artisan industries. Women, limited by their lack of time, skill and capital, used easily available raw materials and locally made crude implements. Consequently, their productivity was low. With the development of transport these commodities became items in a large network of trade involving capital, information and mobility. Their production was easily and profitably mechanized. Women could not compete with the new machines because of their initial low productivity. Factory-produced goods, such as utensils and clothing, gradually replaced women's hand-made products. In addition, commercialization and the pressure on land curtailed access to forests and commons – to food and

---

[25] *BODG*, Cuttack (1933).

[26] *BODG*, Saran (1930), p. 45.

[27] *Census of India* (1911), V, 1, p. 549.

[28] The 1901 Census returned some male midwives who were either dependents or, as in Decca, assistants who cut the cord but took no part in the delivery: *Census of India* (1901), V, 1, pp. 478–479.

[29] *Census of India* (1911), V1, pp. 548–549.

fuel. In 1881, women were engaged in a third of the agrarian occupations and in two-fifths of "making and selling" occupations. By 1921–1931, women's share in the latter occupation had been reduced to a little over a quarter. The biggest losses were in food processing, forest products and caste-specific occupations.[30]

Apart from the secular decline in women's non-agrarian occupations their association with domestic work led to a systematic undercounting of women's work.[31] Only visible work by women in fields or markets was taken into account. A curious and arguable understanding of a direct connection between impoverishment and women's visible work underlay official statements. Government officers tended to use the invisibility of women as an index of the prosperity of a region.[32]

The low workforce participation rates of women in eastern and northern Bengal relative to western and central Bengal and Bihar may reflect only the proportion of women who worked outside the home. In 1911, in Bengal proper, the ratio of workers to dependents was 36:64, while in Bihar and Orissa it was 48:52. This ratio was more marked in the case of agriculture: in Bengal, 1:2 and in Bihar and Orissa, 4.7:5.3.[33] Women's participation in agricultural work would thus seem to be the lowest in eastern Bengal. Yet, in Rajshahi, where "women do not work for wages", they helped in cultivation, in weeding crops, husking rice and weaving gunny bags.[34] In contrast, in Bihar districts, or among the poor of western Bengal, women were active in agricultural operations and petty trading.

Lower wages and the perception that their earnings were secondary meant that women often entered the labour market when they had exhausted other alternatives. Sometimes they were pushed into the labour market by the inadequacy or discontinuation of male earnings. Non-economic reasons like widowhood, desertion or barrenness might force women "to go out to work". In Bihar in the early nineteenth century it was difficult to get female domestic servants except widows and old women "who have lost all their kindred".[35] The situation seemed similar

---

[30] Banerjee, "Working Women in Colonial Bengal", pp. 283–288.

[31] The definition of women's work changed in each Census. The Census of 1881 registered women in the husband's occupation. In 1901 and 1911 "women and children who work at any occupation, of whatever kind, not being merely an amusement or of a *purely domestic character* [were] entered" (emphasis added): *Census of India* (1901), VI, 1, p. 486. In addition, respondents often did not register women's employment. Census figures should be taken as rough guides.

[32] The Magistrate of Tipperah, *General Administration Report for the year 1884*, para 21. Also see Banerjee, "Working Women in Colonial Bengal", p. 289.

[33] In total the female workforce participation rate in Bengal was about two women to seven men, as compared with Bihar and Orissa which had one woman to two men workers: *Census of India* (1911), V, pp. 548–549. For district-wise breakdown see Banerjee, "Working Women in Colonial Bengal", Table 6, p. 289.

[34] Rajshahye Division, pp. 3–4 and Chittagong Division, p. 4, *Dufferin Report*.

[35] Buchanan, *Account of the District of Bhagalpur*.

at the close of the century. Widows and old women without children formed the largest proportion of destitutes in the villages.[36] Such women would have to migrate or hire out their labour.

Married women, especially those with children to support, worked outside the home when male wages were depressed. But they did not work at similar occupations all the year round.[37] They provided labour on family lands during the busy season when wages were higher and the demand for labour was greater. In the lean season, when men could not find work, women would undertake either subsistence activities with low returns or hire out their labour at exceptionally low wages. In twenty-two villages of Muzaffarpur, the supply of labour exceeded its demand by 68 per cent and "only one-third of the female labouring population found work after the male population was satisfied".[38] Women might often enter the labour market when the demand for labour was at its lowest and withdraw when the situation was improving. This not only kept women's bargaining strength in the labour market very low but it also helped maintain women as a flexible supply of labour.

The gender division of labour in agriculture is illuminating. In Bengal, ploughing and sowing were done exclusively by men, while transplantation and weeding were the duties of women. In transplanting, women "are said to be more proficient [. . .] and some women are so proficient, that they will not work for others at daily rates of wages, but will earn much more by taking contracts for definite areas".[39] Such divisions of labour usually appeared in the form of long-established custom. In fact, transplanting was a relatively labour-intensive job and was undertaken when grain prices had risen.[40] In families without stores of grain it was imperative for women to work for hire in this season. Women transplanters were paid either the same rates or less than men depending on the supply of labour. But the rules for such division of labour were not universal. In eastern Bengal, for instance, women were not seen to take part in field work, even in busy seasons.

A CASE OF WOMEN'S EXCLUSION: THE JUTE INDUSTRY IN BENGAL

The decline in women's traditional occupations was symptomatic of a more general agrarian trend. British concern to ensure a steady flow of revenue from the agricultural sector led, in 1793, to the Permanent Settlement in Bengal. The detrimental effects of demographic change, high rev-

[36] Main Report, p. 5, Presidency Division, p. 7 and Burdwan Division, p. 3, *Dufferin Report*.
[37] Report of A.K. Roy, Joint Settlement Officer, p. 6, *Dufferin Report*.
[38] *Stevenson-Moore Report*, p. 364.
[39] *BDG*, Bankura (1908), p. 104.
[40] Noakhally Division, p. 3, *Dufferin Report*.

enue demand and spiralling rent caused repeated crises which, however, were not acute enough to force a very large proportion of poor men, women and children to migrate from the Indian countryside to the cities. Indeed, the relatively small demand for labour generated by private British plantation and industrial capital required no wholesale expropriation of Indian peasantry. In fact, commercialization of agriculture combined with near stagnant production created a more than adequate labour surplus in Bengal's countryside.

Those groups in rural society whose access to capital was limited or non-existent steadily grew more and more impoverished. Their response to poverty was, however, gendered. Though the declining incomes from land, labour and crafts affected women more negatively than men, the need for cash to meet rent and revenue demands propelled men to overseas colonies and to the city to earn a supplementary income. Wives and children were left to work more intensively for subsistence in the rural economy. Only in times of acute distress did families migrate together – including mothers, wives and daughters. Sometimes women, too, came to the city alone, usually to escape familial harassment or destitution in the village. These women were often unable to maintain a link with the village home, unlike most men in the predominantly male urban labour market. The migrant men who retained a "rural connection" devised complex strategies of survival which included resources obtained from both village and city occupations. The typical working-class family was spatially fragmented and was as crucially dependent on the unpaid (or poorly paid) labour of women and children in the rural economy as on men's industrial wages.

Indian factory industry, from its very inception in the mid-nineteenth century, preferred and employed chiefly men. Even the two major textile industries – jute in Calcutta and cotton in Bombay – had about one woman to four men in their workforce. Over time both these industries drastically reduced the number of female workers. Even then, jute was the only factory industry in Bengal to employ a significant proportion of women. Others, such as the metal and printing industries and the railways, did not employ women at all.[41] Bengal was not exceptional in this regard. R.S. Chandavarkar has shown that the same situation existed in Bombay.[42] In the 1930s, C.M. Matheson's investigations into textile centres revealed similar trends. Ahmedabad cotton mills alone employed a relatively large proportion of women.[43] Women played a very minor role in organized "factory" industry, and certainly no "tradition" of women's factory work ever developed in the first century of modern industry's operation.

[41] *Census of India* (1901), VI, p. 83 and (1921), V, 2, pp. 374–376.
[42] R.S. Chandavarkar, *The Origins of Industrial Capitalism in India: Business Strategies and the Working Classes in Bombay, 1900–1940* (Cambridge, 1994).
[43] C.M. Matheson, *Indian Industries – Yesterday, Today and Tomorrow* (Oxford, 1930).

In the case of the jute industry, a predominantly male labour force had in the first instance developed from the character of local labour supply and was then confirmed by the gendered pattern of long-distance migration. Bengal's first jute mill was established in 1855. By the 1880s, jute had become a thriving industry employing about 30,000 workers. In the early years the industry depended on local labour and migrants from Bengal districts. Almost a fifth of its workers were women. Towards the close of the century, men came from Bihar, the United Provinces and Orissa, thus reducing the proportion of women in the workforce. Bengali men were concentrated at the more skilled and higher paid end of the mills, but women's relatively "unskilled" jobs were progressively taken over by migrant men. Women were reduced to about 12 per cent of the workforce.[44]

Jute mill owners made little attempt to interfere in migration or to recruit women. Indian industrial entrepreneurs have been repeatedly evaluated (and usually found wanting) according to the principles of economic rationality that are presumed universally applicable. Less than adequate attention is given to the specificities of their labour strategies. From the beginning and up to the 1970s, one of the chief features of this strategy was a discernible preference for casual and contract labour. Jute mill managers operated with disorganized factor markets and a volatile international market. They were required to maintain high and steady margins of profit in the face of frequent fluctuations in the prices both of raw jute and jute goods. They were not engaged in a relentless quest for ideal standards of competitive production. They preferred casual and manipulable labour, deployable at will and for such short- or long-term periods as suited them, rather than a "settled" and "efficient" workforce.[45]

The industry did not need "individualized" or "proletarianized" workers. Rather, "single" male migrants, who had a buffer in their "rural tie", were best able to provide the casual labour that industry desired. Men, in particular, were preferred because they had control over migration decisions in the household. Generally speaking, familial ideology determined the organization of work according to gender and age. There was no need to "free" labour from family authority.[46] Instead, male heads of household retained their flexibility in the urban labour market by commanding more intensive work from women for an increasingly lower

[44] Report on an Enquiry into conditions of Labour in the Jute Mill Industry in India, S.R. Deshpande (Delhi, 1946).

[45] Sen, "Women Workers in the Bengal Jute Industry"; R.S. Chandavarkar, The Origins of Indian Capitalism, National Commission on Labour, Report of the Study Group for Jute (Delhi, 1968).

[46] Samita Sen, "Unsettling the Household: Act VI (of 1901) and the Regulation of Women Migrants in Colonial Bengal", in Shahid Amin and Marcel van der Linden (eds), "Peripheral" Labour? Studies in the History of Partial Proletarianization, Supplement 4 of International Review of Social History (1996), pp. 135–156.

allocation of resources. Women's cityward migration followed a different pattern. They left their villages when their rural resources were exhausted – either accompanying their displaced families or alone, having been denied access to household resources because of widowhood, barrenness or unchastity. Such women were less prone to pay periodic visits to the village "home". Even if conventional wisdom has exaggerated their abrogation of the "rural tie", there must have been steep hurdles to the deserted or deserting wife's return to the village. Certainly, most women migrants had fewer rural or household resources to draw on by way of insurance. As a result, they were often more "proletarianized" in the conventional sense than men – a disadvantage in the insecure urban labour market.

It was a sudden acceleration of "single" male migration from neighbouring provinces at the turn of the century that began the process of women's marginalization in the jute industry. In this period their employment did not decline in absolute terms. The first significant retrenchment affecting women came in the 1930s. Enormously high war profits had encouraged a rush of investment, and the depression found the industry tremendously over-extended. Mill owners were forced into a sustained reduction of labour deployment.

But their "rationalization" did not affect the workforce uniformly. Mechanization proved more adverse for women. Installation of new machinery enabled a few men to do jobs that had required many women. By long habit, the assumption that women were unable to handle complex machinery had become a conviction. At a time when the economy was shrinking, male-dominated trade unions were happy to encourage this myth. In this, too, the jute industry was not exceptional. In the 1920s women, concentrated in reeling and winding in the Bombay cotton textile industry, were threatened by mass retrenchment. These women were able to unionize and resist mill owners. In the jute industry, however, the effects of the 1930s' crisis and subsequent "rationalizations" did not help to consolidate women's interests.

In the jute industry, despite increasing gender segregation, women were not exclusively departmentalized. No task in the jute industry was considered a female preserve or specifically related to perceived "feminine" skills. Women were neither encouraged to settle as in plantations, nor did they work in male-female units as in coal mines. By the 1920s, however, though there was no work in the mills reserved exclusively for women, some work was designated as men's work, as work women could not do. Women, when employed, were strung across a few of the lower paid jobs. Their "horizontal" segregation sometimes also overlapped with "vertical" segregation. As increasingly fewer women were employed, they were given select jobs across the floor where they worked along with men. Their position, as a result, should have been less vulnerable to specific and systematic threat. However, since the labour-intensive tasks done by women, such as feeding, receiving and sewing were susceptible to mechanization, their jobs did become more precarious than men's. At the same time, since their interests were not obviously cohesive in the workplace, it was difficult for women to find a common cause against the fractional challenges posed by employers.

The attack on women's jobs increased in renewed "rationalization" in the 1950s. Employers wanted gradually to eliminate women: they could not be employed in night shifts, they had to be paid maternity benefit and provided with crèche facilities. Trade unions, faced with spiralling male unemployment, were once again susceptible to these arguments.[47] Since direct retrenchment was difficult, early retirements and "natural wastage" replaced women with men. Some women could be persuaded or coerced into giving up their jobs to a son.[48] Women workers found it difficult to resist the combined onslaught of the family, the unions and the employers. A survey of the National Jute Mill in the 1970s found 2.6 per cent of women in a workforce of 16,386. Almost half of even these women were casual workers.[49]

The periodic changes and sectoral shifts in women's industrial employment can only be understood in the context of wider perceptions of gender that operate within the labour market. Employers draw on varying characterizations of women to sustain their strategies. This can be seen as of the late nineteenth century, when the state began to legislate on employment conditions to "protect" women and children. Government officials, middle-class philanthropists and trade unions, in their zeal to protect the "family" and ensure "family wages", continually emphasized the "supplementary" nature of women's earnings.[50] When employers were faced with buoyant markets and shortage of labour, they countered these with arguments about the need for women's contribution to the household budget. In the 1920s and 1930s, faced with increasingly expensive "protective" legislation, the need to "rationalize" and cut back on labour, they encouraged these stereotypes. Managers argued that there was no point in increasing women's wages or paying maternity benefit because the money was bound to be handed over to a male "protector".[51]

---

[47] Arjan de Haan, "Towards a Single Male Earner: The Decline of Child and Female Employment in an Indian Industry', *Economic and Social History in the Netherlands*, 6 (1994), pp. 145–167.

[48] Interviews, Manager, Bally Jute Mill, September 1989; Personnel Manager, Fort Gloster Jute Mill, August-September 1989.

[49] Sisir Mitra, "The Jute Workers: A Micro Profile", Centre for Regional, Ecological and Science Studies in Development Alternatives (Calcutta, 1981).

[50] "[T]he reason advanced in support of [lower wages for women] has been that while owing to the universality of marriage and the joint family system men have to support a large number of dependents, women workers [. . .] have not to support even themselves fully": S.G. Panandikar, *Industrial Labour in India* (Bombay, 1933), p. 187.

[51] Curjel, D.F., Report of Dr Dagmar Curjel on the conditions of Employment of Women Before and After Childbirth, 1923, unpublished, West Bengal State Archives, Calcutta,

The desirability of a male breadwinner was the basis of "family wage" arguments. An article in *Amrita Bazar Patrika* stated, "millions of bread-winners, men, and women and children are sweated and fleeced off their pitiful wages which are reduced almost to a vanishing point [. . .] How can a man burdened with a family maintain himself on Rs. 10 or 12 a month?"[52] R.N. Gilchrist, government labour officer, suggested to the Indian Jute Mills Association (IJMA), "The incentives to women's work should also be lessened, for the women would be well occupied in the home and in the plot". This was offered as one means of reducing the unemployment problem and avoiding payment of unemployment insurance. Gilchrist suggested,

In respect of both income and expenditure it is the family and not the individual that is important in relation to the standard of living [. . .] It is impossible under the present standards of earnings for the men to be considered the "rice-winner" of the family. The women must go out to work also [. . .] From all parts of India evidence is forthcoming that it was necessity which drove women to work in the mills and mines [. . .][53]

Such existing perceptions of gender influenced employers. These employers also used arguments about women's housework and childcare responsibilities, their physical weakness, their "lack of commitment" to non-familial work and their inability to handle machinery to sustain hierarchies of skills and wages. Thus, employers reinscribed gender hierarchies.

Gender-ghettos became entrenched through personalized and informal recruitment. The role of *sardars* and jobbers in direct recruitment has been repeatedly stressed. While such intermediaries were indeed key players in ensuring labour supply and maintaining labour control, recruitment was usually through myriad social networks based on kin, caste and regional affiliations. This "system" became the norm in large-scale industries at the end of the nineteenth century and remains so even now.[54] For the urban poor, such "ties" played a role in providing access to crucial urban resources: jobs, credit and housing. However, two other significant factors played a role. First, male supervisors' notions of what kind of work was appropriate for women influenced the pattern of their employment. Male values of segregation and male workers' interest in retaining control and use of women's sexuality and labour were written into the hiring practices. Moreover, the supervisors and clerks could extract sexual favours from women in return for access to jobs, which increased the opprobrium of factory work for women and ensured their withdrawal from such jobs

Commerce Department Commerce Branch, April 1923, B77 [hereafter *Curjel Report*], Appendix B, Sl. Nos 7 and 15.
[52] "Politics and Labour", *Amrita Bazar Patrika*, 4 April 1928.
[53] R.N. Gilchrist, *Labour and Land* (Calcutta, 1932).
[54] B. Foley, *Report on Labour in Bengal* (Calcutta, 1905); Mitra, "The Jute Workers". For the Bombay case see Chandavarkar, *The Origins of Industrial Capitalism*.

when higher male earnings allowed them to do so. Second, women rarely had scope for upward mobility: they could neither expect promotion within their own jobs nor shift to other more lucrative jobs.

The better-paid male workers used the informal recruitment system effectively to exclude women from the more prized jobs (such as weaving and spinning in jute and cotton mills). Possibly they feared that the introduction of women would threaten their ability to maintain high wage levels. But why did weavers and spinners not use their "personal" channels to recruit their own mothers, wives, daughters or sisters in well-paid jobs thereby augmenting their household resources? Their "nepotism" was extended to brothers, sons, nephews or fellow villagers rather than to female kin. Obviously, the few who might have desired better incomes for their women relatives were unable to contravene established rules of gender segregation. So, weaving jobs went to male protégés while wives and daughters were given jobs in preparing or finishing. In part, this reflected the preference for male rather than female earners in the family. The better-paid workers were better able to maintain non-earning adult female relatives, and often did so. To have wives living in various modified forms of seclusion and domesticity in the city signalled higher social status, and this prompted better-paid workers to bring their wives to the city. In turn such practices contributed to the clustering of women at the lower rungs of the job ladder. Since their "own women" did not work, the better-paid workers had no obvious interest in promoting women for better jobs.

The employers' arguments about skill, the lower wages they paid to women and their emphasis on domesticity and motherhood enhanced women's marginalization in industry. Employers argued that women married young and they came to work too late for requisite apprenticeship. The demands of housework and childcare hampered women's "career" commitment. Moreover, women had to be apprenticed to men workers, an arrangement not acceptable to either. None of these arguments adequately explains the progressive characterization of women as "unskilled". In jute mills, for instance, the classification of tasks as "unskilled" often bore little relation to the actual amount of training or ability required. Skill definitions were saturated with gender and age perceptions. The work of women and children, usually lumped together, was deemed inferior precisely because it was women and children who did it, rather than because of any intrinsic quality in the work itself. Women and children carried into the workplace their socially subordinate status which served to define the value of their work. Far from being an objective economic fact, calculable from investment or productivity, skill was an ideological category imposed on certain kinds of work by virtue of the social subordination of the workers who undertook them. In turn, the encapsulation of gender and power in the way the notion of "skill" was applied, confirmed, perpetuated and even intensified the marginalization of women's and children's work.

GENDER IDEOLOGIES: THE HOUSEWIFE AND THE MALE PROTECTOR

Employers drew on current gender perceptions shared by the state, the middle classes, male and often even female workers. The gendering of the organized industrial workforce can, therefore, only be appreciated in the context of a wider social phenomenon: the relevance of gender in mediating class identity.

The key to this process was a growing emphasis on marriage. A preference for cheap and malleable labour led employers to recruit young and unmarried women in many areas of Europe, America, China and Japan. South-east Asian development in the 1970s was also heavily dependent on the "feminization" of industrial labour. In India, this strategy has never been of significance. Even in the 1950s, the average age of marriage among the working classes was 7–11 for women.[55] Available single women were widows who constituted about 20 per cent of the female population in Bengal at the turn of the century. But these women were burdened by housework and childcare.[56] Nirmala Banerjee has shown that women's workforce participation peaked after the age of 35 when they were already married and had children.[57]

From the early nineteenth century, a heterogenous range of marriage and cohabitation practices were brought under the scrutiny of the state. Through legislative and institutional means, an attempt was made to impose a singular definition of marriage derived from high-caste Hindu and upper-class Muslim customs. The regulation of marriage was relevant on several counts.

In pre-colonial India, family was the vehicle for the quotidian application of labour where division of labour was based on gender and age, and control over the processes of production was vested in the male head of the family. In colonial India, family continued to play a crucial role in deployment of labour. The informal and casual recruitment practices of industrial employers reinforced the role of family, even in cases where labour was required in greater quantities as in the very large-scale and long-distance migrations to Assam and overseas colonies.[58] But the "pre-capitalist" family could not just be made over to the new needs of colonial capitalism.

It was the supposed immunity of the family from legal regulation that made its labour arrangements more coercive and exploitative. From 1857 the colonial state explicitly abandoned the project of "civilizing" the "pri-

---

[55] *Social and Economic Status of Women Workers in India* (New Delhi, 1953).
[56] *Report on the Census of the Town and Suburbs of Calcutta* (1881), II, p. 50.
[57] Nirmala Banerjee, "Poverty, Work and Gender in Urban India", Occasional Paper No. 133, Centre for Studies in Social Sciences (Calcutta, May 1992).
[58] M.R. Anderson, "Work Construed: Ideological Origins of Labour Law in British India to 1918", in Peter Robb (ed.), *Dalit Movements and the Meaning of Labour in India* (New Delhi, 1993), pp. 87–120.

vate" domain of Indian family. A deviation from this policy, as in the case of the Age of Consent Bill (1891) raised a storm of controversy. But legislative interventions in the direction of Brahminical orthodoxy were not ruled out and indeed happened relatively quietly. Colonial laws repeatedly interceded to elevate the powers of the male head of the family.[59] The role of the paterfamilias was elevated to new heights. Indeed, through the regulation of inheritance and marriage laws, familial control over women's bodies – their labour and their sexuality – was considerably enhanced. Women's ability to resist coercive extraction of labour was reduced. Women were denied the right to escape unhappy or oppressive marriages by flight, divorce or migration. To this end the state appealed, at convenience, to either the contractual or the sacramental understandings of marriage.[60]

Increasingly, from the nineteenth century, a variety of elite discourses delineated marriage and the containment of women as the crucial marks of status. The organization of marriage, motherhood and domesticity and the way these were defined for women became the key, not only to the reproduction of class identity, but also to the quotidian maintenance of class barriers. The separation of the poor and the middle classes became overlaid with distinctions of high and low culture, moral purity and laxity, order and lawlessness. A specific characterization of gender relations was central to such distinctions. The upper castes (usually also upper and middle classes) upheld the sanctity of lifelong female monogamy and the chaste, modest and secluded demeanour of elite women. The home was marked out as women's only proper domain, homemaking and childrearing their only legitimate concerns.

An idealized femininity became further enmeshed in nationalist discourses. These drew on an amalgam of the Victorian "angel of the hearth" ideology and on existing Brahminical standards of women's chastity, segregation and seclusion. The home was the locus of the nation, children its future citizens. Women were the custodians of these two vital national resources. Not only were they charged with a sacred duty; their only possibility of fulfilment lay in the performance of these duties. This reified notion of domesticity became increasingly crucial to characterizations of women and their work. Domestic tasks, subsumed within definitions of femininity, were stripped of their labour content and denuded of their economic value for the household. The physical and social invisibility of elite women's work further denigrated women's remunerated work. However, the effectiveness of the ideology of domesticity as a mark of status lay not in preventing poor women from working, but in promoting

---

[59] Bernard S. Cohn, "Law and Colonial State in India", in J. Starr and J.F. Collier (eds), *History and Power in the Study of Law* (Ithaca, 1989).
[60] Sen, "Unsettling the Household".

the claims of middle-class women to the highly valued domain of exclusive housewifery and childcare.

The "domestication" of elite women in the nineteenth century affected women across various sections and classes. Women's labour was co-opted within "family" economic activity whether in agriculture, manufacturing or trade. Their other occupations were intermittent, often paid in kind and with very little exchange value. The products of women's activities were either directly consumed in the household or regarded as secondary contributions to the family's economic activity. All these activities became extended "housework". The wives of men who migrated to the city found even their paid work subordinated to the cash remittances of the men.

Elite women, too, suffered relative devaluation of their contribution to the household. Middle-class women began to lose direct access to resources – especially food – and their new "domestic" activities were dependent on men's cash earnings. They cooked, cleaned, decorated, learned to maintain household accounts, supervised domestic servants and the education of children. But in all these cases, the resources came from men: food and decorative material had to be bought in the market, education and domestic servants had to be paid in cash. In the village and in the city, access to sources of cash was becoming crucial. The men earned the cash in wage, salary, rent or profit. Their women found significant portions of their labour subsumed within domesticity. Consequently, women's productive role was marginalized and their labour devalued.

But the ideal of domesticity strained against reality. Middle-class male reformers advocated women's education in response to colonial criticism of the low status of Indian women. They pleaded their cause on broad liberal humanitarian grounds, but usually found the need to "train" good wives and mothers a better sell.[61] Within a few decades, however, from the end of the nineteenth century, educated women began to aspire towards professional employment as doctors and teachers. The logic of a gender-segregated culture helped. Women doctors and teachers were required for women patients and students. Moreover, in the case of widowed women or those otherwise denied access to familial resources, access to remunerative work was vital. Middle-class women's employment gathered momentum in the 1930s with rising educated male unemployment. Married women joined widows in a range of formal and informal wage earning. The 1950s opened the floodgates. Between 1951 and 1961, women's participation in educational, scientific, medical and health services more than doubled from 200,000 to 459,000.[62] The partition and the influx of

[61] Women's own writings on the subject are analysed in Himani Banerjee, "Fashioning a Self: Educational Proposals for and by Women in Popular Magazines in Colonial Bengal", *Economic and Political Weekly* (October 1991), pp. WS51–62.

[62] Sinha, *The Indian Working Force*, p. 115.

refugees from East to West Bengal helped familiarize the presence of women across a wide variety of professional and service employment.[63]

The ideal, however strained, also proved remarkably adaptable. The economic compulsions behind women's work and the requirements of family survival allowed an expansion of the concept of the *samsar* (typically, household). So long as a woman justified her waged employment in terms of "need of the family" her commitment remained basically directed towards the home and family.[64] An anonymous article in one of the longest running women's Bengali journals articulated the extension of the household into waged work thus:

if the earning husband falls ill, will women stay crying by their bedside? That day, if necessary, the woman will leave her home to earn money, will stand in the workplace with hundreds and thousands of other men and women. If the husband is weak and the son dead, will the land not be tilled? Will she stand by the door starving with tears in her eyes? [. . .] Today we need women who combine womanliness and *shakti*.[65]

In this way, the concept of *samsar* could be expanded beyond the home. This flexibility strengthened the ideology of domesticity; it became more ubiquitous and almost inescapable. An exceptional economic need, especially that of the family, became the only acceptable justification for women's work across classes and communities. It then became easier to co-opt and appropriate women's waged work within the familial context. As a result, women's ability to wrest any degree of autonomy on the basis of their cash earnings was severely circumscribed. The potential conflict between domesticity and paid employment was resolved to a degree, and the familial control of men over women retained.

Poor women, meanwhile, have to bear the double burden of domestic and paid work. Some women, not surprisingly, prefer to shed a part of their workload. Since domestic work is unavoidable, when they can afford it they choose not to work for wages. For the middle-class observer this is an affirmation of the ideology of domesticity. In a sense they are correct. Working-class women are engaged in ill-paid jobs in poor conditions, most of which are considered demeaning. Since poor (usually also low-caste) women cannot aspire to the "respectable" professions, their aspirations concentrate on domesticity which alone can confer a degree of status to working-class families. Besides most women enjoy little control over their earnings. The majority hand them over to the male "head" of

[63] The image of the working woman became a powerful literary and cinematic device in the 1960s. Satyajit Ray's "Mahanagar" and Ritwik Ghatak's "Meghe Dhaka Tara" are two outstanding examples of the sensitive problematization of this issue.

[64] Mary Higdon Beech, "The Domestic Realm in the Lives of Hindu Women in Calcutta", in Hanna Papanek and Gail Minault (eds), *Separate Worlds: Studies of Purdah in South Asia* (Delhi, 1982), p. 131.

[65] Adarsha Ramani, *Bamabodhini Patrika*, 10 (1913), p. 301.

the household. Their wages, more than men's, are swallowed up in the family budget. They are rarely allowed (or even allow themselves) the luxuries of alcohol or tobacco.[66] Thus women prefer to remain confined to the household when male earnings make this possible. The men in the family are equally eager, when earnings permit, to withdraw women from factory work.

The nature of the work available to poor women – its monotony and its physical demands exacerbated by sexual harassment – tends to push them further into the family. Paradoxically, this trend is reinforced by the difference in the earning potential between husband and wife, but also results in furthering this difference by directing women towards even lower paid home-based work.[67] The 1970s survey of a jute mill reveals that an overwhelming majority of women workers were from the lowest castes and 70 per cent of these women workers believe factory work to be unsuited to women. They preferred "home-based self-employment" as in sewing. This response did not vary by level of income.[68]

For all these women, aspirations for a daughter or a daughter-in-law specifically excluded jute mill employment. Rather, marriage to a man who could afford to keep them out of the mills was more desirable. These attitudes were not universal, but women who preferred to continue to work, rather than hand over their jobs to sons on whose wages they thereafter became dependent, often found it impossible to withstand the combined onslaught of the management and the family. It is, then, not particularly surprising that researchers in the field find "the decline of female labour was not seen as something entirely negative".[69]

In the case of "traditional" industries like jute this trend is particularly noticeable because organized trade union politics has led to significant improvement in workers' wages. Male factory workers can now aspire to upward mobility: education for their sons and dowry marriages for their daughters. The withdrawal of wives from factory work is usually the first step in such a progression. But these confirmations of the domestic ideal create more difficulties for the women who do work in factories – and these women are quite often the primary earners in their family, if not virtually heading the household. It is notable that in the 1890s, women workers told a Commission that only "widowed" women and similar "unfortunates" work in jute mills for this was not considered "respectable".[70] Throughout the 1920s and 1930s observers commented on the

---

[66] Matheson, *Indian Industries*, Appendix II; *Social and Economic Status of Women Workers*, pp. 14–17.

[67] The wife consistently earned less than her husband, but contributed one-third of family income and her job was steadier: Beech, "The Domestic Realm in the Lives of Hindu Women".

[68] Mitra, "The Jute Workers".

[69] De Haan, "Towards a Single Earner", p. 160; *National Commission*, Study Group for Jute.

[70] *Report of the Indian Factory Commission* (Calcutta, 1891).

predominance of "single" women in the factories. These women were "single" not because they lived alone, but because they lived with men "who were not their husbands". The perception that such women were in immoral "temporary" marriages, if not outright "prostitutes" coloured attitudes towards women's work in factories, mills and other urban occupations.[71] The National Jute Mills survey found that more than half the women workers were the sole earners in their family. Usually these women were "single" with children and other dependents to support. Since women's average earnings were lower, it is not surprising that the survey found women-headed households to be poorer on average. But women in these families had a greater say in household decisions and in the allocation of resources. Of the women workers who were not "single", half were "forced" into mill work by the husband's loss of employment. These women were not considered the "head" of their families and were required to hand over their earnings to their husbands. It is not surprising that no women workers considered mill work "suitable" for women and most endorsed the role of the "housewife" as the most desirable for their daughters, even though the price for such desired marriages often crippled poor families.[72] The spiralling of dowry demands among the urban poor was noted by K.P. Chattopadhyay in his comprehensive survey in the 1940s.[73] It is now so obvious as to render "survey" irrelevant. Women interviewed have seen, in their lifetime, the change from "no payment" or brideprice marriages to dowry marriages. These women, who worked in the mill after their marriage, were given a few utensils and a few sarees at their marriages, but they pay cash, jewellery and other consumer items, such as bicycles and watches, to marry off their daughters and granddaughters in the hope that they, at least, will not have the misfortune of having to work in the mills. Basmatia, who bitterly watched her retirement benefit go up in the smoke of the sacramental fire at her granddaughter's marriage, remarked,

Now you have to give so many things – money, furniture [. . .] Earlier this was not there. At my daughter's wedding I gave five utensils and the money she got as presents from family, nothing else [. . .] At my wedding there was nothing.[74]

The Indian woman worker is usually already a wife and mother when she enters the labour market. She has rarely had even a brief spell in her life cycle when she can aspire towards some autonomy. Even most young middle-class working women find "autonomy" elusive. Paradoxically,

[71] *Report of the Royal Commission on Labour in India*, I, V and XI (London, 1931). Margaret Read was a member of this commission. She wrote three books which reflect such perceptions: *Indian Peasant Uprooted* (London, 1931); *From Field to Factory* (London, 1927); *Land and Life of India* (London, 1934).
[72] Mitra, "The Jute Workers".
[73] K.P. Chattopadhyay, *A Socio-Economic Survey of Jute Labour* (Calcutta, 1952).
[74] Interview, Titagarh No. 2 Mill, February 1989.

though women in India are increasingly divided by class and caste, their experiences of these differences remain interdependent. In one sense, the ideologies that underlie their differentiated conditions and shape their diverging experiences are bound in some common hierarchic norms. While in many effective ways, the interrelationship of work and domesticity is being worked out in distinctly different directions for middle-class and working-class women, a pervasive "value" of dependence continues to inhere in definitions of Indian femininity.

CONCLUSION

Women in Bengal were faced with a very different process of industrialization to the one commonly generalized on the basis of European experience. There was no significant separation of production and the household. Factories took men away to the city but left women and children to make a livelihood from the family farm, craft, general labour, foraging and gathering activities. Men's migration enhanced women's involvement in the family's ongoing economic activity. Moreover, industrialization itself was highly enclaved and the majority of Indian workers – men and women – were engaged at a range of informal employment in both rural and urban sectors.

Nevertheless, a gradually pervasive ideology of the male breadwinner emerged in South Asia. Women's economic activities were intermittent, casual and poorly rewarded in comparison with men's. The ownership of capital, assets and tools was vested in men. Migration enhanced already existing wage differentials. Domesticity co-opted large areas of women's work, divesting their work of economic value. Taken together, these factors prompted an implicit and explicit devaluation of women's contribution to the household's maintenance. And this was despite the continuing importance of the family-household economic activity as in the case of the family farm.

Women's contributions were made invisible by the entrenchment of husbands' and fathers' ownership of the labour of their wives and daughters. By extension, South Asian capitalist development became predicated upon familial deployment of labour rather than upon a labour market augmented by young men and women "free" from familial control. Women's family roles included productive and subsistence activities and these took precedence over industrial and plantation capital's demand for cheap female labour. As a result, women did not provide the kind of flexible labour that capitalist employers ideally preferred. Rather, family ideology helped men to acquire greater flexibility through the manipulation of women's and children's labour. Married women – most women entering the labour market were married – "supplemented" male earnings. They entered the labour market on unfavourable terms when a downswing in the economy suspended or reduced men's earnings, they withdrew when employment conditions improved and men were able to "win the bread". Thus the flexible deployment of women's labour benefited the men in the family. Although at times this also benefited the employer by providing him with cheaper female labour, changes in the nature and content of women's work tended to take place in direct response to the changing needs of the men in the family rather than to employers' demands. On the whole, women operated at a remove from the emerging "modern" sectors and the urban labour market which helped entrench the notion of the male provider.

Breadwinning Patterns and Family Exogenous Factors: Workers at the Tobacco Factory of Seville During the Industrialization Process, 1887–1945[1]

LINA GÁLVEZ-MUÑOZ

"TO BE A HUSBAND OF A *CIGARRERA* WAS A PROFESSION"[2]

The organization of production by employers was not indifferent to gender.[3] Labour markets were sexually differentiated,[4] since women and men were considered to be distinct labour forces distinguished by virtue of the differing roles they were supposed to play. The male role was that of the breadwinner, and the fact that this often reflected the reality of the situation should not obscure the point that it was a social construction. Women, on the other hand, were considered as mostly occupied with unpaid domestic work, regardless of whether they were also engaged in work for the market. Breadwinning patterns have been widely debated, particularly with respect to whether the male breadwinner system appeared as a result of industrialization or existed previously as a consequence of a universal system of patriarchy. In parallel with a more cyclical conception of industrialization, recent studies on breadwinner patterns[5] do not support theories based on capitalism or patriarchy but rather support a more historical approach based on the

---

[1] I would like to thank Olwen Hufton, Angélique Janssens, William R. Day Jr, Lavan Mahadeva, Susana García Cerveró and Alfredo Huertas-Rubio.
[2] Interview with J.L.B., retired labour inspector, January 1995.
[3] Recent studies concerning different periods and economic sectors show how employers used different methods depending on the gender of the workers they could hire. E. Jordan's study of the exclusion of women from industries in nineteenth-century Britain is very revealing: "The Exclusion of Women from Industry in Nineteenth-Century Britain", *Comparative Studies in Society and History*, 31 (1989), pp. 273–296. Actually, employers imposed part-time working only when they could hire women. See S. Walby, *Patriarchy at Work* (Cambridge, 1986) and V. Beechey and T. Perkins, *A Matter of Hours. Women, Part-time work and the Labour Market* (Cambridge, 1987).
[4] J. Burnette, "Testing for Occupational Crowding in Eighteenth Century British Agriculture", *Explorations in Economic History*, 33 (1996), pp. 319–345, examining occupational crowding in eighteenth-century British agriculture, demonstrates that men and women were interchangeable in the unskilled workforce. "If the agricultural labour market was not characterized by occupational crowding, this tells us something about where discrimination was located. Gender discrimination originated, not in the competitive market, but in other institutions such as the family, the law, and distributional coalitions" (p. 341). Nevertheless, even if men and women were seen as different labour forces because of differences in productivity rates, it is necessary to study the interaction between the market and the family in order to understand market and family gender differences.
[5] For a reappraisal, see C. Creighton, "The Rise of the Male Breadwinner Family: A Reappraisal", *Comparative Studies in Society and History*, 38 (1996), pp. 310–337.

International Review of Social History 42 (1997), Supplement, pp. 87–128

importance of other exogenous factors[6] such as the regional economy, the local labour market and the customs and associations acting upon it, employers' choices or the legal and institutional framework. The following paper is a case study related to working-class women, the *cigarreras*, who were the main wage earners in the family. It relates to an industry (tobacco) which operated under a monopoly system, and to a particular region (southern Spain), which was fairly underdeveloped in terms of industry. This paper examines from a micro-perspective the universality of patriarchal breadwinner patterns, the discontinuity of the industrialization process, and the importance of other exogenous factors in explaining patterns of bread-winning. *It asks whether changing exogenous factors during the industrialization process make it possible for a female breadwinner and male house-husband model to arise.*

The male breadwinner family was itself a social construct requiring historical explanation. Studies of pre-industrial families, micro-analysis on a comparative basis, and the consideration of alternative sources[7] have emphasized the diversity of routes and outcomes of the male breadwinner family. The choice of a micro-analysis approach to the issue of breadwinning patterns is due to the fact that this type of approach facilitates discussion of a broad range of explanatory factors.[8] Nevertheless, the introduction of such a wide range of factors is not sufficient in itself to explain the interrelationship between the family and the market. It is necessary to study female and male employment rates from the same perspective. Recent studies have demonstrated in particular the importance of the local labour market in explaining female participation. Other elements such as income effects from the husband's earnings, the family life cycle, and institutional constraints have still remained important variables explaining

---

[6] Exogenous factors means factors outside the family economy and outside the family decision-making processes. Although capitalism, as a particular social and economic structure in society, and patriarchy, as a system of values structures and relations, are also family exogenous factors, this paper will name as exogenous factors other factors. These reveal a higher degree of heterogeneity in space and time, such as the regional economy, local labour market, employer's choices, laws, institutions, customs and culture.

[7] The studies by N. Folbre, "Patriarchy in Colonial New England", *The Review of Radical Political Economics*, 12 (1980), pp. 4–75, and C. Sarasúa, "The Rise of the Wage Worker. Peasant Families and the Organization of Work in Modern Spain" (Ph.D., European University Institute, 1995), are especially interesting on pre-industrial family economies. The convenience of using alternative sources is clear in the results obtained by S. Horrell and J. Humphries, "Women's Labour Force Participation and the Transition to the Male-Breadwinner Family, 1790–1865", *Economic History Review*, XLVIII (1995), pp. 89–117, and the contribution by the same authors in this volume.

[8] Creighton has recently voiced the following criticism: "while the increasing diversity of approaches has highlighted a wider range of factors relevant to the problem, we are in many ways further than ever from achieving their integration into a coherent whole. Each account has focused on a narrow range of determinants and has attributed excessive importance to their consequences" (Creighton, "The Rise of the Male Breadwinner Family", p. 333).

women's behaviour. Oddly, however, the same set of variables has not been used to advance an explanation of male participation rates in the labour market. Evidently, the idea that male occupations could be influenced by the wife's employment has not been contemplated, nor has the idea of concentration in particular jobs available in the local labour market and not in others. In most cases, the wife's job will not have been the principal source of household income, but it should not be taken for granted that this was always the case. It is necessary to distinguish among working-class women and to de-aggregate the "statistical category" of women and children. Only by studying women and men from the same perspective is it possible to understand the interrelationship between the family and the market in explaining breadwinning patterns. The *cigarreras* were skilled workers who continued in the workplace until old age and in most cases had the most important job in the family. This fact, in addition to the structure of the local labour market and the set of exogenous factors, conditioned the labour participation rates of the remaining family members, including husbands.

A study of the interrelationship between the family and the labour market which takes into account such a large range of different factors is rendered feasible by the diversity of the sources employed. The documentation consists of national and municipal population censuses, industrial municipal censuses, labour department records, newspapers and photographs, literature, oral history, and above all the comprehensive factory records which contain material relating to virtually every aspect of the tobacco market and industry and the management of the factory. Based on personnel records and other factory records found in the *Archivo de la Fábrica de Tabacos de Sevilla* (AFTS), it has been possible to create a database for 3,000 workers. This information has been cross-referenced with the 1924 municipal census for the most important working-class neighbourhood of the town, Triana, in order to facilitate a detailed analysis of family structure and economy. Owing to the deficiencies of the census data, this analysis reveals the necessity of supplementing these sources of information on working-class families with other kinds of material, such as factory records. For example, only 25 per cent of the *cigarreras* identified were registered as *cigarreras* in the census. In addition, a database of 730 families from the Triana neighbourhood has been created in order to study the differences between *cigarreras'* and other working-class families. Further research based mainly on other factory records of a different labour profile will reveal more about the most common census categories of working-class families: "at home" for women and "day-labourer" for men.[9]

---

[9] This analysis was conducted jointly with Eloisa Baena. The tobacco workers database based on factory records and her research on the pottery industry were cross-referenced with municipal censuses of 1900 and 1924.

This article analyses first of all the *cigarreras*' life cycle, with reference mainly to their working conditions and household model in the context of the Seville labour market. Second, it deals with the interrelationship between the family and the market during the industrialization process and the consolidation of the male breadwinner system.

THE *CIGARRERAS* OF SEVILLE: THEIR WORK AND FAMILIES

The *cigarreras*' household model and its interaction with the market can be understood only in relationship to their labour career: continuing in the factory after marriage and throughout life. An examination of the literature shows that the traditional, or more common, profile of the working woman employed in industry (which is to say young and single) was not universal. Women often continued to work more or less regularly provided the labour market offered opportunities for them to do so, whilst childbearing did not always lead to a separation from the labour market.[10] Some women left the market when their children were able to replace them in work and thus supplement the family income,[11] while others never left, as in the case studied here. Despite this diversity, female industrial time normally appears to have been subordinated to family time, and particularly to the timing of major demographic events.[12] As a general rule, women have been traditionally identified with unskilled labour and their work has always been considered subordinate to family time throughout life.[13] The example of the *cigarreras*[14] shows, however, that when women were in

[10] See especially Horrell and Humphries, "Women's Labour Force Participation' about women's labour force participation and Jordan, "The Exclusion of Women" about the exclusion of women from industry in nineteenth-century Britain. M. Barrett, "Reply to Brenner and Ramas", *New Left Review*, 146 (1984), pp. 123–128, and Creighton, "The Rise of the Male Breadwinner Family", criticize the underestimation of alternative arrangements for female biological determinism. J. Norris, " 'Well Fitted for Females'. Women in the Macclesfield Silk Industry", in A. Jowitt and A.J. McIvor (eds), *Employers and Labour in the English Textile Industries, 1850–1939* (London, 1988), pp. 187–202, demonstrates that the employment of married women in the manufacturing areas in which they were most heavily concentrated actually rose in the second half of the nineteenth century.

[11] See the contribution by Sara Horrell and Jane Humphries in this volume.

[12] "If the term 'industrial time' designates the new time schedules and work disciplines imposed by the industrial system, 'family time' refers to the internal and external timing of family behaviour at different stages of individual and family development, particularly to the timing of major demographic events [. . .]": T. Hareven (ed.), *Family and Kin in Urban Communities, 1700–1930* (New York, 1977), p. 189.

[13] For a critical view of the treatment of women's work in economic theory see the compilations made by Alice H. Amsden, *The Economics of Women and Work* (London, 1980) and recently by Jane Humphries (ed.), *Gender and Economics* (Basingstoke, 1995).

[14] Although analyses concerning *cigarreras*' breadwinning patterns in other Spanish factories have not yet been done, the labour conditions were similar, as shown in C. Candela Soto, "Trabajo y organización en la industria del tabaco: las cigarreras madrileñas, 1890–

demand in the labour market, when they were craft workers and breadwinners, and especially when conditions were favourable to the flexible use of time and to childrearing, women could in the long run be as independent of family time as male workers. In the short run, however, it is more difficult to find evidence of men sharing household work in the day-to-day life of the family.

In order to understand the life patterns of the *cigarreras* during the period studied, it is necessary to analyse their working conditions in the context of the financial and market situation of the company, the legal, institutional and cultural framework of the locality, and their household economy model. It is also necessary to study the opportunities offered by the local labour market to the other members of their families, and more especially to their husbands. This part of the analysis endeavours to avoid the reductionism of explaining the working lives of women solely in terms of gender and likewise the working lives of men solely in terms of labour. Careful consideration is therefore given to the active role played by women's occupations in their husbands' choices of occupation. In such a way, it is possible to address the working conditions and life patterns of the *cigarreras* in conjunction with the local labour market and the household economy.

The factory and life pattern

The factory

From the early seventeenth century, Spanish tobacco production was concentrated in Seville under a centralized manufacturing system.[15] In 1637,

1920", *Sociología del trabajo*, 20 (1993–1994), pp. 91–115; E. Baena Luque, *Las cigarreras sevillanas. Un mito en declive. 1887–1923* (Malaga, 1993); C. Valdés Chápuli, *La Fábrica de Tabacos de Alicante* (Alicante, 1989); L. Alonso Alvarez, "De la manufactura a la industria: La Real Fábrica de Tabacos de la Coruña (1804–1857)", *Historia Económica*, 3 (1984), pp. 13–34; and P. Radcliff, "Elite Women Workers and Collective Action: The Cigarette Makers of Gijón, 1890–1930", *Journal of Social History*, 27 (1993/ 1994), pp. 85–108. The model of the female cigar-maker extends beyond the Spanish border, mainly to France and Italy, where the tobacco industries were state-owned and production was carried out by skilled female cigar-makers. For France, see M. Zylberberg-Hocquard, "Les ouvrières d'Etat (Tabacs-Alluments) dans les dernières années du XIXème siècle", *Le mouvement social*, 105 (1978), pp. 87–107, and J.N. Retière, "Une Entreprise d'Etat Séculaire: Les Tabacs l'example de la 'Manu' de Nantes (1857–1914)", *Entreprise et Histoire*, 6 (1995), pp. 109–127. For Italy, see P. Nava, *La fabbrica dell'emancipazione. Operaie della Manifattura Tabacchi di Modena: storie di vita e di lavoro* (Rome, 1986).

[15] On the history of the Spanish tobacco industry, see J. Pérez Vidal, *España en la Historia del Tabaco* (Madrid, 1959); J. García de Torres, *El tabaco: consideraciones sobre el pasado, presente y porvenir de esta renta* (Madrid, 1875); E. Delgado, *La Renta de tabacos* (Madrid, 1892); and J.M. Rodríguez Gordillo, "La Real Fábrica de Tabacos de Sevilla", in idem, *Sevilla y el Tabaco* (Seville, 1984), pp. 68-75, and idem, "Sobre la industria sevillana del tabaco a fines del siglo XVII", *Cuadernos de Historia*, VII (1977),

the state created a fiscal monopoly. By 1887, which is the start of the period covered by this study, the tobacco industry contributed 12 per cent of state revenues[16] and the over 30,000 workers in this industry represented 3 per cent of the Spanish industrial population.[17] At this date, there were ten factories in Spain, most of them created during the nineteenth century as a consequence of expansion and changes in consumption patterns. The Seville factory, the oldest and most important belonging to the state tobacco monopoly, had around 7,000 workers. However, the cost of sustaining the previous rapid growth in production had by this time become very high. The Treasury was unable to invest in modernizing the factories because the state was interested only in fiscal receipts and in avoiding social unrest regarding a necessary labour reconversion. Instead, it decided to lease the management of the tobacco monopoly to a private company, the Compañía Arrendataria de Tabacos (CAT), which could make the capital investment necessary to achieve further large increases in production. This company managed the monopoly from 1887 to 1945. The legacy of state management was a disequilibrium between market demand and supply of the product, and a fully manual production structure dependent on a skilled female labour force. This case study embraces the period during which management was, in effect, privatized, and in which the company was adapting its production and marketing to mechanized production techniques. As a consequence, the company needed a flexible mode of production and a flexible workforce.

The gendered organization of work

The gendered division of labour was well defined in the tobacco factory at Seville. At the end of the nineteenth century, male *tabaqueros* were in charge of the supervision of the factory building, the services inside the plant, the maintenance of the engines and machinery, and the repair and

pp. 533–552. For the importance of the tobacco monopoly to the state, see F. Comín, and P. Martín-Aceña (eds), *Empresa Pública e industrialización en España* (Madrid, 1990); L. Alonso Alvarez, "La modernización de la industria del tabaco en España, 1800–1935", Working paper, Programa de Historia Económica. Fundación Empresa Pública (Madrid, 1993); and idem, "Estrategias empresariales de los monopolios españoles: de la gestión pública a la gestión privada en el estanco del tabaco, 1887–1936", in F. Comín (ed.), *La empresa en la historia de España* (Madrid, 1996), pp. 383–398. For tobacco consumption, see J. Castañeda, *El consumo de tabaco en España y sus factores* (Madrid, 1936).

[16] The percentage that the tobacco monopoly surrendered to ordinary treasury incomes was 13 per cent in 1850, 12 per cent in 1900, 7 per cent in 1935 and 2 per cent in 1970 (F. Comín, "El sector público", in A. Carreras (ed.), *Estadísticas históricas de España, siglos XIX y XX* (Madrid, 1989), pp. 399–460, esp. p. 404. Under its 1887 contract, the CAT had to pay an annual fee of 90 million Pts. Several changes in the contract established a proportional fee to be paid to the Treasury. During the CAT period, this varied from 90 to 95 per cent of tobacco industry incomes.

[17] See Alonso Alvarez, "La modernización de la industria del tabaco".

maintenance of the factory itself. Processes in the production workshops were carried out exclusively by *cigarreras*. In the factory, there were different types of workshops related to the different products, or to the different stages in the production chain. At the same time, there was a technical division of labour inside the workshops. This specialization was one of the modernizing goals of the CAT, which was realized with the increased mechanization of work. Apart from these differences, all the *cigarreras* had specific tobacco manufacturing skills and all of them (except for the *porteras* and *maestras*) worked in groups on piece-work rates.[18] This gave them a great deal of freedom in their working hours, certainly far exceeding that of the *tabaqueros* who had individualized jobs and were paid fixed salaries. During the period studied, the mechanization of the production process resulted in a dramatic change in the composition of the labour force with respect to gender. In 1896, 5,238 *cigarreras* and 99 *tabaqueros* were employed in the factory, but by 1944 the number of *cigarreras* had dropped to 365 while the number of *tabaqueros* had more than doubled to 191. That is to say, throughout the period – and even beyond it – the *tabaqueros* increased in number while the *cigarreras* declined, mainly because no new *cigarreras* were taken on (except during two periods). *Cigarreras* continued to be employed in production workshops and *tabaqueros* in all areas of work relating to the maintenance of the machines and of the factory itself. The change in the proportion of male to female in the factory was related to a change in capital accumulation and intensification. As shown below, it brought important changes in the *cigarreras'* family labour strategies and household economy model.

Life cycle

Under CAT management, the average duration of employment of *tabaqueros* in the factory was 15 years, while that of the *cigarreras* was 48 years.[19] The duration of the working life and the natural life of the *cigarre-*

---

[18] The organization was the same in all workshops: between six and ten *cigarreras* worked around a table called a *rancho*, directed by an *ama de rancho* who was charged with the distribution of tobacco, tasks and wages, and the maintenance of order and cleanliness on the *rancho*. A number of ranchos made up a *taller*, a workshop, directed by the *maestra*, who was the major authority in the workshop, having sole responsibility for the supervision of production and order. She also had to report the functioning and performance of the workshop to the head of the factory. The oldest maestras became *porteras*, who sat at the entrance of each workshop to register all comings and goings and to inspect all workers leaving the factory to prevent the theft of tobacco.

[19] H.M. Boot, "How Skilled were Lancashire Cotton Factory Workers in 1833?", *Economic History Review*, XLVIII (1995), pp. 283–303, in his estimation of Lancashire cotton factory workers' lifetime earning profiles, subtracted for female workers 7.5 years for childbearing and six months lost through sickness, leaving a working life of 23 years working compared with 35 years for males. For the *cigarreras*, it is necessary to subtract from 48 years, the 18 per cent average absenteeism during this period; the new average working life in terms of earning is then 39 years.

Table 1a. *Average length of the services by marital and family status of* cigarreras

Status	Average years	Sample size
Married	45	462
Single	47	164
Widow	38	5
Married-widow(1)	55	299
Head of household	55	26
Dependent	50	47

(1) Married-widow must be distinguished from those who were already widows when they were hired.

ras were almost identical (Table 1a). Most of them entered the factory as girls and continued there until retirement or death. The majority of vacancies in the factory were due to deaths or transfer to the *Faenas auxiliares* workshop, a euphemism for retirement. Under CAT management, women were not taken on before the age of sixteen and recruitment was concentrated in two periods. As a consequence, the average duration of the *cigarreras'* working lives become shorter. In fact, the recruitment period seems to have been the most important factor determining the average span of a *cigarrera's* working life (see Table 1b). Even if further estimations need to be done in order to establish which variables are relevant in explaining the length of service of *cigarreras* in the factory, a set of simple regressions has been run. First, the dependent variable "years worked in the factory" has been regressed out for each of the regressors separately: husband's profession, literacy, and CAT hiring policy (model 1, model 2 and model 3).[20] Only CAT hiring policy appears to play a role in explaining the variable of interest. Furthermore, R-square values suggest an extremely poor explanatory power of the other two regressors. Second, in another simple exercise, the dependent variable has been regressed with all the regressors at the same time (model 4). As expected, the results confirmed the previous conclusions: the labour policy of the firm seemed to be the sole determinant of the years spent in the factory by the *cigarreras*. Again, both R-square and T values point to a high level of significance. The evidence suggests that the factory's criteria for the recruitment of skilled labour were not related to school attendance, and that a permanent tenure was determined more by the specific skills of the *cigarreras*. There is a positive correlation between the professional category and the years spent in the factory: more responsibility and higher wages mean a longer duration of employment. The average duration was 25 years for *barrenderas* (sweepers), 47 for *cigarreras*, 56 for *amas de rancho*, and 64 for *maestras*, who finished their days working as *porteras* sitting in a chair at the door of the workshop.

[20] See Table 1b for an explanation on how they were constructed.

Table 1b. Cigarreras' *length of service*

	Model 1		Model 2		Model 3		Model 4			
	Constant	Husband's profession	Constant	Literacy	Constant	Hiring policy	Constant	Husband's profession	Literacy	Hiring policy
	3.402	0.032	3.746	0.038	4.571	-0.617	4.221	-0.006	-0.064	-0.761
s.d.	(0.082)	(0.029)	(0.213)	(0.131)	(0.061)	(0.030)	(0.060)	(0.017)	(0.087)	(0.076)
t-ratio	41.371	1.086	17.578	0.293	73.869	-20.109	70.889	-0.360	-0.735	-10.006
R-square	0.010		0.001		0.770		0.596			
Adj R-square	0.001		-0.013		0.768		0.578			
F-ratio	1.180		0.086		404.388		33.443			
Signif. F-ratio (at 5%)	0.280		0.771		0.000		0.000			

Sample size: 400 obs.

Husband's profession: This variable captures the relative value of the *cigarreras'* husbands' professions. In ascendant order to the different jobs the following values were attached: Dependents (Handicapped, ill, retired) – 0; Type C (Day-labourers) – 1; Type B (Semi-skilled industrial workers, *tabaqueros* and service sector) – 2; Type A (Artisans and skilled workers) – 3.

Literacy: This variable takes value 1 when *cigarrera* is literate, and value 2 in the case when she is not literate.

Hiring policy: The entry year has been indexed by three different digits, depending on the factory hiring policy. For those who were hired before the CAT management (before 1887) the index takes value 1; for those who were hired for the semi-mechanical workshops (from 1909 to 1912 included), the index takes value 2; and finally for those hired for the mechanical workshops (from 1922 to 1925 included), the index takes value 3. Entry period = 1 (if entry before 1887; 2 (if entry from 1909 to 1912, both included); 3 (if entry from 1922 to 1925, both included).

Apart from the monopolistic structure of the firm, there are two main sets of reasons explaining why the CAT continued to practise lifetime employment of these workers even while it was modernizing the company. The first relates to labour considerations and the flexibility needed by the company during the mechanization process; the second is political, relating to historical links between the factory and the town, and the state connection.

In so far as the labour considerations are concerned, it was significant that the *cigarreras* were skilled workers. When production was based on manual tasks, they controlled production and the apprenticeship system. During the transition from a manual to a mechanized system, the company did not want to introduce any new workers in the manual workshop. New *cigarreras* were only employed in the mechanized workshops. The factory nevertheless retained the old *cigarreras* in the manual workshops, first because manual production was still important and second, in order to allow for possible consumer preferences for manually produced cigars and cigarettes, which might necessitate the training of new workers in manual techniques. Also, in the context of their skills and the transitional period, the existence of highly suitable workshops made it possible to transfer workers between different workshops, depending on the production needs. Finally, the factory continued to have a demand for the work of elderly *cigarreras* in the *desvenados* (stemmers) workshops,[21] where tasks were relatively easy and less well paid. One of the main managerial strategies was to transfer elderly *cigarreras* to more menial tasks, complementing mechanized workshop production. In order to employ the elderly workers, the *Faenas auxiliares* workshop was created in the Seville tobacco factory in 1905. This workshop was a sort of "nursing home" where old or handicapped *cigarreras* could be sent to perform auxiliary tasks such as the sewing of sacks. From the 1920s, however, this workshop ceased to exist physically in the factory and the term began to be used as a euphemism for retirement, which was still not regulated.

The second set of reasons concerning the continued employment of *cigarreras* relate to the difficulties that the factory encountered in its efforts to displace them. The Seville tobacco factory played an important socio-economic and political role in the city. Because the factory was a state-owned enterprise, it also constituted a link between the government

[21] In the tobacco factory at Seville there were four different types of workshops. The base-workshop was the *desvenado* where the "stemmers" stripped away the midrib of the leaf, leaving the tobacco for the *picaduras* (cut tobacco) and cigarette workshops. It was an unskilled task and for this reason the *cigarreras* who worked in this workshop were the old ones who had lost their ability to make cigars or cigarettes. The other workshops were the *picaduras*, cigarettes and cigars. The cigar workshop was the place where the most skilled *cigarreras* were employed, because cigar-making was a very complicated and specialized task.

and the local elite, which continuously practised a procedure based on *references* trying to send workers to the factory.[22] For this reason, labour measures in the factory always attracted a great deal of attention from both local government and public opinion.[23] In the 1887 contract, the state prohibited the company from firing more than 25 per cent of the work-force. This was an attempt to avoid both social unrest and the local eco-nomic consequences of firing a large number of workers. In fact, whenever the *cigarreras* went on strike, the whole town supported them and shop-keepers, for instance, closed their shops during such periods. Whenever the factory was closed because of internal revolts, local government rep-resentatives always intervened to seek its reopening. These local and gov-ernmental pressures were accompanied by worker and union pressures to preserve the existing labour supply structure.

The loyalty of the *cigarreras* to the factory was three-fold, consisting of a family economy factor (mostly related to gender), a labour factor and a cul-tural factor. The first factor related to the importance of the *cigarreras* to the family economy. As will be illustrated in the next section, the *cigarreras* were in many cases breadwinners and their wages were always central to the family budget. Apart from the unquestionable importance of maintaining a household, if the fact of being breadwinner cannot be differentiated along gender lines with regard to the individual's life cycle, the use of time and childcare did determine female much more than male labour behaviour. In the long run, *cigarreras* could be as independent of the family life cycle as male workers, because they were allowed to bring their children with them to the factory and to work flexible hours. Indeed, their flexible schedule was actually facilitated by the collusion of the factory itself in worker non-

---

[22] See footnote 65.

[23] The strong influence exercised by local elites and the government in their effort to avoid unpopular measures in the factory suggests that the factory itself was used as a stabilizing factor in the labour market. C. Arenas Posadas, *Sevilla y el Estado. Una perspectiva local de la formación del capitalismo en España* (Seville, 1993), pp. 298–305, maintains that the factory did not have a positive spillover effect on the Seville economy except in the labour market. He articulated a theory which partly attributes the survival of some other local industries to the fact that the factory was able to guarantee a secure wage for more than six thousand working women and their families, thus allowing the local bourgeoisie to fix low wages in their own industries and ensure their continued survival. In support of this theory, he has noted that the first newspapers to alert *cigarreras* to the potential con-sequences of the introduction of machinery into the factory, and to the attendant risk of job losses, were those of the bourgeoisie. This author failed in not ascribing importance to the tobacco manufacture in the local economy other than the labour market. During the nineteenth and the twentieth centuries, this huge factory had positive spillover effects on other city industries, even if the tobacco (input) and some complementary inputs together with the machinery came from other places. But even if he exaggerates the importance of the factory to the survival of other local industries because of *cigarreras'* wages, he does show the importance that everything concerned with the factory had in Seville. Therefore, this factory is an ideal place in which to observe how political clientelism worked.

attendance.[24] These circumstances enabled the *cigarreras* to combine their own household work with factory work. These two factors of part-time employment and childcare helped to make it possible for there to be an increase in labour participation rates among married women in the twentieth century.[25] With regard to childcare, the factory provided cradles to allow women to care for their babies in the workshops. When mechanized workshops were established and younger *cigarreras* employed in them, the grandmothers took care of the babies in the manual workshop and the mechanical *cigarreras* went there to breastfeed their children. Finally, a crèche was created in 1943. In addition, maternity leave and job security had always guaranteed flexibility of attendance at the factory, although remuneration for childbirth was not given before 1931.[26]

The *cigarreras* brought to the factory skills[27] specific to the monopolistic enterprise, but their general qualifications were rather poor. There were high rates of illiteracy in the factory up to the 1920s, and it was precisely this high level of specific training and low level of general education that helped to tie the *cigarreras* to the factory. They also had a work culture which anticipated their continued presence in the workplace after marriage and throughout life.[28] The *cigarreras* had an important work culture from childhood, when the factory was presented to them as a

---

[24] See in this article, the section on mothers and work and L. Gálvez-Muñoz, "Management, Labour and Gender: The Use of Time in the Tobacco Factory of Seville", in O. Hufton and C. Sarasúa (eds), *Gender and the Use of Time* (forthcoming).

[25] C. Goldin, *Understanding the Gender Gap* (New York, 1990), p. 158, explains that changes in participation in the labour force among white married women in the period from 1890 to 1980 are in a very important way related to the reduction of hours of work, to part-time employment and, more recently, to childcare arrangements: "Indeed, the increased participation of women over the long run resulted more from a change in the nature of jobs, such as the decrease in hours of work [. . .] than from shifts in social norms and attitudes".

[26] The *Decreto del seguro de maternidad* was implemented by the Republican Regime, 26 May 1931. Years before this, *cigarreras* had already won the right to sick pay for maternity leave. The state paid 90 Pts for six weeks. In the tobacco factory, breastfeeding had always been done in the workshops. A rule of one hour of breastfeeding per day began to be applied wherever possible, particularly among employees in the mechanized workshops where it was forbidden to breastfeed babies inside the workshop.

[27] Following G. Becker, *Human Capital* (New York, 1964), the training the *cigarreras* received was completely specific because it did not endow the worker with any skills that might be utilized in other enterprises, especially in this case because of the monopoly. Among the male tobacco labour force in Spain, only a few workers such as *escogedores*, who were in charge of the selection of tobacco, had specific skills.

[28] Article 6 of the Rules of 1927 provided for all cigar-makers older than 60 to be given the opportunity to retire. Nevertheless, there were still many over-60s who entered the *Faenas auxiliares* workshop after 1927, illustrating the persistence of a work culture of a lifetime in the factory, as well as family economic needs. The earning differences between wages in the *desvenados* workshops, where all the older *cigarreras* were employed and the *Faenas auxiliares* pay were not very high. In any case, the ratio was always variable because the first was piece-work and the second, the *Faenas auxiliares* allowance, was a fixed amount.

"family" (a term that always appears in the oral interviews). They had seen their mothers and their grandmothers combine their work in the factory with their household work.[29]

Finally, an aspect relating to this transitional period has to be addressed. At the end of nineteenth century, the proportion of married women in the Seville tobacco factory was 37.3 per cent (and 17.3 per cent widows), while this rose in the twentieth century to 81 per cent.[30] The difference in the proportion of married women must be explained in part by reference to the labour policy of the company. During the nineteenth century, families provided workers for the factory continuously, from generation to generation.[31] Between 1887 and 1910, the CAT stopped taking on *cigarreras* for the factory in Seville. Daughters could not succeed their mothers, and the proportion of married women remaining in the factory throughout life increased. In 1910, when some daughters were once again admitted to the workshops, their mothers had already passed the critical years of childrearing and some of the new workers were already married. Furthermore, when the next major wave of *cigarreras* was recruited in the 1920s,[32] it was just after the economic crisis at the end of World War I, when a regular wage like that earned by the *cigarreras* was fundamental to the survival of the family.

This combination of elements ensured that the lives of the *cigarreras* were not characterized by the premature abandonment of the labour market

---

[29] By contrast, the *tabaqueros* entered the factory after having worked in other jobs. Thus their work culture was more identified with the culture of the union rather than with the culture of the factory. Arenas Posadas, *Sevilla y el Estado (1892–1923)*, p. 620 and Baena Luque, *Las cigarreras sevillanas*, pp. 123–124, have criticized the lack of solidarity among *cigarreras* in Seville with the rest of the working class prior to the 1920s. These authors have seen this attitude in a negative light, without taking into account that their behaviour diverged from that touted in the patriarchal message of the unions (see S.O. Rose, "Gender Antagonism and Class Conflict: Exclusionary Strategies of Male Trade Unionists in Nineteenth-Century Britain", *Social History*, 13 (1988), pp. 191–208), which exercised a strong influence on the development of the working class (see J. Scott, *Gender and the Politics of History* (New York, 1988)). During World War I, at roughly the same time as the success of the major unions in Seville and the increase of *tabaqueros* in the factory, NICOT, the local section of the national *cigarreras'* and *tabaqueros'* union was founded. This was also the time of the entry of new *cigarreras* into the mechanized workshops, where the noise of the machinery replaced the work in groups chatting around a table. The end of this continuous chat was paralleled by a decrease in skills and the obligatory wearing of a uniform in the mechanized workshops, illustrating how the *cigarreras'* work culture was weakened by mechanization.

[30] AFTS Libro de Personal 1891 (sample size: 5,832) and Personnel dossier 1888–1945 (sample size: 1,655). In the second, because it covers a whole period and not a specific year, the widows are considered together with the married women.

[31] Sara Horrell and Jane Humphries demonstrate this generational relief in the participation rates of married women in nineteenth-century Britain. See their contribution in this volume.

[32] Between 1922 and 1925, around 400 apprentices were admitted to the workshops following a draw among the *cigarreras'* daughters and granddaughters who wanted to work in the factory. They were between 16 and 30 years old and literate.

to assume household duties, but rather by absences resulting from a flexible approach to working hours. This evidence suggests that demand, rather than labour supply, explains trends in recruitment to the factory. From the point of view of the household economy, why did women continue to supply such a high proportion of female labour in the factory even after marriage?

The local labour market and the household economy of the cigarreras

The literature on labour presents women as more unstable workers than men, engaging in the labour market in order to complement regular family income, and therefore justifiably being paid lower wages than men.[33] The fact that women were so frequently engaged in casual labour, various occupations and part-time jobs has resulted in an underestimation of female workers in census figures,[34] which have thus tended to reduce already low female employment rates. Moreover, in twentieth-century Spanish censuses, men engaged in casual work were recorded as *jornaleros* (day labourers), whereas women casual workers were often designated as being *su casa* and thus ascribed no market occupation. The data provided by the 1900 national census indicate that the female industrial population in Seville was 3,112, although the records of the tobacco factory suggest that more than 4,000 women were employed in that factory alone in the relevant year. As already stated, only 25 per cent of the *cigarreras* found in factory records in the 1920s were designated as *cigarreras* in the municipal census of 1924. Even if other sources augmented the proportion, the female participation rates in the Seville labour market were not very substantial.[35]

The effects of industrialization on female participation rates have been widely discussed. Optimistic or pessimistic views, arguments for continuity or discontinuity with pre-industrial behaviour, and the notion of exclusion or segregation by industry have all found a place in the debate.

---

[33] J. Burnette, "An Investigation of the Female-Male Wage Gap During the Industrial Revolution in Britain", *Economic History Review*, 2 (1997), pp. 257–281, has recently demonstrated that in most cases during the Industrial Revolution women were paid market wages and the size of the earning gap should be explained by measurement errors and productivity differences. However, the present article suggests that differences in productivity rates should be explained separately from biological differences, for differences in consumption of calories, human capital and apprenticeship.

[34] For Britain see E. Higgs, "Women, Occupations and Work in the Nineteenth Century Censuses", *History Workshop Journal*, 23 (1987), pp. 59–80, and for Spanish censuses, see L. Gálvez-Muñoz, "Une approche aux sources statistiques. Les recensements à Seville du 1900, 1910 et 1920", paper given at the European University Institute, mimeo (1993).

[35] In the industrial municipal census of 1906, 25 per cent of the industrial population of Seville were women. In the *Padrón de Retiro Obrero* of 1921, 6,560, that is 37 per cent, of the industrial workers were female. For Arenas Posadas, "Sevilla y el Estado (1892–1923)", p. 409, they constituted the "true proletariat of Seville".

Women's employment increased in certain sectors yet decreased in others,[36] in as much as some industries employed women while others did not. Certain occupations became recognized as the preserve of one sex or the other.[37] It is emerging that at least part of the reason lay in the different industrial bases of the various regions or towns. Local traditions concerning both the role of married women in the household economy and the demand for female labour in the context of the local labour market, rather than general theories or new ideas, are now considered fundamental to the explanation of female employment rates.[38]

Labour market in Seville

The main characteristic of the labour market in Seville was its exaggerated size and its dependence on a regional economy based on agricultural exports, always exposed to strong cyclical variations. The city's population grew as a result of immigration, mainly from the Andalusian countryside,[39] an over-populated *latifundio*[40] area where the female monetary con-

[36] Horrell and Humphries, "Women's Labour Force Participation", call attention to the timing in the long run. It seems that the industrialization in Britain first increased female opportunities, only to reduce them later.

[37] In opposition to the view that unions played the main role in the exclusion of women from the labour market, Jordan, "The Exclusion of Women", invokes the gender ideology of the period, based on the gendered division of labour established in the new industries. Employers undoubtedly encountered considerable opposition from male trade unionists when they tried to extend their female workforces, but it was the gender ideology of the period which created an androcentric blindness that prevented them from considering the possibility that some of the tasks within their industries could be performed just as well and far more cheaply by women. J. Burnette, "Testing for Occupational Crowding in Eighteenth Century British Agriculture", *Explorations in Economic History*, 33 (1996), pp. 319–345 and idem, "An Investigation of the Female-Male Wage Gap", refers to differences in productivity among male and female workers.

[38] Rose, "Proto-Industry, Women's Work and the Household Economy", as well as L. Tilly and J. Scott, *Women, Work and Family* (New York, 1978), underline the importance of local traditions and labour market opportunities for family employment rather than new ideologies. The participation of working-class women in the nineteenth century is less the product of new ideas than of the effects of old ideas and pre-industrial values operating in new or changing contexts. Local traditions regarding family employment, rather than new ideologies, may have influenced the reorganization of some industries during the transition to industrial capitalism, resulting in the generation of particular types of employment opportunities for women. See Horrell and Humphries, "Women's Labour Force Participation" and their contribution to this volume; Jordan, "The Exclusion of Women"; and Sarasúa, "The Rise of the Wage Worker", for the Spanish case, have demonstrated the key role of the local labour market in explaining female participation rates.

[39] In the first quarter of the twentieth century the population of Seville increased by 100,000 people – from 140,000 to 250,000. In 1900, more than 40 per cent of immigrants came from the surrounding countryside. The proportion including the rest of Andalusia was 85 per cent, and 95 per cent for 1924. See Arenas Posadas, *Industria y clases trabajadoras*, p. 185.

[40] For the social and economic conditions of *latifundio* in Andalusia, see A.M. Bernal, *Economía e Historia de los latifundios* (Madrid, 1988).

tribution to the household economy is thought to have been only marginal
and temporary. Census figures show very low rates of female participation
in the labour market during this period, especially in the industrial sector
(Table 2). Female employment in the industrial sector almost always
accounted for less than 30 per cent of the total female workforce.[41] The
female industrial population of Seville seems to have been concentrated
in a few large industries, such as tobacco, armaments, textiles, pottery,
and some temporary work relating to the agricultural export industry.[42] As
in the Andalusian countryside, male workers were cheap. As a matter of
fact, this labour market was characterized by a low female participation
and by a significant number of day labourers.[43] The industrial sector in
Seville was still relatively antiquated in the late nineteenth and twentieth
centuries. It was bipartite, with a traditional sector employing artisans and
a modern sector employing a large number of unskilled workers. Local
employers responded to market fluctuations by varying the size of the
workforce rather than by investing in technology. Employment and unemployment were more or less in a constant state of flux, characterized by
periods of inactivity,[44] so that family incomes were determined more by
the number of days worked than by nominal wages. In addition, Arenas
(1995) has shown that workers with higher nominal wages worked more
days a year than those with lower nominal wages.

On average, the factory functioned for about 280 days a year, representing one of the more stable workplaces in the city. As can be seen in
Table 3 and Figures 1–3, the advantages of the *cigarreras'* wages were

[41] The single exception, according to census figures, occurred in 1920. And the reason
seems to be more related with quantification problems than with real changes in the local
economy.

[42] See Arenas Posadas, *Industria y clases trabajadoras*, and E. Baena Luque, "Las trabajadoras sevillanas 1900–1936", in Arenas, *Industria y clases trabajadoras*, pp. 225–245.

[43] The tobacco factory itself could be taken as an example of the way in which this labour
market worked. The factory had established a system of substitutions whereby every morning a limited pool of male workers were admitted into the factory or not according to the
number of absences. As a result, *tabaqueros* endured the pressure of the labour market
every morning at the entrance to the factory. If they were late, other workers might take
their jobs and their wages for the day. This policy was also common in other industrial
contexts: "In a number of cotton weaving sheds in Lancashire, temporary weavers would
come to the mills in the morning and would be given the looms of any permanent weaver
who was late, even though the weavers were employed under piece rates. In one mill, if a
permanent weaver was five minutes late, she lost her looms for the day": G. Clark, "Factory Discipline", *Journal of Economic History*, 54 (1994), pp. 128–257, esp. p. 132.

[44] Arenas Posadas, "Sevilla y el Estado (1892–1923)", studying a sample of the municipal
censuses of 1900 and 1924 and the *padrón del retiro obrero* of 1921, calculates unemployment as between 20 and 40 per cent. The variation was related to the demand for agro-
export customs. For him, these figures are horrific because the only way to survive was
public or private charity. Although these figures are certainly horrific, kinship was still
a fundamental institution. In fact, it was the family who maintained this inflated labour
market.

Table 2. *Occupation ratios in Seville by sex, female marital status and sectors*

		Occupation rates by sex			
Year	*Total*	*Female*	*Male*	*% female*	*% male*
1900	56,902	11,012	45,890	19.40	80.60
1910	59,735	9,125	50,610	15.30	84.70
1920	73,384	8,651	64,733	11.70	88.30
1930	84,110	12,806	71,304	15.30	84.70
1940	113,706	23,058	90,648	20.30	79.70

Marital status (female)

	Single		*Married*		*Widow*	
	Total	%	Total	%	Total	%
1900	7,654	69.50	1,425	12.90	1,933	17.60
1910	6,423	70.40	963	10.60	1,739	19.00
1920	6,503	75.20	827	9.60	1,302	15.20
1930	10,208	79.70	858	6.70	1,740	13.60
1940	18,311	79.40	1,250	5.40	3,490	15.20

Sectors (female)

	Agriculture		*Industry*		*Service*	
	Total	%	Total	%	Total	%
1900	433	3.90	3,112	28.20	7,467	67.90
1910	237	2.50	2,257	24.80	6.631	72.70
1920	12	0.10	4,481	51.80	4,148	48.10
1930	25	0.20	3,445	26.90	9,339	72.90
1940	252	1.20	5,129	22.30	17,627	76.50

more apparent in their annual incomes than in daily wages. In other words, it is necessary to stress the stability of their employment in an unstable labour market. Apart from their annual income, the *cigarreras* were guaranteed future security, not only for themselves (*faenas auxililares* workshop and retirement) but also for their families, in that they were able to arrange work at the factory for their descendants. In addition, they were given free health care, which was also extended in practice to their families. Factory records, literature and oral history suggest that the *cigarreras* often provided the principal source of income for large families. On the other hand, figures based on municipal censuses (Table 4) show that *cigarreras*' families had fewer dependants than other working-class families. This is due to the fact that, thanks to factory records, census figures have been corrected for the *cigarreras*' families. Moreover, the underestimation of female employment in families other than those of the *cigarreras* is still expressed in these figures, and so caution is required in making comparisons. It must be remembered that men who did not work on a regular basis are recorded as day labourers and women in the same situation as having no occupation. For this reason, the majority of women

Lina Gálvez-Muñoz

Table 3. *Real annual wages (in Pesetas)*

Year	Cigarreras	Type-A worker	Type-B worker		Type-C worker	
			Scenario 1	Scenario 2	Scenario 1	Scenario 2
1909	797.88	1,374.00	761.80	609.44	345.80	247.00
1910	907.28	1,575.00	894.40	715.52	393.12	280.80
1911	883.70	1,626.00	889.20	711.36	393.12	280.80
1912	823.77	1,617.00	886.60	709.28	382.20	273.00
1913	726.12	1,479.00	871.00	696.80	349.44	249.60
1914	762.15	1,536.00	865.80	692.64	364.00	260.00
1915	661.64	1,362.00	816.40	653.12	309.40	221.00
1916	670.86	1,458.00	787.80	630.24	318.50	227.50
1917	690.55	1,320.00	735.80	588.64	294.84	210.60
1918	821.13	1,341.00	951.60	761.28	300.30	214.50
1919	844.29	1,260.00	808.60	646.88	380.38	271.70
1920	899.45	1,389.00	884.00	707.20	420.42	300.30
1921	918.30	-	824.20	659.36	393.12	280.80
1922	835.86	-	889.20	711.36	433.16	309.40

Source:

Cigarreras: Average daily wages of Cigarrillos Superiores workshop multiplied by number of days worked in a year.

Type-A worker: Arenas' (1995) estimates of craftsmen, mechanics and skilled industrial workers' daily wages multiplied by full employment (290 days per annum).

Type-B worker: Semi-skilled workers:

   Scenario 1 (optimistic = Arenas' estimates multiplied per an average of 4.5 days per week per annum);

   Scenario 2 (pessimistic = Arenas' estimates multiplied per an average of 3.5 days per week per annum).

Type-C worker: Day labourers:

   Scenario 1 (optimistic = Arenas' estimates multiplied per an average of 3.5 days per week per annum);

   Scenario 2 (pessimistic = Arenas' estimates multiplied per an average of 2.5 days per week per annum).

The number of days worked per annum are constant for the whole period studied, except for the *cigarreras'* case.

Both optimistic and pessimistic scenarios are based on different information related to different years, occupational categories and companies collected by Arenas (1995). Therefore, the trends in annual wages of all type-A, B and C groups are the same as the daily ones.

Table 4. *Number of income-less family members, 1924*

	Type	% of income-less
Families with at least one *cigarrera*	1	23.4
Householder: female	2	74.0
Householder: day labourer	3	54.9
Householder: semi-skilled and skilled industrial	4	54.7

in working-class families appear as dependants. Moreover, the estimates are based on individual households. The evidence of many working-class households without income substantiates the existence of families extending beyond a single household: families were not always united under a single roof.

Cigarreras' husbands

The fact that neither marital status[45] nor position in the household seems to have affected the length of *cigarreras'* working lives (see Tables 1a and 1b)[46] corroborates the notion that their positions were as independent as those of men with respect to the family life cycle in the long run, and suggests that their jobs were often the main source of family income, whether they were married or single. This model concurs with the male model in which the job is considered to have been an important variable explaining the course of male workers' lives. In explaining breadwinner patterns, married *cigarreras* seem therefore to be more interesting subjects of study than single ones. From a sample of the professions of 400 husbands of *cigarreras* (see Figure 4), 42 per cent (type C) were *jornaleros* (day labourers); 25 per cent (type B) were either semi-skilled workers (11.5 per cent), *tabaqueros* (5.5 per cent) or employed in the service sector (8 per cent); 28 per cent (type A) were skilled workers; and 5 per cent were otherwise employed, handicapped or dependent for some other reason. Based on the information provided by the municipal census and wages data in Table 3, the earnings of the married *cigarreras* were probably the principal source of income for their households. The proportion of married *cigarreras* contributing the main source of income to the family economy varies from 72 per cent of total married *cigarreras* according to a pessimistic estimate (scenario 2) to 47 per cent in a optimistic estimate (scenario 1).[47] Table 4 shows that the proportion of *cigarreras'* wages to family income were similar to that of the householder's income in the other working-class families, except in those families where the householder was a woman. These figures show the scarcity of employment for both male and female workers. The *cigarrera*'s job was often the main

[45] However, it may be more interesting to study fertility rates than marital status to explain the length of the *cigarreras'* working lives. Neither the municipal census of 1924, referring to a specific year, nor the personnel dossier are reliable sources of this information. The only source which gives information about the number of children of *cigarreras* is oral history, but these data are not susceptible to computation because they are approximate. It seems that the fertility was high according to the rates at the time, and it was encourged by the facilities of the factory.

[46] For an explanation of the construction of Table 1b, see the section on the factory and life pattern, pp. 91–100. Only cases where the husband's profession is known have been used for this regression.

[47] Pessimistic and optimistic estimates are considered in relation to the number of days worked per week. For the construction of both scenarios, see Table 3.

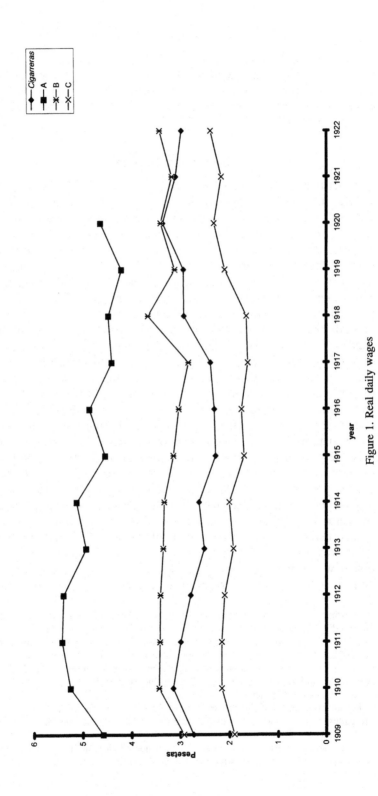

Figure 1. Real daily wages

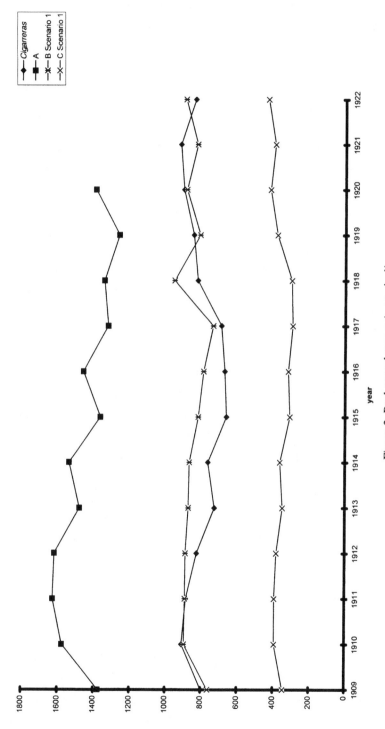

Figure 2. Real annual wages (scenario 1)

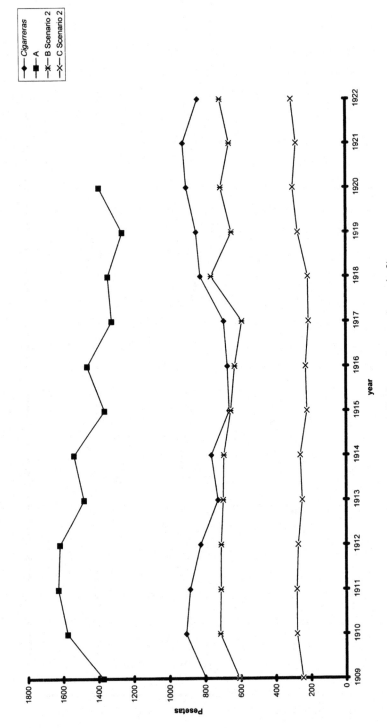

Figure 3. Real annual wages (scenario 2)

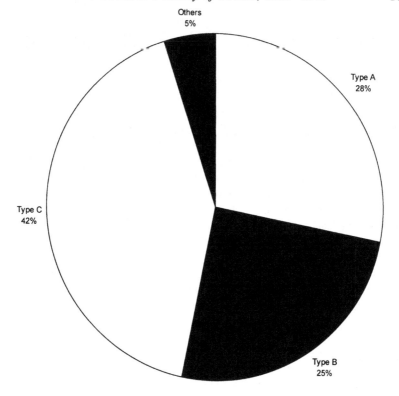

Figure 4. *Cigarreras'* husbands by type of job

source of employment in the family, not only in terms of actual income, but even more importantly in terms of security. Compared to other local industries in the private sector, the tobacco factory, operating under a monopoly system, constituted the most dependable source of employment in town.

The lack of professional stability of the majority of the *cigarreras'* husbands helps to explain why *cigarreras* were attractive prospective marriage partners. The factory exit was always crowded with men waiting to see the women emerge, as in the representations by Merimée and Bizet. Whatever the importance of the Carmen myth to the *cigarreras* and the collective identity of Seville, it seems that other kinds of interests were also at work in this custom. This can be illustrated not only quantitatively but also qualitatively on the basis of such diverse sources as factory records, literature and oral history. In the period up to 1920, the boss of the factory operated a policy of firing any apprentice who got married. This was illegal under the rules of the company and those fired during these years were readmitted during the 1920s. Personnel records on one cigar-maker dismissed after marriage and later readmitted explain that she was never formally married but simply left her mother's house to live in that of her fiancé; for the boss of the factory, however, the arrangement was equivalent to marriage. When her fiancé discovered that she had been dismissed by the factory, he left her because he wanted to marry a *cigarrera*.[48] Literature,[49] and more especially oral histories, are even more explicit than the factory records. In their interviews, *cigarreras* emphasized that not all of their husbands were lazy drunkards but that some certainly were; they speak of *bad luck*. Perhaps the most revealing statement is that of a labour inspector charged with the task of determining which *cigarreras* were entitled to receive a family subsidy in the 1940s: "*Ser marido de una cigarrera era una profesión*" (to be a husband of a *cigarrera* was a profession),[50] he declared. If so, then it is possible to say that the wife's job – if the main one in the family – could determine her husband's occupation. Nevertheless, as in explaining female participation in the workforce, the employment behaviour of a *cigarrera*'s husband should not only be related to his wife's employment, but also to the opportunities offered by the local labour market. Arenas (1993) shows that, out of a sample of 4,864 industrial workers in 1921, 41.12 per cent were skilled and 58.88 per cent unskilled.[51] The same author estimates the rate of unemployment during the first quarter of the twentieth century at between 20 per cent and 40 per cent.[52] When the *cigarreras*' daughters ceased to be taken on for work in the factory, they began to press for their sons and also their husbands to be employed there.

The example of the *cigarreras* shows that a female breadwinner model could exist, and not only in female householder families. But the sexual division of work was not immutable; is the figure of the breadwinner free of household tasks therefore independent of gender?

Cigarreras' households

The reverse image of the breadwinning wife – the house-husband – did not exist. Instead of *cigarreras*' unemployed husbands performing household work, there is evidence of *cigarreras* coming to the factory later in the morning and being absent in order to perform household tasks (see

[48] AFT Personnel dossiers, 1921. Angeles Castaño Reina.
[49] In Palacio Valdés, *La hermana San Sulpicio* (Madrid, 1887) the confidant of the main character is a *cigarrera* and her husband is shown in the story as an alcoholic and an idler.
[50] Interview with J.L.B., January 1995.
[51] For Arenas Posadas, "Sevilla y el Estado (1892–1923)", pp. 431–432, the estimates have only a superficial statistical value. He defines this proportion as the arithmetical value of a dual reality in the labour market showing a duality in industry, employing workers with different characteristics.
[52] In the municipal poverty census of 1904, families with less than 3 Pts a day were considered poor. There were 16,158 families and 64,632 persons in this category, 60 per cent of the population. Measurement changes reduced this percentage, but it still remained very significant: *ibid.*, p. 418.

section on mothers and workers, pp. 118–126 below). The interview with an elderly shopkeeper in the Triana neighbourhood[53] corroborates the idea that these women were in charge of everything relating to the household. He remembers seeing them always going about with their children and selling them food already half-prepared for cooking. Although the *cigarreras* did not share their household tasks with their husbands, conditions in the factory, assistance from female family members and facilities in the neighbourhood seem to have helped them to cope with their double working day. The factory permitted them to bring their babies into the workshops and, in addition, they belonged to extended families who assisted with childcare and other household tasks. Finally, the neighbourhood also helped to mitigate the strain of a lengthy working day in both factory and home. The type of housing in which *cigarreras* lived, *corrales* and *casas de vecinos*, was such that many daily tasks could be collectivized. This included that of caring for children, who were always together in the yard under the supervision of a neighbour. In addition, the religious communities' census of 1900 shows that the *Hijas de la Caridad de San Vicente de Paúl* declared that their occupation was to take care of *cigarreras'* children while these women were working.[54]

Nevertheless, during the twentieth century the *cigarreras'* family model became a minority one and began to change. With the CAT's new labour policy of not hiring new apprentices (except in the periods from 1909 to 1912 and 1922 to 1925), many potential *cigarreras* were excluded from the factory. A reduction both in the number of families dependent on the tobacco industry and in the number of *cigarreras* per family resulted in a reduction in the financial contribution of *cigarreras* to the family economy. This loss of family income was in part mitigated by the gender change in the labour strategies that came about as a consequence of the new factory policy and changes in the production process. When it became impossible for the *cigarreras* to introduce their daughters to the workshops, they began to promote their husbands and sons as prospective factory employees, as can be seen from the many applications for jobs made to the factory. Arenas (1995) sees the diversification of family incomes as common throughout the working classes of Seville during this period, and believes that this has to be related to the process of degradation[55] of

---

[53] Interview with F.V.G., July 1996.

[54] Archivo Municipal de Sevilla, Sección estadística.

[55] The idea of de-skilling with industrialization has been substituted by that of heterogeneity with regard to changes in the workforce. First, with a redefinition of the concept of skill in the pre-industrial period, M. Berg, *The Age of Manufactures. Industry, Innovation and Work in Britain, 1700–1820* (London, 1985) has demonstrated that, with the division of work, skill was sometimes identified with ability or speed. In the majority of cases, the de-skilling process was actually a re-skilling process and in only a few cases was the de-skilling process accompanied by a loss in wages. See W. Lazonick, "Industrial Relations and Technical Change: The Case of the Self-Acting Mule", *Cambridge Journal of Economics*, III (1979), pp. 231–262, and P.L. Robertson and L.J. Alston, "Technological Choice

pre-industrial skilled workers.[56] The *cigarreras* certainly suffered a process of de-skilling, but this did not result in a diversification of family incomes but rather in a shift to the male breadwinner system.[57] Under CAT management, the workforce of more than 6,000 women was reduced to 300. This decrease and changes in the ratio between the sexes in the factory workforce should be related to a new phase of capital accumulation, demanding fewer workers directly engaged in production workshops and more engaged in the maintenance of the plant.

Once their daughters could not enter the factory, the *cigarreras'* families had to face not only the problem of redundant workers but also the necessity of changing the family economic system. As already mentioned in this article, this brought about a gender change in the family labour perspective towards the factory. Further research is required to analyse whether diversification also affected the *cigarreras'* daughters who were unable to enter the factory.[58] Although definitive results are not yet available, it seems that these daughters continued waiting to enter the factory and did not seek permanent employment in other industries, so encouraging the slow imposition of the male breadwinner system. This fact must be linked not only to the *cigarreras'* work culture and the CAT hiring policy, but also to the scarcity of opportunities for women in the Seville labour market. The CAT's new labour policy brought about a decline in the importance of the *cigarreras* and the female industrial worker over the period studied, and destroyed the traditional family economy model of *cigarreras*, which may have been one of the very few examples of female breadwinner family models. Even if the fact of being the breadwinner did not imply a reduction in responsibility for household tasks, it did give the women concerned great control of family incomes. Descriptions of the

and the Organization of Work in Capitalist Firms", *Economic History Review*, XLV (1992), pp. 330–349. That was not the trend in the female skilled labour force, which suffered a pure process of degradation.

[56] Arenas Posadas, *Industria y clases trabajadoras*, p. 219, maintains that the importance of complementary wages to the overall family income increased during the first quarter of the twentieth century. During this period the contribution of the main wage fell from 78 to 73 per cent of total family income, which seems to confirm the degradation of work. Nevertheless, Arenas considered the diversification of family income and the degradation of skilled workers a negative phenomenon. But in many cases this degradation made it possible for women to have a job and to make a contribution to the family economy, and subsequently changed power relations within the family unit.

[57] The idea of re-skilling with industrialization is represented by the adoption of new labour roles, mostly related to supervision in the workshops by the old skilled workers. But the consequences of industrialization in a female labour force appear to have been a purely de-skilling process. Because of patriarchy, women were not considered capable of supervising other workers.

[58] It is necessary to analyse the *cigarreras'* family economy in the post-Spanish Civil War period.

way they dressed,[59] the factory records punishing market exchanges in the workshops and records demonstrating the opportunities open to them to leave their husbands or to arrange the adoption of their children after they died all show that in most cases they controlled their wages. The industrialization process made this model a thing of the past. It continued to be important in the collective memory of the town but disappeared as a representative reality. How this happened is examined in the next part of this article.

THE INTERACTION BETWEEN THE INDUSTRIALIZATION PROCESS AND FAMILY STRATEGIES

The industrialization of the tobacco factory in Seville was gradual but effective.[60] The lease contract established that the CAT had to pay an annual fee of 90 million Pts to the Treasury.[61] As a consequence of this high annual fee and the market disequilibrium inherited from the state, the company had a negative financial balance during the first three years and this imposed a low investment policy. To make a profit, the CAT needed to increase production by replacing labour with technology. However, a total mechanization of the factories would have required a large capital expenditure and would probably have provoked a popular uprising. Obviously, the state had an interest in preventing such occurrences and did not permit the company to make any radical change in the production process. In fact, the state's contract expressly stipulated that the CAT could not fire more than 25 per cent of the factory's personnel. The size of the industry also made it impossible to invest in technology on a massive scale. During the CAT's first few years of running the industry, there was no major investment in technology. The only investments made focused on two newly established factories, and on the *picaduras* workshops in the older factories. Workshops producing cigars and cigarettes, where the majority of *cigarreras* were concentrated, did not experience this investment boost.[62] This was partly because the Spanish consumer did not easily

---

[59] Photographs and literary descriptions reveal a beautiful way of dressing. *Cigarreras* were highly concerned about the way they dressed.

[60] Jordan, "The Exclusion of Women", p. 276, says that in nineteenth-century Britain women continued to be employed in industries where the transition to industrialism was gradual, but were excluded from new fields and from industries that underwent radical reorganization.

[61] Contract of Lease of the Tobacco Monopoly for the Production and Sale of Tobacco in the Peninsula, Balearic Islands, Ceuta and the rest site in Northern Africa, 16 June 1887. AHFT, Expedientes generales, Leg. 628.

[62] The CAT already knew that it had to be very prudent in introducing machines to the workforce. For example, the Luddite-inspired revolt of 1885 in the factory at Seville was still a very recent experience. The reason for this insurrection was the rumour of the arrival of cigarette machines. The actual arrival took place more than thirty years later.

accept mechanically-produced cigarettes, and the quality of manually-produced cigars, in particular, far surpassed that of mechanized ones. Apart from these technical and financial constraints, it seems to have been market deficiencies – the mismatch between supply and demand – that determined the rate of mechanization. Many of the tasks performed in the factory related to products for which there was little consumer demand. In addition, the market value of these products was inconsistent with the cost of production. This mismatch was so great that the main goal of the CAT was to eliminate it. The CAT tried to produce by both mechanical and manual methods new goods that corresponded better to consumers' tastes at a lower price. In a market where consumers' habits were essentially based on custom, changes had to be introduced slowly and with caution; in fact, only some of the new CAT products were accepted by the market.

This slow path towards modernization, influencing customers' habits whilst avoiding social disorder, was largely possible thanks to the firm's monopoly structure[63] and to flexibility in the mode of production and the labour force. Nevertheless, during the period that the CAT was running the company, the production process was eventually mechanized, resulting in an 80 per cent reduction in personnel and the loss of production control by the workers, but also in a 7.5 per cent increase in productivity. In fact, the main strategy of the CAT was to modernize all areas of the tobacco industry: raw materials market, production, marketing, distribution, and so on. Regarding production and labour organization in the factories, the CAT adopted a two-pronged strategy: the mechanization of the workshops and the adaptation of the workforce to the number of *cigarreras* needed for the new mechanical order. To achieve this second aim, the CAT chose to abstain from firing *cigarreras*, and rather to limit the number of new hires and wait for this slow conversion to happen by itself. As a consequence, this process has passed into history as non-traumatic: there was no massive firing process and no violent workers' demonstrations. It has been suggested that the company displayed a paternalistic attitude due to the state connection and that the workers' passivity was due to lack of unionization at the time. The limited nature of this interpretation lies first in the fact that it takes the individual, rather than the family, as the unit of analysis and that it considers the worker in isolation from the family. The reduction in personnel due to the ending of a continuous hiring policy was indeed traumatic, in that it fundamentally destroyed the household economy model of the *cigarreras*. Second, this interpretation fails to ana-

[63] Independent of the lease of the right to a state monopoly by a private company, the fiscal monopoly involves a distortion in the allocation of resources relative to the competitive model. In fact, when the management of a monopoly is run by a private company, the subjection of the company to private law does not mean that the company develops a private activity; the main characteristic of the company activity is derived from the existence of the monopoly, which determines its dominant position in the market.

lyse the relationship of capital and labour always in terms of conflict.[64] In the short run, the workers benefited from this slow conversion, through the maintenance of a flexible labour organization.

The main family strategies of the *cigarreras* can be characterized by two major features: professional opportunities for family members and a trade-off between wages and time for household tasks. How did mechanization interconnect with these two main strategies in the consolidation of the male breadwinner family? Were these family strategies, representing mostly pre-industrial values and labour conditions determined by the gender of the workers, a marginal or an integral component in the process of industrialization in the tobacco factory at Seville?

Mothers of workers

During the nineteenth century, when the factory was hiring personnel on a regular basis, entry took two forms: through a relative (the family route) or as a result of a recommendation (the political route). While the second route was promptly eliminated by the CAT[65] so far as the *cigarreras* were concerned, the influence of family ties on the recruitment of new workers was never eliminated, despite the changes in production conditions under CAT management.

The manual apprenticeship system

When production in the factory was manual and labour could be considered a quasi-fixed factor of production, the recruitment system was very convenient for the factory. The *cigarreras* provided their own apprenticeship system, based on the fact that the *cigarreras* brought their young daughters with them to the factory to tend the babies. The babies lay in cradles provided by the factory inside the workshops themselves. As *cigarreras'* daughters grew up in the workshop context, they learnt how to make cigarettes[66] and how to be a *cigarrera*: mother and worker. The

---

[64] See P. Joyce, *Work, Society and Politics* (London, 1982), and M. Burawoy, *The Politics of Production* (London, 1985).

[65] The boss of the factory wrote the following to the director in Madrid in May 1922: "I could observe, with the biggest and most intimate protests, that all requests for personnel moves, leave of absence, promotions and the like are made by demanding recommendations from referees who are most of the time not related to the factory and unknown to me [. . .]. I am aware that all these workers are observing an old and well-established custom. However, I beg them to desist from these practices. No more policies based on influence, but rather on good behaviour." The political route was resurrected during the Civil War and post-war period because the factory employed ex-soldiers and collaborators of Franco.

[66] T. Hareven, *Family Time and Industrial Time* (Cambridge, 1982), p. 200, describes a similar case. In the Amoskeag Company, even though young workers did not actually enter factory work before the age of 16, children were socialized to the work experience in the mill at an early age. Industrial labour became part of their life even before they actually worked.

factory took advantage of this system, which provided a means by which to acquire a ready-made skilled workforce without having to invest in an apprenticeship programme requiring several years of training.[67] These apprentices had only to achieve a certain proficiency in their tasks before they could be sent to any workshop. Factory rules – from 1834 right through to 1945 – provided that any apprentices taken on should be descendants of previous workers.[68] In addition, the factory usually preferred the daughters of *cigarreras* because they were already familiar with the work[69] and because it was easier to control the workforce if the whole family was dependent on the factory. The cigar-maker work culture fostered in the factory among the daughters of *cigarreras* also made them more attractive as potential employees.

Family work and mechanization

The family unit also profited from this system, because positions available in the factory were always reserved for daughters of the *cigarreras*. After

---

[67] M. Prus, "Mechanization and the Gender-Based Division of Labour in the U.S. Cigar Industry", *Cambridge Journal of Economics*, 14 (1990), pp. 63–79, maintains that the beginning of mechanization in the American tobacco industry was due to the interest of the employers in controlling production, thus depriving cigar-makers of the importance of their skills and eliminating the apprenticeships which had been a powerful weapon of these skilled workers.

[68] To reserve positions in the factories for the workers' relatives was very usual from the beginning of industrialization, in part because of the control exercised over the workers through this practice, and in part because of the role played by the family in the apprenticeship and recruiting system. Joyce, *Work, Society and Politics*, gives the example of Lancashire factories' bosses who obliged workers to bring their wives to the factory. Another example is the Amoskeag Company in Manchester, New England. Hareven, *Family Time and Industrial Time*, shows first that for the company the workers' families constituted an elastic reserve workforce adaptable to changing circumstances; second, that the factory saved on the apprenticeships because the workers were instructed by their relatives; third, that the workers developed a sociability in the factory to avoid conflicts; and finally, that the factory hired workers with a particular work culture learnt from childhood, and who therefore saw a job in the factory as the only possibility. Furthermore, the families profited from these practices because they found jobs for new family members coming into the city, and knew that the family would have sufficient employees in the factory to allow them to find lifetime employment in some capacity. The kinship system and these "labour rights' produced a comfortable atmosphere for the workers. For the economic origins of paternalism, see M. Huberman, "The Economic Origins of Paternalism: Lancashire Cotton Spinning in the First Half of the Nineteenth Century', *Social History*, 12 (1987), pp. 177–192, and for some objections of his theory see M. Rose, P. Taylor and M.J. Winstanley, "The Economic Origins of Paternalism: Some Objections", *Social History*, 14 (1989), pp. 89–103.

[69] The boss in Seville was not in favour of recruiting *cigarreras'* daughters, but company management and the state preferred this option to a social uproar: "Apprentices for the manual workshop? If you take account of my modest opinion, do not oblige me to hire apprentices for manual tasks; here and now, in this factory, it is better to talk about machines, mechanized workshops, apprentices for new tasks and cigarreras 'of the future'

the CAT took over the factory, there was no recruitment of new labour for more than twenty years until new mechanized workshops were created. In fact, it was only during two very specific periods – 1909–1912 and 1922–1925 – that *cigarreras'* daughters were once again recruited to the factory after the new mechanized workshops had been introduced. Although the factory demanded no specific skills for staff in these mechanized workshops, it continued to hire daughters of *cigarreras* in preference to outsiders. The practice continued because, apart from maintaining manual production, it was considered the only means of avoiding strikes and a consequent paralysis of the workshops and production shortfall.

In fact, the recruitment of daughters was the main demand made by the *cigarreras*, because their labour strategies were almost exclusively focused on the factory. *Cigarreras'* acceptance of machines in order to maintain their household economy model is an example of how family strategies could be more important than craft strategies. The same women who wrecked the factory in 1885 in response to a false rumour concerning the arrival of cigarette-making machines actually asked for such machines in 1909, after a period of over twenty years during which there was no new recruitment of *cigarreras* to the factory. The management let it be known that the only way it could admit apprentices was through the introduction of the new mechanized workshops. In fact, the *cigarreras* changed strategies of behaviour in order to maintain the family labour model, even if it was to be destroyed in the long run. Another example is the way in which the *cigarreras* became literate. The CAT imposed certain restrictions on the admission of new workers: they had, for instance, to be between 16 and 30 years old and must be literate. This actually changed the literacy rates among *cigarreras* before and after CAT.[70] The factory's demand for literacy encouraged workers' families to educate their daughters. To send daughters to school was not a substitute for sending them to

with other manners and education; do not talk about the cigarreras' daughters trained by their mothers or grandmothers in the infamous tasks which ultimately manipulated their families, and introduced them to the customs and vices of older cigarreras": AFTS, Leg. 636. Exp. 12, Seville, 10 September 1909.

[70] The factory began to demand cigar-makers who knew how to read and write, so the *cigarreras* began to send their daughters to school: "[. . .] I said before that the apprentices should not be older than 20, and that all of them should know reading and writing. Since then, you see all the daughters of the cigarreras learning at the schools and colleges of Seville, as a result of the mothers' objective of seeing their daughters being recruited on the same terms as the first 24 apprentices used to implement smoothly and peacefully, the reforms needed to transform the factory from manual tasks to mechanical ones without excessive protests": AFTS, Leg. 636. Exp. 12, Seville, 10 September 1909. So literacy became a means by which to broaden professional opportunities. This accords with the thesis of C.E. Nuñez, *La fuente de la riqueza. Educación y desarrollo económico en la España Contemporánea* (Madrid, 1993) on differences in literacy by region and by sex in Spain, which shows that the literacy rates depended on the modification in labour opportunities that the parents decided for their children in response to the changes in the labour market.

the factory, but a consequence of labour family strategies and factory labour demand plans.

The gender change in family labour strategies

While all *cigarreras* were descendants of tobacco factory workers, this was not until the 1930s the case with the *tabaqueros*. In 1925 recruitment of *cigarreras* ceased. At this point, the *cigarreras'* family labour strategy switched to the promotion of their sons instead of their daughters as factory workers and the proportion of *tabaqueros* descended from factory workers increased, although it remained less than that of the *cigarreras*. The reason is related to the kind of work performed by *tabaqueros* in the factory. It did not involve specific skills passing down from generation to generation within the family. Moreover, from 1936 onwards, the factory was obliged by the Franco regime to hire war veterans. These men probably occupied some jobs that would otherwise have been taken by *cigarreras'* sons.

The changes in the production process converted the nineteenth-century demand for a female workforce[71] into a twentieth-century demand for a male one. During the nineteenth century it was cost-effective for the factory to take on *cigarreras'* daughters, but during the twentieth century such measures only continued as a means to avoid social protest and to smooth the way for the introduction of machinery. For the *cigarreras'* families, mechanization meant the end of their household economy system and a slow shift to the male breadwinner system, although even today most workers in the factory, both male and female, are descendants of former workers.

Mothers and workers[72]

Childcare and work outside the home were not incompatible with each other under the conditions obtaining in the industry. Even if being a mother was not crucial in explaining the female employment rates, as some authors have seen,[73] particular conditions were needed to make these tasks compatible. It is necessary to study women in the labour force at the limits of what is possible given the options open to them.

---

[71] Under CAT management, it was possible in theory for *cigarreras* to bring only their very young babies with them to the workshops. This led to a loss in the transmission of skills, since in the former period older children – those over two years of age – were also in the factory caring for the little ones and learning the job.

[72] This part of the article is mostly based on Gálvez-Muñoz, "Management, Labour and Gender".

[73] For J. Brenner and M. Ramblas, "Rethinking Women's Oppression", *New Left Review*, 144 (1984), pp. 37–71, childcare and work outside the home were impossible to combine under the conditions of capitalist production.

The working day

Under CAT management, the start of the *cigarreras'* working day continued to be flexible, as it had been under state management. They could start between 8 and 10 o'clock in the morning, but – as previously – it was quite common to come in later. In fact, one of the reasons underlying the *cigarreras'* strike in 1896 was the inconvenience caused by the CAT's new rule prohibiting arrival after 11 o'clock. This could be difficult because by then the women had to finish household tasks such as "to dress their children, cook, clean their houses and perform other maternal duties".[74] The maintenance of a flexible working day was also the reason why the *cigarreras* opposed the introduction of the eight-hour working day,[75] contrary to union demands.[76] After the introduction of the eight-hour day, in October 1919, the tobacco factory at Seville allowed the *cigarreras* to come in between 8 and 10 o'clock in the morning. Nevertheless, it continued to be usual for some *cigarreras* to arrive at the factory after 10 o'clock.[77] In fact, flexible hours and the frequent tolerance of non-attendance by *cigarreras* constituted a tacit recognition of the domestic role of women.[78] At the same time, this flexibility responded to the necessities derived from the general organization of production. Because the *cigarreras* worked on a piece-work system,[79] hours were arranged on the

[74] The *Baluarte* of 28 January 1896, quoted in Baena Luque, *Las cigarreras sevillanas*, p. 76.

[75] The *Real Decreto* of 23 April 1919 introduced the eight-hour working day. The CAT introduced the eight-hour working day from October, 1919: "[. . .] According to this law that [. . .] has harmonized the uses and conditions of each town with the familial necessities of thousands of working mothers, wives and daughters [. . .] the daily work time has been made more human in terms of average working time per day since this does not exceed 8 hours [. . .] according to the opinion of maestras and cigar makers thus reforming the internal rules of the factory [. . .]": AFTS Correspondencia, Leg. 19, 23 September 1919.

[76] *Cigarreras* opposed to the eight-hour working day went on strike in December 1919 and January 1920. The law imposed a fixed working time and *cigarreras* considered they lost money because they used to arrive later in the morning. They asked for an increase in piece-rates of 50 per cent. The conflict ended when the company increased the piece-rate to 25 per cent, even though it felt 15 per cent would have been enough: AFTS, Correspondencia, 22 January 1920.

[77] In January 1922, Seville suffered a very severe flu epidemic which affected a lot of factory workers. During this time, the factory was running at a loss, and the directors of the company issued the following rule: "To balance this deficit [. . .], some measures will be established in order to improve punctuality in the factory: first, admission to the Factory ends at 11, which increases the time entrance band by one hour with respect to the official one. Despite the inconvenience of this rule to the cigar-maker, it will increase cigarette production by at least 10 per cent [. . .]": AFTS, Correspondencia, Leg. 21, 25 January 1922.

[78] Toleration of non-attendance among *cigarreras* in order to take care of other members of the family was reported in the 1927 rules, article 8. They received the fixed part of their wages for an maximum of eight days. This article did not apply to *tabaqueros*.

[79] The pure piece-work system ended in 1917, when workers started to receive a fixed portion of their daily wage.

basis of production plans, individual productivity[80] and the trade-off
between wages and time for the household economy. The fact that many
cigarreras came into work after 11 o'clock in the morning meant that,
under conditions of manual production, the *cigarrera* was in charge of her
own factory working time. This flexibility was transformed by mechanization. The introduction of mechanized workshops divided the *cigarreras*
working in the factory into two categories: young ones who arrived punc-
tually to work in the mechanized workshop and older ones who were less
punctual in the manual workshops.[81] Once mechanical production became
the norm, the manual workshops became a place for *cigarreras* who could
not be fired and a precaution against a possible change in consumption
patterns. Mechanization spelt the disappearance of the *cigarrera* as a
skilled worker in control of her own factory working time. In spite of this,
starting times and attendance continued to be flexible for many of them,
a policy of tolerance reflecting a company strategy of accommodating a
manual system to a mechanical one while avoiding unpopular adjustments
for existing staff.

A culture of absenteeism[82]

The flexible pattern of attendance and persistent absenteeism in the factory
during the industrialization period illustrates the interaction between the
family and the market better than the flexible daily use of time. Sometimes
this was because of a collusion between the flexibility needed by the company[83] and the flexible use of time needed by the *cigarreras* to accomplish

---

[80] Among the *cigarreras*, there was a high degree of solidarity and mutual support. One
cigarrera (C.M.A., interviewed in March 1994) said that she was more productive than her
sister and used to help her to reach the quota every day. P.A. Cooper, *Once a Cigar Maker:
Men, Women and Work Culture in American Cigar Factories, 1910–1919* (Urbana, 1987),
on work culture between men and women in the American tobacco industry, has also
encountered this solidarity among women who worked in groups: "Women created a bank
so that they could share tobacco with each other out of the foreman's sight and help
everyone meet quota, which reflected a collective, rather than individual, approach to shop-
floor discipline" (p. 321).

[81] This double use of time was sanctioned in the 1927 rules, when the company knew that
the end of the manual workshops was only a question of few years. Article 40 of the 1927
rules established that: "The official number of working hours at the factory will be established as 8, which can be adapted to any special personal and town circumstances. In the
manual workshops, considering that their members are mostly aged, the time of entrance
to the workshops can be more flexible but, given that the exit time is fixed, they will work
less than the 8 hours when they arrive later."

[82] Because *cigarreras'* absences were a real problem for management, as reflected in company records, it is possible to use the term absenteeism when referring to the *cigarreras'*
absences.

[83] Through the study of the financial aspects of the companies, it is possible to know
whether or not companies profited from non-attendance. See T. Barmby, C.D. Orme and
J. Treble, "Worker Absenteeism: An Analysis Using Microdata", Discussion paper series,
Centre for Economic Policy Research (London, 1990), and idem, "Worker Absence Histo-

their household tasks, and sometimes the practice was seen as the lesser of two evils: preferable to the alternative of firing workers and creating social uproar. The continued toleration of these practices by the factory, even after the workshops were mechanized, has to be understood from within a monopoly system and in relation to a company strategy derived from the flexibility needed in this transition period. The maintenance of these practices related to the family has to be understood within this historical context and through a gender analysis. In past centuries, household work involved a greater number of tasks than it does nowadays and, in the context of the living conditions of working-class families, absenteeism could be understood as enabling the part-time running of the household.[84]

The *cigarreras* maintained a level of non-attendance during this period equivalent to around 20 per cent of total attendance at the beginning of the period of CAT management, 10 per cent in the years following World War I, and nearly 30 per cent in the 1930s. This variation was mostly in response to the factory's demand for production. The collusion between company strategies and custom, motivated by both labour and family considerations, needs some explanation. During the nineteenth century, increasing consumption of cigars and cigarettes provoked continual recruitment of personnel, mostly descendants of *cigarreras*. Cigar-making was a semi-autonomous profession. The women worked on a piece-work system and had to bring their own tools to the factory.[85] No control was exercised over attendance in the workplace.[86] This production context, together with the state monopoly structure of the factory and the fact that the skilled workers were women who needed time for household tasks, encouraged the development of a culture of absenteeism. In contrast to

---

ries: A Panel Data Study", Working paper, School of Accounting Banking and Economics (University of Wales, Bangor, 1994), who have demonstrated the potential importance of considering the financial aspects of the firm and attendance control in explaining persistent absenteeism.

[84] Nevertheless, part-time jobs continued to be performed by women. In fact, studies of household labour beginning in the 1910s and continuing through to the 1970s show that the amount of time a full-time housewife devoted to her housework remained virtually unchanged over a 50-year period, despite dramatic changes in household technology (see N. Folbre and B. Wagman, "Counting Housework: New Estimates of Real Product in the United States. 1800–1860", *The Journal of Economic History*, 53 (1993), pp. 275–288). J. Schor, *The Overworked American. The Unexpected Decline of Leisure* (New York, 1991), p. 8, explains that over time, new responsibilities were created, such as the need to pay more attention to the education of children and to personal care.

[85] The 1835 rules said that: "[. . .] workers should carry with them chairs, scissors [. . .]: *Obligaciones y Facultades del Superintendente*, 1835. AHFT (Archivo histórico fábrica de Sevilla), Expedientes generales, Leg. 628.

[86] M. Perrot,"De la Manufacture à l'Usine en Miettes", *Le mouvement social*, 125 (1983), pp. 3–12, esp. p. 5. The piece-work system did not demand a continuous control as did work in the textile factories because piece-work labourers enjoyed a flexible use of time. The disciplinary crisis at the beginning of the twentieth century was in part a consequence of the application of a "textile" discipline to other industries.

the *cigarreras'* flexible use of time, the *tabaqueros'* working day conformed to conventional standard working hours. *Cigarreras* had different patterns of attendance from those of *tabaqueros* not only because they were female workers but also because of their working conditions, given the remuneration system.[87] *Tabaqueros* did not have this flexible use of time but enjoyed higher wages than the *cigarreras*. The organization of the factory recognized the role of men as breadwinners and the domestic role of women, even if the *cigarreras'* jobs were actually the most important to the household economy. The firm divided its profits amongst its workers as required by society, compensating men in terms of money to perform the breadwinner role and women in the terms of time to perform "their"[88] household tasks. As a result of mechanization, men and women eventually switched importance in the factory's labour plans[89] and in their contribution to family incomes.

[87] For example, when comparing the Spanish tobacco industry with its American counterpart, in which the skilled cigar-makers were men, the influence of the labour conditions on the different use of time between women and men becomes more apparent. Cooper, *Once a Cigar Maker*, has shown how male tobacco workers (unionists) in the US, because of their level of skill, had a higher piece-rate and enjoyed greater freedom in their use of time than women using moulds and machinery (team work). W.D. Evans, "Effects of Mechanization in Cigar Manufacture', *Monthly Labor Review*, Report No. B-4 (1938), pp. 1–21, in his report on the American tobacco industry, writes for the Department of Labour: "[. . .] hours of labour in factories making cigars by hand especially before the introduction of machines, were in general somewhat informal [. . .] many cigar-factory employees do not work all the hours the factory is open and work afforded. The work is so largely individual in many factories that the coming and going of employees does not interfere materially with the work of others – this information is related to 1911–12 [. . .]" (pp. 18–19). The remuneration system is very important in explaining the absence behaviour of workers. J. Treble, "The Wages Book of Garesfield Butepit, County Durham: Data Description and Summary Statistics, June 1890 to June 1892" (Labour Economics Unit, Research Papers 90/2, University of Hull, 1990), a study of the Durham mines workers, established the way in which workers were remunerated as an important determinant of absenteeism: as important as labour conditions in the different areas of work in the mines, such as humidity, depth, etc.

[88] Their house or their tasks were the terms under which women with no market occupation are recorded in twentieth-century Spanish censuses prior to the advent of democracy.

[89] Control of production in the workshop was no longer exercised by the *cigarreras* but by the mechanics. Comparing the models of the evolution of the sexual division of labour in the Spanish tobacco factories and those in the United States (see Prus, "Mechanization and the Gender-Based Division of Labour"), it is possible to observe that the homogenization of both models was only accomplished with complete mechanization. In the US, the skilled workers were men, and women joined the tobacco industry at the end of the nineteenth century, parallel to the application of the first semi-mechanical techniques. When factories became fully mechanized, the women took over the men's posts. As in the Spanish case, workers making cigars mechanically lost the importance in the production process possessed by the manual cigar-makers. In both tobacco industries, the new key job in the workshops was that of the mechanic, and in both this was the province of men. While in Spain control over production passed with the mechanization from women to men, in the US – even though there was a switch in duties – the transition was man to man. See Gálvez-Muñoz, "Management, Labour and Gender".

Modernization plans and flexible use of time

The flexibility required during this period and the maintenance of a skilled but frequently absent workforce was a second-best strategy, employed due to the impossibility of eliminating the labour surplus created when the *cigarreras* were replaced by machines but social, financial,[90] technical and market constraints prevented their dismissal. Flexibility was needed, on the one hand, to match tobacco supply to demand and, on the other, to begin the process of mechanization and modify the workforce in a way which would avoid social unrest. It was achieved first because the monopoly system permitted a slower and more secure transition; and second because the workers' flexible use of time provided an available skilled labour force when it was needed.

The state and the firm's monopolistic structure played an essential role in allowing the mechanization of production to coexist with the *cigarreras'* absenteeism. Although the state could be expected to be more interested in maintaining social stability (more especially, in this case, because of the importance of tobacco factories to their various local labour markets), it was the monopoly structure of the firm more than the interventionist power of the state that explains the caution employed in the implementation of the CAT's two main strategies: mechanization and the reduction of the labour force. On one hand, the monopolistic character of the business permitted price control, while also pursuing a cost-based pricing policy. On the other hand, apart from the direct effect of public paternalism on the rise of absenteeism rates,[91] the fact that the tobacco factories were real instruments of political clientelism led local forces to express strong opposition to any mass firing policies as a consequence of the investments in modern technological equipment.

The toleration of absenteeism in the tobacco factory at Seville and the plans to rationalize production could coexist due to the following factors. First, absenteeism did not affect relative wage costs under a piece-work system of remuneration. Second, the CAT's need for flexibility to meet the demand for tobacco during the mechanization process was reinforced by the fact that tobacco was a perishable product ruined by long storage. Flexible production to solve the mismatch between supply and demand

---

[90] The high rent that the CAT had to pay to the state was due to the importance of fiscal monopolies, and especially the tobacco monopoly, to the Spanish Treasury. It has to be related to the insufficiency of tax resources and Spanish backwardness in refusing modern tax systems. About the fiscal monopolies, see F. Comín, "La empresa pública en la España contemporánea: formas históricas de organización y gestión", in Comín, *La empresa en la historia de España*, pp. 349–367.

[91] G. Esping-Andersen, "Decommodification and Work Absences in the Welfare State", Working paper, IUE, no. 367 (Florence, 1988), studying absenteeism in the Scandinavian countries, has demonstrated that the state promoted non-attendance more as an employer than as a legislator.

inherited from state management also required a flexible labour force. For this reason, during the first decades of CAT management, before the introduction of semi-mechanical and mechanized workshops, the firm implemented a labour hoarding strategy.[92] The maintenance of more *cigarreras* than production needs required helped to lower the hiring and firing costs if the market changed. Because of the *cigarreras*' culture of absenteeism, it was necessary to have 15–20 per cent more cigar-makers in the workshop in order to maintain production. The specific skills of cigar-makers and the existence of highly substitutable workshops eased internal labour mobility, mitigating the effects of absenteeism on production. This system also permitted the coexistence of absenteeism and mechanized workshops where the investment in technology (in capital) required a continuous flow of personnel. These practices became an alternative to firing workers since, at the same time, the company did not exploit its right to dismiss 25 per cent of the labour force. Indeed, the firm's inaction in this respect constituted a conscious policy of avoiding social unrest by transferring all responsibility to the worker. This gradual transition to industrialism would have been impossible with a male labour force.

The market, production plans and absenteeism

The CAT used incentives to attract *cigarreras* to the factory in order to tailor the number of workers to production needs in response to market changes and production plans. For instance, from 1917 onwards, the firm added an attendance incentive component to the *cigarreras*' pay in order to solve the problem of insufficient tobacco production. As a matter of fact, the lowest absenteeism rates occur from this date through to 1925. The policy of freezing new recruitment after 1887 was reasonable as long as labour was being replaced by machines. However, the number of employees in the factories dropped considerably over this period. The

---

[92] The concept of labour hoarding comprised the company strategy applied during the economic recessions, mostly among workers with specific skills. This strategy consists of maintaining more workers than production needs rather than firing them, because of the transaction costs that the company has to suffer, not only for the fired workers but more for the cost of the substitution of these workers on the labour market when the economic situation changes. This idea has its origins in the variability and uncertainty of modern economies, and in the concept of work as a quasi-fixed factor of production. This implies that managers have an incentive to consider workers as capital when they have taken on part of the training of the worker. The first person to sustain the idea of work as a quasi-fixed factor of production was W.Y. Oi, "Labor as a Quasi-Fixed Factor", *Journal of Political Economy*, 70 (1962), pp. 538–555. The Marxist concept of excess army could not be used in this model. This concept implies the existence of an excess labour population which worked as crowbar for capitalist accumulation: see H. Braverman, *Labor and Monopoly Capital* (New York, 1974). Nevertheless, this concept saw the worker as exploited, while the *cigarreras* profited in terms of time from this company strategy, which was in itself mostly an adaptation of the earlier situation.

beginning of the attendance incentive payments in 1917 changed the remuneration system, introducing a mixed model of payment consisting of a fixed part and a variable part depending on individual production.[93] At the same time, the new payments acted as an incentive to attendance in the workplace because workers received them only if they turned up at work. As a result, the opportunity cost of absenteeism to the household economy was now higher. By contrast, during the 1930s the factory encouraged non-attendance by the *cigarreras* by allowing sick leave regardless of whether *cigarreras* were really ill. The introduction of apprenticeships in the 1920s and the mechanization of the majority of the workshops resulted in an excess of workers, which also affected the mechanized workshops.[94] Until this time, the manual workshops with skilled workers had been maintained to allow for any shift in consumer preference towards manually produced cigars and cigarettes. This meant that some new workers could be trained in manual techniques. However, the definitive acceptance of machine-made cigars and cigarettes made the manual workshops and their workers practically redundant. The average daily wage of a cigar-maker in 1930 amounted to 7.17 Pts. Sick leave reduced this to 5 Pts per day. Since workers could not be dismissed because of state pressure, absence brought double benefits to management: it reduced average wages and limited the excess production of tobacco, which would otherwise have had to be stored and possibly thrown away. Doctors gave unlimited leave of absence for illness. Sick leave gave the *cigarreras* money and time. In fact, in 1933 when the *cigarreras*' and *tabaqueros*' union denounced the doctors for negligence in granting leave of absence, only two women obeyed the union and signed the protest, although the *cigarreras* constituted 80 per cent of union members. As in the case of the eight-hour working day, they defended family strategies against union strategies.[95]

A change in the nature of the absenteeism occurred when there was a break in the previously direct link between time needs for household tasks and job attendance. When the CAT started to subsidize *cigarreras*' absenteeism through sick leave (because it could not fire them), the company also took control of *cigarreras*' absences. The company was expecting the

[93] The fixed part was 0.25 Pts a day when it was established in 1917. It was raised to 0.5 Pts in 1918; to 1 Pts in 1919; to 2.5 Pts in 1930; and to 3 Pts in 1933.
[94] In an inspection of the workshops made on 18 May 1931, the administration made a list of *cigarreras* in the workshops and *cigarreras* taking any kind of leave. For example, in the mechanized cigarette workshops, it was calculated that the number of workers needed for production was 54, but there were 65 on the list. These 11 *cigarreras* were an excess of supply which smooth the functioning of the workshop when other cigar-makers did not attend. If the number in attendance exceeded 54 they were employed in other workshops: AFTS, Leg. 917.
[95] In 1919, the *cigarreras*' opposition to the eight-hour working day could be understood as an opposition to a general working-class demand. But on this occasion, the opposition is specifically to the *cigarreras*' and *tabaqueros*' union. The Seville section, NICOT, denounced the doctors because they refused to become members of the union.

government to pass a compulsory retirement law for tobacco workers in order to rid itself of the excess workers who could not be fired. When legislation was passed introducing a compulsory retirement age of 67 for CAT employees, the necessary adjustment in staff size was finally made. The number of workers in the company at last approximated to the optimal number required for mechanized production. It was only after the retirement law for the tobacco workers came into effect that the age of workers in the factory was limited to 67.[96] This law was mainly a necessary instrument to adjust the size of the staff to the new mechanical order.

The flexible use of time and the gender of its workers formed an integral component of the industrialization process in the tobacco factory. The maintenance of the female labour force's opportunities was closely related to the gradual way in which the company imposed industrialization. The gender of workers not only permitted this flexibility, but also helped to make the transition less traumatic. Precisely because women were not supposed to be breadwinners, a labour adjustment involving as much as 80 per cent of the workforce in a factory linked with the public administration would have been more difficult and violent with male workers rather than female.

CONCLUSIONS

Through the analysis of a wide range of exogenous factors, this essay shows the necessity of employing a more historical approach to explain breadwinner patterns. Nevertheless, although the local labour market, regional economy, company labour policy, institutions, laws and customs all played a fundamental role, both patriarchy and capitalism continued to provide strong explanations for the consolidation of the male breadwinner family. On one hand, the study of *cigarreras'* labour and household models demonstrates the strong explanatory power of patriarchy. In this historical context, a breadwinner-wife was possible but a house-husband was not. In fact, the model of the *cigarrera* was only possible because of the special working conditions which allowed these women to bring their babies to the factory, to enjoy a flexible use of time and to control the apprenticeship system, and because of the high rates of unemployment in

---

[96] This law was promulgated on 2 July 1936. But the law came into force only when the Civil War ended and the management of all Spanish tobacco factories was reunified. That retirement was beneficial for the workers and for the company is shown by the fact that the company managers and the tobacco workers' union jointly petitioned the government for it. The company expressed itself in these terms: "This workforce is mainly aged and has imposed a constraint on technical development. We have compensated for this economically by intensive production and redistributing work spaces in order to reduce pressure on some workshops, as well as by better discipline and supervision [. . .] Socially, we have observed moral responsibility towards those workers who have devoted all their lives to the factory": quoted in Valdés Chápuli, *La Fábrica de Tabacos de Alicante*, p. 73.

the local labour market. On the other hand, the industrialization of the Spanish tobacco monopoly spelt a change in the *cigarreras'* family economy system at three different levels: first, as a result of the reduction in female staff employed by the CAT, the number of families associated with the system declined. As a matter of fact, there was a reduction in the percentage of wives occupied and an identification of the female workforce with unskilled and temporary workers in the Seville labour market. Second, the number of *cigarreras* per family decreased. Following the freeze on recruitment to the workshops, only two cohorts of female descendants were able to enter the factory during the period studied. The result was a gender change in the composition of the factory's workforce and in the family labour supply. After mechanization, the company stopped hiring female tobacco workers but increased its demand for male workers. As a consequence, the family labour supply changed from a female to a male workforce by promoting sons as the most eligible candidates for factory jobs. As a consequence of industrialization, the *cigarreras'* family model changed to a male breadwinner family system. And third, parallel to the de-skilling process experienced by the *cigarreras*, the labour supply model (or the transmission of jobs from one generation to the next) ceased to be a necessity imposed by the family apprenticeship system, and became a concession by the company in response to worker pressure. In addition, there was a breakdown in the transmission of skills from mothers to daughters, resulting in the end of this skilled female labour model.

This article has tried to demonstrate the interactive relationship between the family and the market. The joint analysis of company strategies and family strategies during the industrialization process at the tobacco factory of Seville shows how the *cigarreras'* family strategies were an integral component in this process, apparently helping to render the transition to industrial capitalism less traumatic, even while destroying the traditional *cigarreras'* family economy model. The mechanization of the factory under CAT management was gradual but effective, thanks to the firm's monopoly structure and the flexible organization of production. This process was interconnected in a different way with the two main family strategies. If the flexible use of time needed for the running of the family unit colluded with the labour flexibility needed by the company during this transitional period, the maintenance of hereditary hiring policies was due more to political than to economic considerations. The recruitment of new apprentices coincided with the start of the mechanized workshops. Even if the company did not benefit economically from this practice since the apprenticeship system was no longer essential to mechanical production, its use of apprenticeship may be explained first by the fact that it helped the firm to avoid social unrest and second on the basis that it helped a group of workers to accept the machines which they had traditionally opposed.

Lina Gálvez-Muñoz

Table 5. *Sample of cigarreras census bias*
(730 households in Triana, census 1924)

In census	23
Total	87
% in the census	26.4%

Table 6. *Average income share, 1924*

Type	Code	All *cigarreras*	One *cigarrera*	Rest
Families with at least one *cigarrera*	1	55.7%	68.5%	31.5%
		Householder		Rest
Householder: female	2	3.1%		96.9%
Householder: day labourer	3	62.6%		37.4%
Householder: semi-skilled and skilled industrial	4	63.9%		36.1%

Finally, this paper calls for the use of the same approach in analysing female and male labour behaviour. Since the interrelationship between the family and the market is a gendered construct, men and women should both be studied in the family and in the market. Scholars should avoid explaining the working life of women solely in terms of gender, identifying women with unskilled work, and explaining the working life of men solely in terms of labour, identifying men as the breadwinners. General theorizations need to be reconsidered in favour of a more historical approach.

Family, Work and Wages: The Stéphanois Region of France, 1840–1914[*]

MICHAEL HANAGAN

Exploring issues of the family wage, this paper examines labour markets, family employment patterns and political conflict in France.[1] Up to now, the debate over the family wage has centred mainly on analysing British trade unions and the development of an ideal of domesticity among the British working classes, more or less taking for granted the declining women's labour force participation rate and the configuration of state/trade union relations prevailing in Great Britain.[2] Shifting the debate across the Channel, scholars such as Laura Frader and Susan Pedersen have suggested that different attitudes to the family wage prevailed.[3] In France, demands for the exclusion of women from industry were extremely rare because women's participation in industry was taken for granted. But a gendered division of labour and ideals of domesticity remained and made themselves felt in both workforce and labour movement.

In France, conditions of labour supply contrasted sharply with the UK, for it was far more difficult to recruit factory labour in France than in Britain. As a result of the difficulty of recruiting males, many of whom remained in peasant agriculture, female participation in the French labour force grew rapidly at a time when it was declining in England; in France, even a significant number of married women with children worked in factories. Censuses indicate that 24.7 per cent of the total female population of France was economically active in 1866, compared with 27.2 per cent in Great Britain in 1871, and 9.7 per cent in the US in 1870. However, forty or more years later, France had 38.7 per cent in 1911, Britain 25.7 per cent in 1911 and the US 16.7 per cent in 1910.[4] With female labour

[*] I would like to thank Miriam Cohen, Louise Tilly and Angélique Janssens.

[1] Derived from Seecombe, the definition of the "family wage" employed here is the "notion that the wage earned by a husband ought to be sufficient to support his family without his wife and young children having to work for pay": see Wally Seecombe, "Patriarchy Stabilized: The Construction of the Male Breadwinner Wage Norm in Nineteenth-Century Britain", *Social History*, 1, 11 (1986), pp. 53–76, esp. p. 54. Seecombe prefers the term "male breadwinner norm" to "family wage", but the concept of "norm", as we shall see, has its own problems.

[2] C. Creighton, "The Rise of the Male Breadwinner Family: A Reappraisal", *Comparative Studies in Society and History*, 38 (1996), pp. 310–337, esp. p. 330.

[3] Laura Frader, "Engendering Work and Wages: The French Labour Movement and the Family Wage", in Laura L. Frader and Sonya O. Rose (eds), *Gender and Class in Modern Europe* (Ithaca, 1996), pp. 141–164 and Susan Pedersen, *Family Dependence and the Origin of the Welfare State* (New York, 1993).

[4] P. Bairoch, *The Working Population and Its Structure*, vol. 1 (Brussels, 1968). It is very likely that French female labour force participation is underestimated because the

force participation in France high and growing in the second half of the nineteenth century, it was much harder to foster an image of "domesticity" as a "norm" for working-class women.

French labour unions were also generally less formally organized than their British counterparts and less able to carry out exclusionary practices had they so desired. In France, even in the 1900s, such flourishing British institutions as collective bargaining and strongly-organized national craft unions were almost non-existent – with one exception. By far the best-known case of the exclusion of women from the trade unions was the Couriau affair of 1913 and, in this case, the printers' union's effort to exclude women from skilled work was not upheld by the French national trade union, the CGT.[5] But the affair really underscores the irrelevance of craft; the French printers' union was explicitly modelled on craft unions of the American and British types, with relatively high dues, strike funds and mutual aid functions, but it was practically the only French trade union so organized. Highly paid skilled workers might laud the benefits of domesticity, but the structure of French unionism with its fluctuating duespayers, its weak national federations, and its unpaid local officials whose participation was based on political zeal, was unsuited to exclusionary policies.[6]

Finally, the relationship between the French labour movement and the state was fundamentally different from that in the UK. In both countries, the labour movement had long made itself a champion of universal manhood suffrage. Opposed by their own peers, manhood suffrage and the long sought republic were achieved in the 1870s, but republican triumph had seriously divided French elites, influential segments of which were firmly anti-republican. As a result, French republicans had to acknowledge their dependence on the working classes in a manner different from that of British Liberal reformers. Republicans could not afford to see reactionary anti-republican industrialists carry out massive repression of workers; sustained working-class defeats in a region sooner or later meant the advent of an anti-republican deputy. French labour organizations could remain decentralized and radical because, despite their weak national organization and their radicalism, they could count on a measure of government support.

This paper focuses on a single region of France and looks at the context for the emergence of demands for a "family wage". Unlike studies that seek to support their argument by searching for cases which illustrate it,

participation of women in peasant agriculture is not fully incorporated into census estimates.

[5] Charles Sowerwine, "Workers and Women in France Before 1914: The Debate Over the Couriau Affair", *Journal of Modern History*, 55 (1983), pp. 411–441.

[6] Michelle Perrot, "L'éloge de la ménagère dans le discours ouvrier français au XIXe siècle", *Romantisme*, 13–14 (1976), pp. 105–122; Edward Shorter and Charles Tilly, *Strikes in France, 1830–1968* (Cambridge, 1974); and Gerald Friedman, "The State and the Making of the Working Class", *Theory and Society*, 17 (1988), pp. 403–430.

this study selects an area and surveys the ways in which workers used the demand for a family wage. Unlike artisanal and craft workers, many workers in large scale or heavy industry were still illiterate in late nineteenth-century France. Industrial workers were usually consigned to the periphery of those reading circles, debating societies and independent newspapers that enthralled more prosperous and better educated artisans – and little written record remains of their beliefs. To gauge industrial workers' opinions, a variety of sources and contexts must be examined. The region chosen is the area around Saint-Etienne in south-eastern France, the so-called Stéphanois region, one of the earliest centres of the Industrial Revolution in France, an important site for the growth of French heavy industry, but also an old ribbonweaving centre possessing thriving garment industries.

BEYOND THE FAMILY WAGE DEMAND: RHETORIC AND DAILY LIFE – THE PRE-INDUSTRIAL EXPERIENCE

In the Stéphanois the idea that wife and young children of "respectable" workers should belong to a household that was a refuge for weary male workers had weak roots. To understand the perspective of Stéphanois working-class families on the place of work and family in daily life between 1840 and 1914, account must be taken of the experiences that migrants brought with them to the industrial city or acquired growing up in the city before the advent of heavy industry in the 1840s. First, rural dwellers were committed to economic diversification; second, they were accustomed to a gendered division of labour; and third, they were reared in a culture in which the role of the male as household head was at least publicly acknowledged.

Economic diversification was characteristic of pre-industrial labour in the Stéphanois. Conscious of economic frailty, peasants planted a variety of secondary crops in case a main crop would fail, so wherever possible, rural families in the migrant-sending regions combined waged work and farming or one type of domestic industry with another.[7] Students of "proto-industry" have described it as the royal road to proletarianization because, by investing all their resources in domestic industry, producers could be swept away by a downturn in demand or by technological obsolescence. Families engaging in rural domestic industry seem to have been at least dimly aware of this danger because, when they could, they avoided concentrating in a single industry.[8] The rich diversity of rural industries

---

[7] This kind of division of labour seems to have been quite general: Harriet Bradley, *Men's Work, Women's Work: A Sociological History of the Sexual Division of Labour in Employment* (Minneapolis, 1989).

[8] A point well made for the commune of Marlhes by James Lehning, "Nuptuality and Rural Industry: Families and Labour in the French Countryside", *Journal of Family History*, 8, 4 (1983), pp. 333–345.

present in the Stéphanois in the first half of the nineteenth century made this possible.

In the first half of the nineteenth century, between 1806 and 1856, the cities almost continuously lining the valleys to the north-east and south-west of the city of Saint-Etienne on the eastern edge of the Massif Central grew rapidly: Rive-de-Gier's population increased almost three times to around 15,000, and neighbouring Saint-Etienne grew at the same rate to 180,000. The population of the Stéphanois valleys were largely migrants from the nearby mountainous countryside to the west, south and north-west. Before 1840, tens of thousands of households of the *arrondissement* of Saint-Etienne in the *département* of the Loire, the *arrondissements* of Yssingeaux and Le Puy in the Haute-Loire, and the *arrondissement* of Ambert in the Puy-de-Dôme had participated in a regional economy that combined the cultivation of rye, domestic industry and seasonal labour. Indeed, agricultural and industrial work long remained complementary even as industrial work moved from countryside to city. The manpower requirements of the harvest season in rye were concentrated in July, August and September when the water-powered mills of the mountain hamlets and the cities in the valley, consumers of rye bread, slowed to a trickle due to seasonal drought; the long winters provided plenty of time for agriculturalists to participate in industry – at least as long as the cold did not freeze the mountain streams.[9]

These mountainous areas were poor agricultural terrain, but the opportunities for seasonal labour and domestic industry promoted population growth. Incredible as it may seem for someone who visits this terrain today, in the 1840s the *arrondissement* of Ambert in the Puy-de-Dôme was one of the fifteen most populous *arrondissements* in all of France – rural or urban. This population was no stranger to industry. For at least a century before 1840, the current generation, their parents and their parents' parents had engaged in industrial labour. Countrymen and women had pursued silkweaving, lacemaking, or ironmongering in their own rural environment, while others, mainly men but sometimes women, had taken the road down to the valley to market their farm goods, to bring their loads of bolts, scythes or knife blades to the urban merchant, to obtain seasonal work in urban construction or as industrial day labourers, or to work as domestics in ribbonweavers' households. In the city, migrants prepared their return to rural life, women worked for their dowry, men to round off the piece of land they expected to inherit.[10]

---

[9] The importance of looking at the ecological relationship between proto-industrialization and industrialization is stressed by Joyce M. Mastboom, "Protoindustrialization and Agriculture in the Eastern Netherlands", *Social Science History*, 20, 2 (Summer 1996), pp. 235–258.

[10] Michael Hanagan, *Nascent Proletarians: Class Formation in Post-Revolutionary France, 1840–1880* (Oxford, 1989). On seasonal migration, Jan Lucassen, *Migrant Labour in Europe 1600–1900: The Drift to the North Sea* (London, 1987).

Second, while migrants from these regions were utterly familiar with a gendered division of labour and an individual wage, they were unaccustomed to a division between men working for wages and women performing exclusively unwaged work outside of markets. Commonly, men and women performed different types of labour, but even when they performed the same basic type of labour, there was almost always some distinction between the work performed by women and that performed by men. Later on, we shall look more closely at ribbonweaving, but a gendered division of labour can be seen in the mills and factories, generally located in the countryside, both up- and downstream of the weaving process; in the preparatory stages, the reelers (*dévideuses*), the warpers (*ourdisseuses*), and the silkthrowers (*moulineuses*) were all women, while the dyers (*teinturiers*) were male. In the finishing stage the dressers (*dresseurs*) were male and the folders (*plieuses*), female.

Many combinations of wage work and market participation were common. In an area like Saint-Amant-Roche-Savine, a small commune in the *arrondissement* of Ambert, north of the Stéphanois, that contributed many migrants to the industrialized region, the economy was based on seasonally-migrant male "sawyers" who travelled down the mountainside together in bands offering their collective services to farmers or builders. Their mothers, wives and sisters tended the farm. Women, sometimes supervised by fathers or fathers-in-law, were in charge of hiring labour and managing the farm between the planting and harvest periods and marketing. At times, men's seasonal absence could extend to several years, and women's responsibilities multiplied.

In areas of the mountainous Haute-Loire, due east of Saint-Etienne and a prodigious population donor to the Stéphanois, a gendered division of labour followed the rule "The exterior to the men, the interior to women":

This great distinction, general in the region, dominates everything: working the land, cultivation, is reserved for men: never, except for haymaking do the women intervene: their role, along with domestic responsibilities, is butter and cheesemaking, strongly reduced by the export of milk, wetnursing [. . .] and ribbonweaving.[11]

Concentration on domestic activity often meant that women organized and supervised textile production. In 1867 Jules Vallès wrote that: "the women of the Haute Loire reveal themselves as energetic. They are small businesswomen, small farmers' wives, or important tradeswomen who are the head, soul and sometimes the arms of the house." He explained that "the country lives by lacemaking and as the workers are young and fresh peasant girls who embroider the lace [. . .] the wives prefer not to let their husbands talk with the embroiderers or tradeswomen".[12] In the wintertime,

---

[11] Pierre du Maroussem, "Fermiers Montagnards du Haut-Forez", in *Les Ouvriers des Deux Mondes*, vol. 4, Deuxième Serie (Paris, 1892), p. 421.
[12] Jules Vallès, "La Situation, 22 septembre 1867", in Roger Bellet (ed.), *Oeuvres* (Paris, 1975), p. 979.

with agricultural work reduced, husbands could be found spending entire days in nearby cafés while their wives supervised work in the household.

Finally, despite female participation in wage work and markets, men still asserted their role as household head and the particular responsibility of women for domestic affairs. Peasant customs insisted on this point. For example, in Forez, the mountainous region of the Loire *département* west of the Loire river, when the young bride returned to her home from the church, she often found a broom across the door and was expected to sweep with it to demonstrate her mastery of household tasks and responsibility for its chores.[13] In one Forézien village, during the marriage banquet, a chorus lectured the groom about the dangers of marital relationships. The groom responded with his own song including the lines, "I wish to be always master of the house".[14] All such rituals, as Martine Segalen reminds us, are polysemic and subject to different interpretations, and other customs suggest that, even after marriage, questions of familial authority were not entirely closed, but the public facade of male household headship and female domesticity was at least maintained.[15]

Migrating to the urban centres of the industrial valley, rural dwellers found continuity with rural divisions of labour as well as important differences. In some communities, such as Firminy, on the north-eastern edge of the industrial valley, urban life in the first half of the nineteenth century was not so different from rural. One of the Stéphanois industrial cities, which would soon become a largely coalmining town, Firminy was dominated by nailmaking and silkweaving. In domestic workshops, men and boys heated iron ingots and shaped them on an anvil into nails. Meanwhile, above the smithy, women wove plain silk fabrics.[16]

In Saint-Etienne and Saint-Chamond, centres of skilled silk production, a true "family economy" prevailed. Workshops in which the household was both the unit of production and reproduction were more likely to be found in cities. Saint-Etienne was the predominant French centre for the production of silk ribbons. Ribbonweaving was a fashion industry, tied closely to the rhythm of Parisian garments, and skilled weavers congregated together to keep abreast of fashion trends and to learn the new techniques they required.

Ribbons produced in family workshops on large silk looms were expensive and required substantial skills. The master/father directed the labour of his wife and children, although in many households where wives had grown up in the silk trade they were as knowledgeable as their husbands. In more prosperous households, masters were assisted by young

---

[13] Marguerite Gonon, *Coutumes de mariage en Forez* (Lyon, 1979), pp. 67–68.

[14] *Ibid.*, pp. 98–99.

[15] On the ambiguities within the rituals, James R. Lehning, *Peasant and French: Cultural Contact in Rural France during the Nineteenth Century* (Cambridge, 1995).

[16] Albert Boissier, "Essai sur l'histoire et sur les Origines de l'Industries du Clou Forgé dans la Région de Firminy", *Revue de Folklore Français*, 12, 2 (1941), pp. 63–109.

apprentices and journeymen learning the trade. The fluctuating demands of fashion led to rapid changes in the requirements for silk goods. The contractors (*commis de barre*) who were the intermediaries between the *fabricants*, who took orders from Paris, and the master silkweavers, generally arranged production so as to preserve their relationship with highly skilled masters who might be needed in the next fashion swing.

In one city in the industrial valley, Rive-de-Gier, almost alone in the Stéphanois, an industrial economy developed in which women were not expected to engage in wage labour. The idea that women would not engage in wage labour was so remarkable that it was enshrined in a proverb. The saying went: "Rive-de-Gier is hell for horses, purgatory for men, and heaven for women."[17] The logic of this saying was that: horses were lowered into the mines, never to see the light of day; men working in the glassworks were in contact with fire much of the day and miners descended into the ground for most of the daylight hours; and women were in paradise because they did not work for wages.

Because early coalminers came from the countryside around Rive-de-Gier and possessed land for farming or gardening, the only conspicuous group of workers with wives involved in unwaged work were the glassworkers. Theirs was a well-paid elite whose standard of living was celebrated in song and story, and stories convey perhaps better than anything how unusual these workers' families were, not only at the time but in succeeding decades. Forty years after the glassworkers' trade union had been broken and twenty years after the disappearance of most glassworking from the Stéphanois, a local storyteller told of glassworker improvidence. "What stories did they not tell of the glassworkers whose wives went to the countryside with aprons heavy with ecus? Certain of them, for dinner, ate only chicken filets and threw the carcasses out the window to the family's dog pack, waiting in the street, which fought over the pieces."[18] In the 1920s, this cuisine of dainty worker housewives partook of the fabulous.

BEYOND THE FAMILY WAGE DEMAND: RHETORIC AND DAILY LIFE – THE INDUSTRIAL EXPERIENCE

The new working-class families developing in the Stéphanois came from backgrounds where female domesticity was exceptional and, given the miserable conditions confronting early urban proletarians, had no incentive to demand the exclusion of women from industry. After 1848, Stéphanois workers, particularly miners, rhetorically, demanded a "family wage" and,

---

[17] The saying probably originated in a description of Paris. Louis-Sebastien Mercier referred to survival rates of women, men and horses in urban environment of the capital, quoted in Jeffrey Kaplow (ed.), *Le Tableau de Paris* (Paris, 1982), p. 31.
[18] M. Fournier, *La vie d'une cité: Impressions de Rive-de-Gier* (Saint-Etienne, 1936), pp. 8–9.

publicly, lamented the heavy responsibilities of supporting an entire family. At the same time, in everyday life they sought, through the employment of family members, to avoid the burden that they bore so publicly. Workers' demands for a family wage were not inconsistent with sending very young children, daughters, and even wives to work. But it was not always possible to find employment for many family members. Except for a reticence to send married women to work outside the home, and this was often overcome, family employment patterns ultimately depended not on workers' fancied respectability or aggrieved masculinity but on the availability of jobs. While the industrial transformation of the Stéphanois began in the 1810s and the region was a principal centre of the first Industrial Revolution in the European continent, it was the second Industrial Revolution, after 1840, that really threatened to transform the character of popular life. Over the next seventy-five years, however, Sté-phanois workers held fast to multi-stranded ties to wage work, a gendered division of labour, and male household headship and feminine domes-ticity – all legacies of their proto-industrial past.

The great change in the everyday conditions of workers' lives began in coalmining and built on proto-industrial traditions while reshaping them in significant ways. In the 1840s, the newly established coal monopoly completely reorganized the Stéphanois mines, ending the small-scale exploitation whose unsystematic character had led to a dangerous proxim-ity of pits and to the flooding of poorly maintained mines. The monopoly invested large sums of capital, consolidated production into a few newly excavated mines and restructured the labour force. Between 1846 and 1854, coal production doubled, and the workforce more than doubled from about 3,200 to a little under 8,000.[19] No longer recruited exclusively from among the older miners' kin, management officials now hired the work-force. The result of the reorganization was the appearance of a new kind of worker. The large-scale exploitation of the mines made possible by greater capital investment required a larger number of miners who would work on a year-round basis. As the opportunity for year-round work became available in quantity, working-class mining families sprang up in the urban industrial valley drawn from landless agricultural migrants and workers in declining domestic industries.

As the mines expanded rapidly, they recruited far beyond the region in which peasants or tenant farmers could walk to the mine, and the urban population grew. In Rive-de-Gier, many miners' wives became primarily housekeepers, although many also became coal sorters working above ground sorting the coal, separating out rock and washing it down (these were the women celebrated in the song, "The Carbon Flower"). They

---

[19] Pierre Guillaume, "La situation économique et sociale du département de la Loire d'après l'Enquête sur le travail agricole et industriel du 25 mai 1848", *Revue d'histoire moderne et contemporain*, 10 (1963), pp. 5–34.

were temporary workers, hired by the day. But the importance of shiftwork in the mines and, later, in metalworking, created new connections between work and households. If a household was old enough to have sons working in the mines then the responsibility devolved upon mothers and daughters to make sure that food, clothing and bed were ready for workers toiling at very different times. Some Stéphanois women worked at home in domestic industry, while others laboured as less skilled machine tenders in machine construction, but the rapid growth of a mining population produced a less skilled or unskilled urban labour force in which women's waged work (both mothers' and daughters') played a peripheral or even non-existent role.

Here a focus on the small industrial towns that followed the industrial valleys on either side of Saint-Etienne is invaluable. The wide variety of employment combinations that emerged in different towns shows how Stéphanois male workers and their families responded to different employment opportunities. If employment patterns in the three Stéphanois industrial towns are compared in 1876, at the highpoint of rapid growth during the second Industrial Revolution, the variation in women's employment is striking. In 1876, the refined activity rate for men, standardized for age, runs from 0.776 in Le Chambon Feugerolles to 0.856 in Rive-de-Gier, a difference of about one-tenth (0.103); for women it runs from 0.152 in Rive-de-Gier to 0.423 in Saint-Chamond, a factor of about one and three-quarter times (1.782), more than seventeen times the discrepancy for males.[20]

While much was new, old employment patterns also recapitulated themselves. As in pre-industrial labour, women's work experience in industrial labour was fundamentally different from men's. Garmentmaking and other cottage industry employed women and young girls, while metalworking and mining employed men and boys. Because garments and domestic labour employed younger children, girls typically began to work for wages a year earlier than boys. Young girls were also likely to be kept at home to help their mother in her domestic chores, but only after more essential family needs were fulfilled. Logistic regression of the determinants of child employment in the three towns in 1876 shows that girls were likely to be kept at home where there were young siblings needing care, where boarders needed service, or where the presence of older employed siblings provided sufficient income to allow mothers to recruit helpers.[21] None of these considerations affected the employment of young boys.

While there was nothing new about the employment of men and women, boys and girls in different industries or the involvement of girls and married women in industry, the growth of a non-working female population among the wives of less skilled workers is worth remarking. To understand

[20] Hanagan, *Nascent Proletarians*, p. 160.
[21] *Ibid.*, pp. 142–143.

this development, it is necessary to explore mining and metalworking. The second half of the nineteenth century witnessed the growth of a true industrial proletariat in the Stéphanois. Metalworking plants and mines offered wages above those of casual day labourers, and the huge investment in machinery required that these plants run continually on a year-round basis – usually for twenty-four hours a day. These newly reorganized industries employed males almost exclusively. In part, Stéphanois workers were not tempted to demand the exclusion of women from industry because employers in heavy industry had already excluded them. There were a number of obvious reasons for this, not least of which was that tradition played a decisive role. Metalworking in the Stéphanois, even in domestic industry, had generally been male dominated, although not exclusively so, and mining had never employed women in underground labour. Male bias may play a partial role here because all the metal and mining employers were male.[22]

But an equally important explanation for the exclusivity of the male presence is due to the scarcity of year-round, long-term labour and the assumption, correct enough, that year-round, long-term labour was most likely to be male. In times of rapid expansion, Stéphanois employers urgently sought to recruit workers from other regions and were horrified by rumours that employers from other regions had sent recruiters to the Stéphanois. Employers were not interested in temporary workers – these they had in abundance. In the winter, they were besieged by job-seekers, and they were frustrated when reliable workers disappeared for good to the countryside after only a few years. What Stéphanois employers required were continual, long-term workers. Given their assumptions that male household heads were less mobile than single males, married women should and would be consigned to childcare, and working-class families should bear the entire cost of childrearing, married male workers were the ideal labour force.[23]

The overwhelming predominance of adult males in large-scale heavy industry created new employment problems for their family members. Heavy industry employing male heads of household paid the highest wages and called the tune; families formed alongside factories and mines; if domestic industry or light industry was inadequate, than families were unable to earn supplementary income. In fact, such problems were inevitable, because small-scale industry was always subject to greater fluctuations than heavy industry. Indeed the major appeal of such industry was its low capital requirements which accounted for its flexibility and adaptability; labour bore the brunt of seasonality and fluctuating demand.

---

[22] Samuel Cohn, *The Process of Occupational Sex-Typing: The Feminization of Clerical Labour in Great Britain* (Philadelphia, 1985).
[23] Johanna Brenner and Maria Ramas, "Rethinking Women's Oppression", *New Left Review*, 144 (1984), pp. 33–71.

The point is well illustrated by the case of Le Chambon Feugerolles. Between 1840 and 1880, Le Chambon underwent a transition from multi-stranded family labour to dependence on a male wage. If we look at employment patterns in Le Chambon in 1856 we find that most adult males were miners or metalworkers. Many of these male workers had daughters and wives who worked at home as ribbonweavers. Alongside these workers, a minority of the working population was engaged in knifemaking in family workshops. By 1876, hardware manufacturing still survived, but mining and metalworking had grown and loomed even larger in the city's economy, for ribbonweaving had almost entirely disappeared – a victim of economic contraction and changing taste. But perhaps the contraction in ribbonweaving was only a fortunate coincidence, a pretext that allowed adult male workers to withdraw their wives and daughters from a domestic industry that threatened a growing sense of respectability?

Such an interpretation makes no sense at all of Le Chambon in 1900. Domestic industry and women working in factories had returned to the city with a vengeance, employing more women and children workers than formerly, and many daughters were employed in the small factories that had grown up in the interstices between domestic industry and heavy industry. The dynamic force in the city's evolution was the relationship between filemakers in medium-sized factories and filecutters in domestic industry. These had evolved out of the pre-existing blademakers who had switched their attention to files and spread their skills to other sections of the population. Their presence had enabled the town to take advantage of a new need for industrial tools such as files and for industrial products such as bolts. Adult male miners and metalworkers allowed their wives and children to work in domestic and in light industry with alacrity. The metalworkers' daughters, returning home from bolt factories, their clothes covered with grease, reveal how easy it is to confuse changing employment opportunities with the growth of respectability.[24]

A very different pattern emerged in Saint-Chamond. As ribbonweaving declined in the 1850s, it was replaced by the manufacture of braided trimmings – a textile industry that employed large numbers of women. Given the opportunity to send their daughters to work, metalworkers and miners sent them in large numbers as Elinor Accampo has shown.[25] In Saint-Chamond, some workers' wives also found work in the mills. Because censuses underestimate women's work, it is difficult to get a good idea of the extent of women's, particularly married women's, participation in the

---

[24] The infiltration of a miners' quarter of Saint-Etienne, Côte Chaude, by ribbonweaving is another example of this process. On domestic work in another Stéphanois miners' community, see Jean-Paul Burdy, *Le Soleil noir: Un quartier de Saint-Etienne, 1840–1940* (Lyon, 1989).

[25] Elinor Accampo, *Industrialization, Family Life, and Class Relations: Saint-Chamond, 1815–1914* (Berkeley, 1989).

labour force; in 1876, the manuscript census showed that about 8 per cent of wives were employed.[26] In 1911, metalworkers in the large *Aciéries de la Marine* in Saint-Chamond petitioned their employer to change the time of their midday break. The midday break had changed to noon in the braidmaking factories and workers wanted their employer to adjust his schedule similarly so that they could dine *en famille*.[27]

The braiders of Saint-Chamond were extremely poorly paid; their wages clearly provided only a meagre supplement to family income. Dormitories operated by the larger textile companies provided supervision for young girls from the countryside who also worked in the mills, and also three servings of broth per day. The girls were expected to bring their own meat and vegetables to give the broth substance, and usually brought these stores back when they returned from their visits to the countryside.

The concept of the family wage had an impact on these young women; following the model of a gendered division of labour in which males were responsible for supporting families, the women and young girls did not demand a family wage, but simply a wage adequate to support a single woman. This demand won wide support in Saint-Chamond and provoked the biggest strike of women workers in the town's history. In 1877, the advent of the republic temporarily shook the political order of conservative Saint-Chamond. Male workers played an important role in initiating and supporting the strike; skilled male dyers had been challenging their employers and, working together with a group of braiders, encouraged the growth of unionism among the braiders.[28] As part of their campaign, in 1878, they brought a union organizer from Lyon, Marie Finet, labelled the *"Grande Emancipatrice Lyonnaise"*, who helped form a local branch of *Chambre syndicale des dames*, an organization then spreading throughout the south of France. The organizing committee of this union produced a poster which contained an address, "To the Working-Women of Saint-Chamond". One of its demands ran: "It is time, Citoyennes, that an end may be put to this barbarous exploitation, worthy of ancient times. Let us unite [. . .] to demand our right to live, a right contained in work detached from all arbitrariness, pay sufficient to permit a working women to live honestly, by the sweat of her brow."[29]

The evolution of the demand for a "living wage" in braiding was a shrewd strategy designed to promote solidarity among a disparate labour force. Without reliance on paternalistic housing, heating and some food, women did not receive and could not earn a wage that would enable them to live independently in the city. Only a few unmarried women spent their

---

[26] Hanagan, *Nascent Proletarians*, p. 141.

[27] "Rapport n. 240, commissariat de police de Saint-Chamond au préfet", 27 March 1911, ADL 93/M/11.

[28] On alliances, Carol E. Morgan, "Women, Work, and Consciousness in the Mid-Nineteenth Century English Cotton Industry", *Social History*, 17, 1 (1992), pp. 23–41.

[29] Archives de le Prefecture de Police, 4 juillet 1878, no. 47, Ba 171.

entire lives in braiding, but these were a strategically important group who were loyal to the employers who granted pensions to those of them who were diligent and submissive. The demand for a living wage might appeal to these women while it would also have greatly benefited the mass of young female workers who did not expect to spend their lives in the industry.

At the same time that the wives and daughters of metalworkers and miners worked in domestic industry and in factories in Le Chambon Feugerolles and in Saint-Chamond, they continued to concentrate in unwaged labour in Rive-de-Gier. Lacking any ties to domestic industry, Rive-de-Gier found it impossible to develop new ones; new domestic industry seems to have evolved through channels created by old domestic industry. In Rive-de-Gier there was very little in the way of wage work for the daughters of metalworkers and miners, and here the adult male's wage truly had to be a family wage, supplemented mainly by the work of sons when they grew old enough to work in the factory or the small sums earned by sending boys off to the countryside to tend cattle.[30]

Rive-de-Gier illustrates another aspect of the demand for a "family wage"; it was a political issue with a strong resonance in public opinion, and it unified miners and metalworkers across the Stéphanois who participated in very different types of family economies.[31] Napoleon III had broken up the coal monopoly in 1854, but Stéphanois employers had transformed themselves into an oligopoly with five major employers in the region; the same companies which ran mines in Rive-de-Gier and paid wages to many male miners who might be the sole support of their families, also ran mines in Saint-Etienne and Saint-Chamond where female employment was possible.

The defence of the "family wage" was a powerful rejoinder to attempted wage reductions precisely because it drew miners together throughout the region. Striking workers demanded that employers pay the same wages in all the mines that they operated, and the large size of the mining companies meant that most mining companies employed both large numbers of workers belonging to families with working dependants and also workers whose families depended solely on the wages of the male head. Workers' leaders quickly realized the advantage of framing strike demands in terms of the situation of workers with non-labouring dependants; they were the most impoverished and pitiful section of the workforce, yet orienting strikes towards winning a basic wage sufficient for them would benefit all workers. The defence of the "family wage" rallied the poorest miners and metalworkers to the union banner, and the power of the appeal to the family wage against company attacks could only

---

[30] Hanagan, *Nascent Proletarians*, pp. 98–101.
[31] Marcel van der Linden, "Connecting Household History and Labour History", *International Review of Social History*, 38 (1993), Supplement 1, pp. 163–173.

benefit workers in the other towns – workers who did not rely solely on the wage of a male household head.

THE DISCOURSE OF WORKING-CLASS FAMILISM

The French discourse on working-class familism differed markedly from that of Britain, where it is claimed that wives and young children of "respectable" workers did not perform waged work. To understand the evolution of the demand for a family wage in France, it is important to understand this context. By 1900, whether they called for social revolution or mild reform, French working-class leaders and middle-class social reformers more or less took for granted the presence of working married women. This assumption was shared by employers and governments who sought to recruit and govern a stable working-class population. Male workers were not slow to adopt the language of familism to raise demands and make claims on the state, the local middle class, and their employers but, as workers applied it, familism also took on working-class associations.

This new discourse arose to interpret and to deal with the emergence of a new type of working-class family – and the Stéphanois region was one of the earliest sites of its development. The growth of a mining monopoly between 1836 and 1846 was crucial; the dilemmas of working-class familism were first represented in reformist discourse by the image of the coalminer and his family. When social reformers first raised the issue of the "working-class family", they did not have in mind such families as those of the skilled silkweavers, long established in Stéphanois cities, or the families of casual labourers, temporary migrants, who often returned to rural families; rather they imagined the families of the mining proletarian, and later the less skilled factory worker.

The Catholic church was first to locate the working-class family as a key point of intervention; it laid little emphasis on the fact of female employment but stressed the disorganization and degradation of working-class life and the need to moralize it by promoting marriage and religious observance. In 1844, Cardinal de Bonald, the powerful conservative leader of the Lyonnais church, whose see included the *département* of the Loire, refused to condemn a miners' strike, and wrote a letter to the curé of Notre Dame in Rive-de-Gier inquiring whether the families of workers injured in a confrontation with French troops needed aid.[32] In 1844, also, the *Société charitable de St-Jean-François-Régis* was formed in Saint-Etienne to promote the marriage of the working-class couples and the legitimation of their children.[33] The society lamented that:

[32] Paul Droulers, "Le Cardinal de Bonald et la grève des mineurs de Rive-de-Gier en 1844", *Cahiers d'histoire*, 3, 6 (1961), pp. 265–285.
[33] For a discussion of the origin of the society and its Parisian operations see Barrie M. Ratcliffe, "Popular Classes and Cohabitation in Mid-Nineteenth Century Paris", *Journal of Family History*, 21, 3 (July 1996), pp. 316–350.

In the frame of mind where they find themselves, they are ready to welcome avidly all the doctrines, which may, for a time at least, get rid of their inquietude, their doubts, and their remorse for their circumstances. Ideas of order, the love of property, the desire of acquiring and transmitting which doubles the force of the hardworking labourer, has nearly no influence on their spirits.[34]

Governments also began to concern themselves with these workers. The Labour Committee of the Luxembourg Commission, set up in the early days of the 1848 revolution and containing many socialists and trade unionists, prepared a questionnaire (*l'Enquête sur le travail agricole et industriel*) to be filled out in each canton. The decree was approved on 25 April 1848 and much of it was carried out in the Loire in late May.[35] The questionnaire inquired about the number of men, women and children under sixteen employed in industry, requested that respondents compile an annual budget for a working-class family of four ("at the average price of consumer goods") and wanted as well a report about the condition of housing, nourishment and clothing.

After its consecration by the state itself, it is no wonder that discussions of family budgets and concerns with child and female employment show up in subsequent protests! To answer the question concerning family needs, miners from Rive-de-Gier drew up a family budget demonstrating that, for many categories of workers, their own wages were inadequate to support a family. The mining companies made their own budget estimate which, when compared with the wages they paid their miners, revealed that workers could easily support a two-child family.[36] Although the assumption was not explicit, the joint response to the inquiry conveyed the impression that a miners' wage *should* support a family of four people.

An early theorist who helped set French government policy was Frédéric Le Play who stressed the instability of working-class life due to the absence of elders in the household and the prevalence of partible inheritance. Deprived of those ties of property or skill that had attached earlier generations to their parents, working-class children would, he feared, "leave their parental firesides as soon as they gained any confidence in themselves". Even in good times, Le Play asserted, such conduct could not preserve either the individual's welfare or the moral order, but his crowning argument was that such selfish individualism turned to despair when faced with industrial downturns and the loss of employment that could produce only "destitution and misery".[37] In England, industrial conditions had created a new type of "unstable" working-class family such as the miners, where employers "unscrupulously drew the workmen from

---

[34] ADL 28/M/1.
[35] Hilde Rigaudias-Weiss, *Les Enquêtes Ouvrières en France entre 1830 and 1848* (Paris, 1936), pp. 184–203.
[36] "Enquête de 1848 – mineurs de Rive-de-Gier", AN C956.
[37] Frédéric Le Play, *The Organization of Labor in Accordance with Custom and the Law of the Decalogue* (Philadelphia, 1872), pp. 41 and 167.

all rural employments by offer of the most tempting wages without giving them any guarantees of security".[38]

Le Play was consulted by Napoleon III on issues of social policy regarding families and his influence can be seen in some important imperial projects for dealing with the working class. Napoleon III attempted to build a reputation as a friend of the worker; one of his leaflets assured workers that he was interested in their fate from the "cradle to the grave".[39] Much of Napoleon's policy focused on establishing savings banks for workers and encouraging the development of government-controlled mutual aid societies to tide workers over periods of unemployment and to provide for their old age. Such public concern for the working-class family encouraged workers to couch appeals in familist terms.

Workers' interpretation of industrialization and its effect on family life was strongly influenced by the desperate visions of working-class family life advanced by Social Catholics and Le Play, lingering memories of the controversies of 1848, as well as by their own too evident difficulties in making ends meet. The repression of trade unions – reduced briefly in the final years of Louis Napoleon's reign – intensified again after the Commune and continued through the early Third Republic, gave workers relatively limited experience with trade unionism and encouraged the spread of revolutionary alternatives. In turn, socialist revolutionaries were hardly inclined to paint a rosy vision of collective bargaining; they portrayed strikes in the manner of Zola's *Germinal* (1885) as the despairing actions of hungry and cruelly oppressed workers. Throughout the whole of the nineteenth century, the major currents of French socialists, including syndicalists such as Fernand Pelloutier, but particularly the Marxist Guesdists, accepted the idea, put forward by the German economist Karl Rodbertus (1805–1875), of the "Iron Law of Wages". With the inevitable and irresistible force of economic law, Rodbertus argued, workers' wages must decline to a "survival wage", the sum necessary to reproduce himself and his family.[40] In 1878, Jules Guesde wrote of working-class families:

To get by they must have more children, but while the small excess of their wages or of subsistence will permit them to snatch a greater number of their children from death, workers will soon see their wages reduced to the last degree by the appearance on the market of these children become men.[41]

The widespread acceptance of the "Iron Law of Wages" tended to conflate workers' demands for a "family wage" with the idea of a "survival wage".

[38] Le Play, *The Organization of Labor*, p. 155.
[39] David Kulstein, *Napoleon III and the Working Class: A Study of Government Propaganda under the Second Empire* (Los Angeles, 1969).
[40] For Pelloutier's defence of the "Iron Law of Wages", see *L'ouvrier des deux mondes*, 1 February 1898.
[41] Jules Guesde, "La Loi des Salaires et ses consequences", *Collectivisme et révolution* (Paris, 1945; 1st pub. 1878), pp. 43–44.

Although Guesde's basic position on pauperization grew more sophisticated with time, it did not change fundamentally in the pre-World War I period. A study of Guesdist ideology has commented on the degree to which "The theory of pauperization, often in its most simplistic form, dominated the Guesdist conception of the revolutionary class interest."[42] However dogmatic and inflexible we might regard such talk, it was hardly the kind of rhetoric that would justify a cult of respectability among French workers or encourage feelings that married women belonged at home.

Guesde's *Parti ouvrier français* (POF) was strong in the Stéphanois, but its local leaders were not as intransigent as Guesde. Nevertheless, the idea of pauperization found its Stéphanois supporters. In 1893, a metalworker from Rive-de-Gier wrote to the Guesdist newspaper, *Le Socialiste*, documenting the decline of metalworkers' wages relative to "the time of my father" and, by means of detailed budgetary comparisons, showed how his father had been able to provide for his children, concluding that now one can hardly "make ends meet".[43] This article provoked considerable discussion in the local press and even stirred a local administrative inquiry.

Guesdist assertions of a declining or stagnating standard of living were wrong and by the 1890s their inaccuracy was increasingly apparent, but French workers still refused to acknowledge their rising living standards publicly and so the familism of the French labour movement differed from that of British workers and white American workers who were then embracing the ideal of the non-working wife.[44] In France, as in the US and Great Britain, there was a growing concern with the condition of childhood.[45] French reformers too, particularly dissatisfied with that country's unusually high infant and child mortality rates, reinforced the importance of childhood by glorifying it, but however much they urged increased care for children, they also assumed that many working-class wives would

---

[42] Robert Stuart, *Marxism at Work: Ideology, Class and French Socialism During the Third Republic* (Cambridge, 1992), p. 466. For the Guesdist attitude towards women workers, see Patricia Hilden, *Working Women and Socialist Politics in France, 180-1914, A Regional Study* (Oxford, 1986).

[43] *Le Socialiste*, 5 March 1893.

[44] For US studies which suggest that appeals to a domestic ideal had little purchase among African-American women who had high labour force participation rates, see Eileen Boris, "The Power of Motherhood: Black and White Activist Women Redefine the Political", in Seth Koven and Sonya Michel (eds), *Mothers of a New World: Maternalist Politics and the Origins of Welfare States* (New York, 1993), pp. 213–245 and Linda Gordon, *Pitied But Not Entitled: Single Mothers and the History of Welfare* (New York, 1994), pp. 112–114. On poor women in London's East End, see Andrew August, "How Separate a Sphere? Poor Women and Paid Work in Late-Victorian London", *Journal of Family History*, 19, 3 (1996), pp. 285–309.

[45] Carolyn Steedman, *Childhood, Culture and Class in Britain: Margaret McMillan, 1860–1913* (New Brunswick, NJ, 1990).

remain at work.[46] French intellectuals such as Jules Simon might lament female labour in factories and hope that it could be confined to homework, but the distinctively French contributions to social policy ameliorated working mothers' plight without prohibiting mothers' working. For example, in the 1880s, government-sponsored child care, the *crèches*, provided invaluable aid for working mothers as did the maternity leave bills of 1909 and 1912 which forbade employers from dismissing mothers for a two-month absence from work and provided assistance to needy working mothers.[47]

Although male workers articulated their own familistic demands, women were absent from the dialogue; while they may have supported and even died in defence of male workers' demands, women remained, by and large, on the periphery of the labour movement and never came to identify themselves fully as workers. Lacking the vote, Stéphanois women workers were concentrated in industries that were low paid, temporary and notoriously difficult to organize. While evidence is more fragmentary than for males, women workers often seemed interested in combining domestic and wage labour, frequently expressing their preference for cottage industries because "one works in one's own home". An old Stéphanois woman interviewed by Jean Burdy indicated that as a mother she had worked "to keep the pot boiling" and suggesting an association of work with household responsibilities. Perhaps Burdy's most interesting finding concerns what he labels the "obscuring" of women's work. Reminiscing about their past, many women initially identified themselves as "housewives", yet as the reminiscences lengthened, so did memories of participation in the labour force; few women participated continuously but many had participated irregularly over many years.[48] None the less, their years of work had not given them a sense of themselves as "workers", and the Stéphanois labour movement had done nothing to deepen their sense of identity.

EVOLUTION OF THE FAMILY WAGE DEMAND

In the Stéphanois region, the presence of working women did not affect the development of demands for a "family wage". Increasingly male workers who led local trade unions and political parties asserted that men were responsible for their families' welfare and that the male wage should be sufficient to provide for the existence of their family. Strike demands, songs and speeches conjured up an image of a working-class family whose existence depended solely on adult male earnings.

---

[46] See Alicia C. Klaus, "Babies All the Rage: The Movement to Prevent Infant Mortality in the United States and France, 190–1920" (Ph.D. thesis, University of Pennsylvania, 1986). See also, Elinor A. Accampo, Rachel B. Fuchs and Mary Lynn Stewart (eds), *Gender and the Politics of Social Reform* (Baltimore, 1995).

[47] Klaus, "Babies All the Rage".

[48] Burdy, *Le Soleil noir*, pp. 133–154.

The miners played the key role in introducing the concept of the family wage in the Stéphanois. They viewed a family wage as a minimum survival wage necessary to keep the family together and to provide for the rearing of young children. In May of 1848, the miners of Saint-Etienne composed a petition complaining of wage cuts that they attributed to the coal monopoly asserting that "The consequences of these arbitrary measures have been misery for the miners and their families".[49] The miners' response to the government questionnaire stressed their plight as fathers. They pleaded for support "for the household where there are 4, 5, and 6 children who are not able to work [. . .] These poor children are covered with rags and sometimes go barefoot for lack of money to buy clothes". The miners lamented the deprivation that forced them to send their children to work at an early age: "education among the miners is totally neglected because the miners who are fathers of families are forced to make their children work because their own wages are insufficient to support an education". And they reported that "fathers of families are obliged to impose upon themselves rigorous privations".[50] By mid-June the tone of the miners in the western part of the coal basin, around Le Chambon Feugerolles, became urgent: "We are devoted to the republic [. . .] we are men of order and of labour, but our children ask us for bread, and the best sentiments must give way to necessity in order that our families do not die of hunger."[51]

Despite the threat, the miners as well as most Stéphanois workers remained loyal to the republic supporting it through repression and *coup d'état*; the rate of abstentions in the 1851 plebiscite ratifying Louis-Napoleon's coup was among the highest in the nation.[52] In an effort to win the support of Stéphanois workers who remained committed to republicanism, the imperial government transferred to Saint-Etienne a prefect known in the north for establishing a working-class mutual aid society. Encouraged by the government in 1866, a miner who had been on the committee that responded to the 1848 questionnaire started a mutual aid society, *La Fraternelle*. Workers responded enthusiastically to a society that would insure them against accidents and provide for their families in case of their death or incapacity. The administration sought to use the society's popularity and its leaders' prestige to win electoral support. But the victory of the imperial candidates in the 1869 elections was put in doubt by rumours of a miners' strike. The strike itself threatened because company efforts to keep nearly exhausted mines in production lowered wages, and workers also wanted some say in the compulsory company-run insurance programmes maintained by the mining companies.[53] The prefect

[49] *Le Mercure ségusien*, 21 May 1848.
[50] "Enquête de 1848 – mineurs de Rive-de-Gier", AN C956.
[51] *Le Mercure ségusien*, 16 June 1848.
[52] Hanagan, *Nascent Proletarians*, p. 21.
[53] *Ibid.*, pp. 191–196.

called in representatives of *La Fraternelle* and at least hinted that after the election he would intervene in their favour with the companies. As a result miners' leaders lobbied their members passionately to vote for the imperial candidate. At stake, the leaders insisted in highly gendered rhetoric, was the fate of the family:

Long live the miners! Long live the brave and honest fathers of families who, in peril of their lives, painfully tear each day from the bowels of the earth the daily bread of industry [. . .] LONG LIVE LIBERTY WITH THE EMPEROR.[54]

Unfortunately, after the imperial victory, the coal companies refused to make the concessions suggested by the prefect and a long and bitter strike ensued that resulted in the "Massacre of the Ricamerie" in which soldiers fired into a crowd and killed fourteen people. The massacre ended whatever chance the Empire had of securing the loyalties of local workers.

The image of the adult male wage earner as crushed by his responsibility for the economic well-being of his family spread quickly. By 1868 it was already incorporated into the Stéphanois ditty entitled "The Worker":

> He marries and soon becomes a father
> And must provide bread for his children.
> Then he bows under labour and age;
> At fifty years old, he holds out his hand,
> Somber, ashamed, his face blushing.
> for the worker, this is the real road.[55]

While the inadequacy of the adult male household head's wages for his family was highlighted in such stories, the inadequacy of his family's pension (and the need to make it adequate) was underlined by a Stéphanois coalminer delegate to the Marseilles Congress in 1879:

If the widow's pension was brought to 1 franc, and that of the orphan to fifty centimes per day, one would see fewer prostitutes among the widows, and the children would be able to learn a little morality; in place of becoming vagabonds, they would be honest citizens who would be able to serve the republic with honor and fidelity instead of peopling the prisons.

By 1891 even proud glassworkers reinforced their wage claims by familist appeals:

There is a heart which beats in the great family of labour [. . .] Don't be insensible to those who call for help, for aid, let your contributions come to help us, let the women think of her sisters, the child break his piggy bank to help his brother glassworkers, let mothers think of the enfants who, themselves innocents, will themselves suffer from the inhuman conduct of capital *vis-à-vis* the producers.[56]

---

[54] *L'Eclaireur*, 4 June 1869.
[55] Eugène Imbert, *Chants, Chansons et poésie de Remy Doutre* (Saint-Etienne, 1887), pp. 24–25.
[56] ADL 92/M/41.

By 1911, metalworkers appealed to soldiers occupying Le Chambon Feugerolles not to fire on: "Workers [who] in order to feed their wife and family demand wage raises."[57]

Although the demand that large employers pay adult men wages adequate to feed a family was well established in the Stéphanois, it was not associated with demands for the withdrawal of female wage labour. In 1902 grumbling male silkweavers complained that "The grand potentates of industry are destroying the family, for the mother works in their prisons for 1.25 F., while the father, unemployed, goes to the bistro and the unsupervised children run in the streets." The article concluded that: "the cause of our misery is feminine labour, let us join together to suppress it or at least to prevent its increase".[58] But they suggested no concrete measures for action and their resistance died aborning.

A serious demand for female exclusion from industry did not emerge even though Stéphanois working women were, in some respects, better advantaged than many French working women. The dowry contract, general in the countryside, even for poor women, survived transplant to the city. In 1870, in Rive-de-Gier where there was little work for married women and in Saint-Chamond where there was considerable, a correspondent to a local newspaper, Dr Hervier, estimated that about 75 per cent of all marriages involved a dowry contract.[59] For working women, such a contract meant that they could spend their income as they chose except that they could be legally required to contribute to the maintenance of the household.[60]

Demands for a family wage for miners and for insurance to provide for their families were not the product of trade union organizations divorced from their community and male workers' demands for a family wage met with widespread popular support in the Stéphanois. Before 1914, the roots of unionism were local, and the growing centrality of labour exchanges controlled by municipalities, the *Bourses du travail*, reinforced the importance of the locality. Before 1914, all the mass strikes in the region were led and initiated by local organizations.

Mass strikes, the most important tool of industrial worker trade unionism in France, depended on the mobilization of the entire working-class community. Large-scale, mass strikes generally took the form of the "turn-out" in which the major social actor was the "crowd"; this crowd marched down what one author called "the great road of uprisings", passing through the centre of the valleys intersecting Saint-Etienne to the

[57] Leaflet distributed July 1911, ADL 92/M/185.
[58] Cited in Mathilde Dubesset and Michelle Zancarini-Fournel, *Parcours de femmes: Réalités et representations, Saint-Etienne 1880–1950* (Lyon, 1993), p. 115.
[59] *L'Eclaireur*, 23 April 1870.
[60] Frances Ida Clark, *The Position of Women in Contemporary France* (London, 1937), pp. 165–168.

south-west and north-east.[61] This whole effort depended on a community consensus as to the legitimacy of the cause.

A classic example of the community character of mobilization was the great strike of 1869 – a strike that shook the Empire. In a tense atmosphere caused by rumours of betrayal and high-handedness on the part of authorities and the leaders of the workers' mutual aid society, the strike was begun by an informal clique of workers in Firminy, at the western end of the basin, who stood up on the billiard tables of several cafés and called the miners out to strike. A crowd of miners emerged from the cafés, pouring out into the streets and marching eastward towards the local mines in the direction of Saint-Etienne. Shutting down the mines and factories in its path, the crowd marched through the centre of the adjacent towns and their market-places, picking up the workers, housewives and children who lived along the main road or who attended its markets.[62]

Women and children participated in strikes hinging on familist demands, such as those of 1869, because these were incorporated into a militant working-class culture that portrayed itself as the defender of the entire local community and appealed to long-held community traditions.[63] In the Stéphanois, the demand for a family wage was often equated with a survival wage and was usually a response to a reduction in the wages of adult male workers. In 1848, 1869 and 1893 workers, in reply, claimed that the newly reduced wage was insufficient to support a family, appealing to local public opinion and to elites that the result of a wage decrease would be social catastrophe. Many Stéphanois working women were undoubtedly convinced that they were right. Except when troops were called out against workers, as in Le Chambon in 1911, workers never invoked family issues in strikes that involved proactive demands such as shorter hours, union recognition, or the firing of an unpopular foreman – or to demand the exclusion of women workers. The attempt of the national CGT to do so in the eight-hour campaign of 1906 met with little response although the campaign itself was pursued vigorously in the area. By 1906, the family wage had become a familiar item in the workers' strike repertoire – it was firmly attached to attacks on the status quo.

---

[61] Léon de Seilhac, *Les Grèves du Chambon* (Paris, 1912), pp. 5–7. On the "turnout" and the "crowd" see Mark Steinberg, "Riding the Black Lad and Other Working-Class Ritualistic Actions: Towards a Spatialized and Gendered Analysis of Nineteenth-Century Repertoires", in Michael P. Hanagan, Leslie P. Moch and Wayne te Brake (eds), *Challenging Authority: The Historical Study of Contentious Politics* (Minneapolis, forthcoming 1998).

[62] L.J. Gras, *Histoire économique générale des mines de la Loire,* vol. I (Saint-Etienne, 1910), p. 315.

[63] On different framings for gendered protest see "Providers: An Exploration of Gender Ideology", in Alice Kessler-Harris, *A Woman's Wage: Historical Meanings & Social Consequences* (Lexington, 1990), pp. 57–80.

CONCLUSION

Our survey of work and family in the Stéphanois has shown an extremely wide variety of family strategies in both the countryside surrounding the industrial valley and the valley itself. No simple formula can capture these relations except to note that Stéphanois working families were hungry for wage work and diversified the work which family members performed when they could. The rhetoric of familism spread in the 1840s and even as late as the 1930s French elites became alarmed about the conditions of working-class family life. Workers used this alarm to argue against wage reductions and to forge solidarity among workers belonging to a variety of different family economies. But workers' rhetoric about families was not a fair representation of their family experiences. Workers' concerns about their family circumstances expressed itself in both the rhetoric of the "family wage" and the determination to develop multi-stranded relationships to work.

In the nineteenth century, the situation of working-class families in the Stéphanois was too economically precarious for workers to narrow the scope of wage earning and, thus, enlarge the number of family dependants. For workers, to contemplate withdrawing family members from the labour force required the redefinition of the family wage from a kind of "survival wage", preventing family disintegration, to a more generous standard of living that recognized a wider range of human necessities, including stronger protection against accident, injury and old age.[64] A fundamental step in this direction was the growth of a welfare state that had hardly existed in France before 1914. Only in the twentieth century, as a welfare system developed based on male wage earning and rights to social security based on male wage earning did such a "family economy" become feasible in the Stéphanois. At the same time, as the family became less indispensable in the battle against risk and uncertainty, other less repressive alternatives to the male-dominated family beckoned.

---

[64] See Amartya Sen, "The Standard of Living Lecture 2, Lives and Capabilities", in Geoffrey Hawthorn (ed.), *The Standard of Living* (Cambridge, 1989), pp. 20–38.

Welfare State Attitudes to the Male Breadwinning System: The United States and Sweden in Comparative Perspective

LENA SOMMESTAD*

Human reproduction is a basic economic activity in every society. It includes activities such as maternal care, childcare, old age provision, poor relief, healthcare, and labour protection. In pre-industrial times, human reproduction was typically a part of kin-based household economies, but since the onset of industrialization two new institutional solutions have developed: the male breadwinning system and the welfare state.[1]

In historical perspective, the male breadwinning system builds on earlier household-based reproductive practices. It constitutes a basically private approach, marked by a female specialization in reproductive activities. According to male breadwinning ideology, men are primarily providers, responsible only for professional and financial aspects of the reproductive process. Married women, by contrast, are supposed to perform most of the work needed to reproduce the population. This work is unpaid and consequently married women are economically dependent on their husbands.

In practice, of course, male breadwinning systems diverge more or less from the strict gender division of labour prescribed by male breadwinner ideology. In particular, married women have often participated in breadwinning activities. More importantly, however, there is no industrialized society in which the male breadwinning system has been capable of carrying out the national reproductive process without public support. Along varying institutional paths, public institutions have intervened to take on responsibility for smaller or larger parts of the national reproductive burden. Welfare states have taken shape.

Welfare states have differed markedly in their attitude to the male breadwinning system, and although all welfare states have modified their adherence to the male breadwinning model in recent decades, important distinctions remain. In residual welfare states, such as the United States, the guiding principle has been to rely as much as possible on private, male breadwinning arrangements. Social spending has been limited and access to benefits largely gendered. Other, more extensive welfare states, such

* I am grateful to Christina Bergqvist, Daniel A. Cornford, Angélique Janssens, Bo Malmberg, Sally McMurry, Lynn Karlsson, Grey Osterud, Wendy Sarvasy and Ulla Wikander for helpful comments and to Michael Brown and Görel Granström for valuable information.

[1] A.F. Robertson, *Beyond the Family. The Social Organization of Human Reproduction* (Cambridge, 1991), pp. 1–5.

as Germany and the Netherlands, have also relied heavily on the male breadwinning system but, in contrast to the United States, these welfare states have more actively supported male breadwinning practices. This active support has resulted in strong male breadwinner states with gendered social rights. Finally, in a few cases, welfare state development has partly served to undermine citizens' dependence on the male breadwinning system. Sweden is a case in point. In the post-war Swedish model, the costs of human reproduction were increasingly socialized, and a dual breadwinner norm was explicitly established in the early 1970s. At this time, the government initiated separate taxation, a new and generous programme of parental leave, and a rapid expansion of public day-care provision. Today, the only major entitlement that is still provided exclusively to women in their capacity as wives, widow's pensions, is gradually being phased out.[2]

How can we explain the fact that most welfare states have continued to rely on the male breadwinning system, while Sweden has not? In this article I suggest that we need to study early welfare state institutionalization, up to the 1930s, in order to understand the distinctiveness of the Swedish case. I argue that nationally specific economic and demographic conditions during this formative period shaped distinctive social policy solutions, and that these solutions in turn affected subsequent welfare state developments. In order to support my argument, I compare Sweden with the United States, a contrasting case in Western welfare state history.

My discussion centres on three main aspects of social policy: the public inclination to intervene in the sphere of reproduction, the gendered structures of social provision, and state attitudes towards gainful work by single mothers and married women. Tax policies are not considered. In the American case, I focus on the European American population, whose representatives were predominant in shaping social policies and defining national goals. My analysis ends with the 1930s, when Roosevelt's New Deal and the social democratic breakthrough in Sweden initiated a new era.

THE MALE BREADWINNING SYSTEM AND THE RISE OF WELFARE STATES

It has been a widespread assumption in feminist welfare state research that the early European welfare states were designed to fit and to reinforce the male breadwinning system. Only recently has this assumption been

[2] Jet Bussemaker and Kees van Kersbergen, "Gender and Welfare States: Some Theoretical Reflections", and Anette Borchorst, "Welfare State Regimes, Women's Interests and the EC", both in Diane Sainsbury (ed.), *Gendering Welfare States* (London, 1994), pp. 8–44; Jane Lewis (ed.), *Women and Social Policies in Europe. Work, Family and the State* (Aldershot, 1993), pp. 15–20; and Diane Sainsbury, *Gender, Equality and Welfare States* (Cambridge, 1996), pp. 9–14, 49–72 and 190–194.

challenged, primarily with reference to developments in France and Sweden. Susan Pederson has suggested, for example, that the French welfare state is built on a "parental" rather than on a male breadwinner welfare logic, and Diane Sainsbury has shown that Sweden early developed social policies that were at odds with the male breadwinner model. As regards the rise of the distinctive American welfare state, the early period in particular has evoked different interpretations. Theda Skocpol describes American social policies up to the 1920s as "maternalist" in character, in contrast to the more "paternalist" welfare states of contemporary Europe. By contrast, studies by Linda Gordon and Alice Kessler-Harris confirm the view that the early American welfare state, like major European welfare states at the time, was built in accordance with a male breadwinner model. However, institutional solutions in this residual American welfare state differed from models of social provision prevalent in Europe.[3]

A pioneering theoretical contribution on the historical relationship between welfare states and the male breadwinning system was presented by Jane Lewis in 1992.[4] Lewis classifies a number of European welfare states according to the strength of the male breadwinner model. Her scheme includes strong male breadwinner states (Britain and Ireland), "modified" male breadwinner states (France), and "weak" male breadwinner states (Sweden). Lewis points to the fact that modern welfare state formation coincided with a historical period when the ideology of male breadwinning was particularly strong, and she argues that all welfare states have subscribed to some degree to the idea of a male breadwinner model.

How, then, can the development of different state attitudes to male breadwinning practices be explained? Lewis does not deal explicitly with this question, but she does point to distinctive features in Irish and British as opposed to French and Swedish welfare state history. Her analysis of France and Sweden, where the male breadwinner model is "modified" or "weak", is of special interest. In the French case, economic and demographic factors stand out as particularly important. On the basis of broad scholarly agreement, Lewis observes that pro-natalism and high female labour force participation, in particular in the large rural sector, led at an early stage to the modification of the male breadwinning system in France. As regards the rise of the weak Swedish male breadwinner state, by contrast, Lewis gives less weight to economic and demographic factors.

[3] Linda Gordon, *Pitied But Not Entitled. Single Mothers and the History of Welfare 1890–1935* (New York, 1994); Alice Kessler-Harris, "Gendered Interventions: Exploring the Historical Roots of U.S. Social Policy", *The Japanese Journal of American Studies*, 5 (1993–1994); Susan Pederson, *Family, Dependence, and the Origins of the Welfare State. Britain and France 1914–1945* (Cambridge, 1993); Sainsbury, *Gender, Equality*, pp. 49–72; and Theda Skocpol, *Protecting Soldiers and Mothers. The Political Origins of Social Policy in the United States* (Cambridge, MA, 1992).
[4] Jane Lewis, "Gender and the Development of Welfare Regimes", *Journal of European Social Policy*, 2 (1992), pp. 159–173.

Instead, she focuses on the ideological and political role of the Social Democratic party and argues that it was not until the late 1960s and early 1970s that successive Social Democratic governments consciously moved towards a dual breadwinner model.[5]

Lewis's divergent approaches to French and Swedish welfare state history points to the need for more developed analyses of the Swedish case. To understand the rise of the weak Swedish male breadwinner state, we need to pay more attention to economic and demographic developments as well as to actual policies enacted during the early period of welfare state institutionalization. In fact, Sweden and France experienced to some extent similar economic and demographic developments before World War II. As will be shown below, a closer examination of early Swedish social policies also reveals that Sweden – like France – was early marked by a comparatively weak adherence to the male breadwinner model.[6]

In this paper, I suggest an economic and demographic approach to the study of welfare state attitudes towards the male breadwinning system. This approach focuses on the male breadwinning system as an economic structure. It should be remembered that female participation in breadwinning activities does not necessarily imply female autonomy or emancipation. I designate Sweden as a weak male breadwinner state and the United States as a residual variant of the strong male breadwinner state.

In most recent feminist research on the rise of welfare states, a leading question has been to what extent political variables determine variations in welfare state development.[7] My analysis of the American and Swedish cases takes account of some insights from this polity-centred approach, and I have also built to some extent on other theoretical approaches, such as the role of industrialization and class mobilization.[8] However, my primary aim in this article is not to develop a broad explanatory framework, but rather to point to the hitherto largely neglected role of national reproductive experience in the gendering of welfare states.

---

[5] Compare Jane Jenson and Rianne Mahon, "Representing Solidarity: Class, Gender and the Crisis in Social-Democratic Sweden", *New Left Review*, 201 (September/October 1993), pp. 77–91; and Yvonne Hirdman, "Genussystemet", in *SOU 1990: 44. Demokrati och makt i Sverige* (Stockholm, 1990), pp. 73–112.

[6] Compare Sainsbury, *Gender, Equality*, pp. 63–67.

[7] For example Seth Koven and Sonya Michel, "Womanly Duties: Maternalist Politics and the Origins of Welfare States in France, Germany, Great Britain, and the United States, 1880–1920", *The American Historical Review*, 95 (1990), pp. 1076–1114; Pederson, *Family, Dependence, and the Origins of the Welfare State*; and Skocpol, *Protecting Soldiers and Mothers*.

[8] For theoretical overviews, see for example *ibid.*, pp. 11–62; and John B. Williamson and Fred C. Pampel, *Old Age Security in Comparative Perspective* (New York, 1993), pp. 5–19.

AN ECONOMIC AND DEMOGRAPHIC APPROACH TO
WELFARE STATE DEVELOPMENT

I suggest that conditions in the sphere of human reproduction have shaped state attitudes towards the male breadwinning system in decisive ways. In order to analyse the impact of reproductive conditions, we may distinguish between, on the one hand, a country's capacity to make investments in human reproduction, its *capacity for reproductive investments*, and, on the other hand, the specific *reproductive challenges* that occur during the formative period.

A country's capacity for reproductive investments is closely related to per capita income. If per capita income is high, the reproduction of the population can largely rely on a male breadwinning system. In this situation, it is possible to allocate large private resources to reproductive investments, and reproductive activities can be separated into specialized, typically female spheres of activity. When incomes are low, however, the amount of resources that can be spent on reproductive investments is more limited. Women will tend to share their time between productive and reproductive activities, often giving priority to the former, and men's role as providers will be less marked.[9]

The term "reproductive challenges" refers to demographic changes that diminish a society's supply of labour power, either in absolute terms or in relation to dependent age groups. In Western welfare state history, *emigration* constitutes one such important reproductive challenge. Typically, people emigrate as young adults. When this happens, the national supply of labour power is immediately reduced. *Low or falling fertility* represents a less dramatic phenomenon, but when countries experience low or declining birth-rates there is reason to fear future labour shortages. *An ageing population*, finally, is a reproductive challenge that eventually affects all countries that go through the demographic transition. When the proportion of old people increases, the reproductive burden on the economically active population will weigh more heavily.[10]

How, then, does national reproductive experience affect state attitudes to the male breadwinning system? I suggest, first, that reproductive experience shapes living conditions and everyday practices, thereby fostering political demands and strategies with distinct class and gender characteristics. An ageing population, for example, might encourage demands not

---

[9] For this approach, compare Bussemaker and van Kersbergen, "Gender and Welfare States", p. 20.

[10] Low fertility and ageing, though not migration, have attracted substantial attention in welfare state research: see, for example, Gisela Bock and Pat Thane, *Maternity and Gender Policies. Women and the Rise of the European Welfare States 1880s to 1950s* (London, 1991), pp. 10–11; Peter H. Lindert, "The Rise of Social Spending, 1880–1930", *Explorations in Economic History*, 31 (1994), pp. 6–7 and 16–28; and Fred C. Pampel and John B. Williamson, *Age, Class, Politics and the Welfare State*, (Cambridge, NJ, 1989), pp. 5–9 and 165–168.

only for old age insurance and old age care but also for increased support to other reproductive activities strained by scarce resources, such as childcare. Second, reproductive experience affects state concerns about national strength and survival. Only so long as a nation's supply of labour power is perceived as satisfactory, in both quantity and quality, will human reproduction be seen as a purely private concern.

THE UNITED STATES: THE RISE OF A RESIDUAL MALE BREADWINNER STATE

The most distinctive feature of the United States around the turn of the twentieth century was its high capacity for reproductive investments. In 1913, the United States had the highest per capita income in the world. Only the United Kingdom and Australia came close to the American figure.[11] Economic growth and urbanization proceeded rapidly. Industry, commerce and administration expanded at the expense of agriculture.[12] However, inequality in wealth and income was also great. By the time of early welfare regime institutionalization, the relative economic distance between the middle ranks and the poor was probably greater in the United States than in almost any other industrial country.[13]

In this distinctive economic setting, signs of a strong male breadwinner system were to be found at an early date. In the eastern, most commercialized parts of the country, reproductive strategies of male breadwinning had already grown increasingly important in the 1820s and 1830s. By this time, rising numbers of urban middle-class women no longer needed to take an active part in family businesses, wage work or extensive home production of food and textiles. A discourse on motherhood, domesticity and gender difference unfolded, stressing women's private caring responsibilities, moral superiority and emotional capacities. According to influential opinion-makers, women and men should act in *separate spheres*.[14] In other social settings, such as agriculture, male breadwinning practices were less developed, but even here norms of female domesticity were spreading.[15]

---

[11] Angus Maddison, *Dynamic Forces in Capitalist Development. A Long-Run Comparative View* (Oxford, 1991), pp. 6–7, table 1.1.

[12] *Ninth Census of the United States taken in the year 1870. Volume III*, pp. 808–809; *Thirteenth Census of the United States taken in the year 1910. Volume VIII*, p. 238.

[13] Jeffrey G. Williamson and Peter H. Lindert, *American Inequality. A Macroeconomic History* (New York, 1980), pp. 75–132; Lindert, "The Rise of Social Spending", pp. 26–28.

[14] Nancy F. Cott, *The Bonds of Womanhood. "Women's Sphere" in New England, 1780–1835* (New Haven, 1977); and Mary P. Ryan, *Cradle of the Middle Class. The Family in Oneida County, New York, 1790–1865* (Cambridge, MA, 1981).

[15] Jon Gjerde, *The Migration from Balestrand, Norway, to the Upper Middle West* (Cambridge, MA, 1985), pp. 192–201; Joan Jensen, *Promise to the Land. Essays on Rural Women* (Albuquerque, 1991), pp. 11–21: Lena Sommestad and Sally McMurry, "Farm Daughters and Industrialization: A Comparative Analysis of Dairying in New York State

Female labour force participation in the United States was comparatively low. By 1910, only 23.4 per cent of all adult American women – including agrarian women – were in gainful occupations, while female participation rates in major European nations at the time exceeded 35 per cent.[16] Among married European American women, only 6.5 per cent were registered as gainfully employed in 1920.[17] In addition, American society was marked by a strong male breadwinner ideology. Although married women in lower-income families had in practice to contribute to the family economy – if not by wage work, then by taking in boarders, supplementing the limited incomes of wage earners, or by doing odd jobs for pay – this female economic contribution was seldom recognized in the social policy discourse.[18]

I suggest that the comparatively high capacity for reproductive investments in early twentieth-century America shaped state attitudes towards the male breadwinning system in decisive ways. Most importantly, high reproductive capacity served to diminish the demand for all sorts of state interventions in the sphere of reproduction. As argued by historian Daniel Levine, a deep-rooted perception of the United States as a land of plenty meant that most Americans saw poverty as something unnecessary, even among workers. It was believed that people should normally be able to manage critical states such as parenthood, sickness or old age without public support. Those who failed were seen as deviants to be cared for through philanthropy or poor relief, not through comprehensive systems of social security.[19]

Second, the great confidence in the male breadwinning system formed the basis for a gender-divided model of citizenship. In this model, men were regarded as independent breadwinners, normally capable of protecting themselves and providing for their families without public support. Women, on the other hand, were in principle to be protected and provided for by male breadwinners. Only if they lacked male protection, because they were widows or worked unprotected in factories, for example, were limited state interventions seen as legitimate in order to guarantee prevailing norms of motherhood and domesticity. This gender-divided model of citizenship had a profound impact on welfare thought in the United States. As noted by Alice Kessler-Harris, the recognition of women's

and Sweden, 1860–1920", *Journal of Women's History* (forthcoming, vol. 10, Summer 1998).

[16] *Thirteenth Census of the United States taken in 1910. Volume IV*, p. 37; Bock and Thane, *Maternity and Gender Policies*, p. 16, table 0.2.

[17] Teresa L. Amott and Julie A. Matthaei, *Race, Gender and Work. A Multicultural Economic History of Women in the United States* (Boston, 1991), p. 303, table 9.3.

[18] *Ibid.*, pp. 297–307; Jensen, *Promise to the Land*, pp. 11–21; Alice Kessler-Harris, *Out to Work. A History of Wage-Earning Women in the United States* (Oxford, 1982), pp. 108–141; and by the same author, *A Woman's Wage* (Lexington, 1990), pp. 57–80.

[19] Daniel Levine, *Poverty and Society. The Growth of the American Welfare State in International Comparison* (New Brunswick, NJ, 1988), pp. 15–23 and 151–179.

gender-specific need for state protection only strengthened the widespread suspicion of state intervention. Male citizenship was equated with self-reliance and men of all classes tended to associate freedom from state intervention not only with independence, but also with manliness.[20]

Finally, high capacity for reproductive investments encouraged the belief that women should specialize in reproductive activities. An important expression of this belief was the early social policy ambition to provide American widowed mothers with "mothers' pensions". While the United States was a laggard in other fields of social policy, American states pioneered pensions for single mothers (primarily widows) as early as the 1910s. By 1930, mothers' pension laws had been passed by forty-four states.[21]

In a comparative perspective, the limited scope of public interventions in American social provision is indeed striking. With some exceptions, comprehensive programmes of social security or income maintenance were largely lacking up to the 1930s. The United States had neither sickness insurance nor old age insurance on the federal level. Public assistance was typically means-tested and directed towards the very poor. No labour regulations for male workers were passed other than special laws applying to particularly dangerous occupations. In addition, no extensive public services were provided in relation to caring activities or motherhood. Among the few successful programmes enacted before the New Deal was Workmen's Compensation, an insurance programme dealing with industrial injury, passed by forty-two states between 1911 and 1920.[22]

Instead, widespread prosperity provided the basis for voluntary structures of social provision, in particular philanthropy. Great numbers of wealthy Americans had the economic and temporal resources successfully to organize large-scale private support for the marginalized needy. This philanthropic movement was a multifaceted phenomenon. It developed into an inclusive voluntary grass-roots movement as well as into a business of benevolence with employed social workers, stretching from traditional charity to social case work. Cooperation with public institutions was widespread.[23]

---

[20] Kessler-Harris, "Gendered Interventions", pp. 3–22; and by the same author, "The Paradox of Motherhood. Night Work Restrictions in the United States", in Ulla Wikander, Alice Kessler-Harris and Jane Lewis (eds), *Protecting Women. Labor Legislation in Europe, the United States, and Australia, 1880–1920* (Urbana, 1995), pp. 337–357; and Robyn Muncy, *Creating a Female Dominion in American Reform 1890–1935* (New York, 1991), pp. 3–37.

[21] Skocpol, *Protecting Soldiers and Mothers*, pp. 3–11 and 424–479.

[22] Michael B. Katz, *In the Shadow of the Poorhouse. A Social History of Welfare in America* (New York, 1986), pp. 113–205; Levine, *Poverty and Society*, pp. 151–179; James T. Patterson, *America's Struggle Against Poverty 1900–1980* (Cambridge, MA, 1981), pp. 20–34; Skocpol, *Protecting Soldiers and Mothers*, pp. 3–11, 226–229 and 285–286.

[23] Robert H. Brenner, *American Philanthropy* (Chicago, 2nd ed., 1988), pp. 72–135; Frank Dekker Watson, *The Charity Organization Movement in the United States. A Study in American Philanthropy* (New York, 1922), pp. 65–443.

Women played a crucial role in the institutionalization of the limited and gendered American male breadwinner state. Most importantly, middle-class women with plenty of time took on responsibility for vital reproductive activities both inside and outside their own families, such as childcare, poor relief, public health campaigns, and the operation of orphanages and playgrounds. They coordinated philanthropic activities in *charity organization societies*, engaged in philanthropic field work as "friendly visitors", or developed more radical alternatives such as the settlement house movement. These activities reduced the demand for state interventions and encouraged the belief that domestic work and "social housekeeping" are intrinsically private and female duties. In addition, more reform-minded women engaged in social policy-making, primarily by lobbying for public interventions in favour of women only. They gathered in influential organizations, such as *The General Federation of Women's Clubs*, and they concentrated successfully on carrying through programmes of mothers' pensions, maternal and child welfare, and protective labour legislation for women. In the period from 1908 to 1920, 39 states passed hour laws for women, 13 states passed minimum wage laws for women, and 16 states explicitly forbade female night work. It was rarer, however, for female reformers to extend their interventionist ambitions to include more extensive public support for the process of human reproduction.[24]

How, then, was this residual male breadwinner state influenced by our second explanatory factor, *reproductive challenges*, during the early, formative phase of welfare regime institutionalization? In brief, I suggest that the American tendency to rely on the private male breadwinning system was for a long time significantly strengthened by the comparative weakness of reproductive challenges (such as emigration, falling fertility and ageing). Only during temporary periods of military, economic or demographic crisis, such as World War I and the Depression, did problems of human reproduction for some time attract greater political attention. The breakthrough for old age security on the federal level, for example, came during the Depression, a period of temporary emigration and a growing proportion of elderly people in the population.[25]

[24] Paula Baker, "The Domestication of Politics: Women and American Society, 1780–1920", in Linda Gordon (ed.), *Women, the State and Welfare* (Madison, 1990), pp. 55–91; Brenner, *American Philanthropy*, pp. 72–84; Kessler-Harris, "The Paradox of Motherhood", p. 338; Levine, *Poverty and Society*, pp. 28–36; Muncy, *Creating a Female Dominion*, pp. 3–211; Skocpol, *Protecting Soldiers and Mothers*, pp. 8–10, 95–96 and 321–524. For more radical outlooks among American female reformers, see Wendy Sarvasy, "Beyond the Difference Versus Equality Debate: Postsuffrage Feminism, Citizenship and the Quest for a Feminist Welfare State", *Signs*, 17 (1992), pp. 329–362.
[25] *Historical Statistics of the United States, Colonial Times to 1957. A Statistical Abstract Supplement*, US Department of Commerce, Bureau of the Census (Washington DC, 1960), p. 8, Series A 20 and p. 10, Series A 84; Julian L. Simon, *The Economic Consequences of Immigration* (Oxford, 1989), pp. 31–35; Edward D. Berkowitz, *America's Welfare State. From Roosevelt to Reagan* (Baltimore, 1991), pp. 15–28.

The great American confidence in the male breadwinning system was particularly encouraged by extensive immigration. Immigration peaked in the first decade of the twentieth century, when it accounted for almost 40 per cent of total population increase. It was dominated by men with a high rate of labour force participation, and – except during the World War I period – it remained important up to the mid-1920s.[26]

Immigration shaped American class and gender relations in significant ways. As regards state attitudes to the male breadwinning system, the most important effect was to reduce national interest in female labour and in more – or healthier – babies. With a steadily growing population and an abundant male labour supply, it was hard to get support for extensive public efforts to support childbearing and childraising or to help mothers combine their duties as workers and mothers.[27] Only during World War I did demand for female labour rise considerably, and the war situation also opened up some possibilities for child welfare reform. As healthy children were increasingly regarded as a vital resource for the nation, female reformers could use temporary currents of patriotism and state-interventionism to advance the cause of maternal and child welfare, a social policy effect of warfare well known from other countries. The result was the first federal programme of maternal and child welfare in the United States, the Sheppard-Towner Act (1921–1929).[28]

The lack of support for mothers and children is indeed one of the most striking features of early American social policy. In spite of extensive female activism and strong currents of maternalism, American reformers did not succeed in carrying through any universal programmes of maternal and child welfare. Only mothers in need could get support, and the programmes enacted were limited in scope. Under the 1921 Sheppard-Towner Act, for example, public nurses could offer maternal and infant health education but no direct services. For working mothers, there were no paid maternity leaves, and the issue of childcare provision did not attract much attention. The enactment of mothers' pension laws did for some time nurture more radical visions of social reform, but in reality benefits were small and means-tested, and only a minority of single mothers got any aid at all.[29]

---

[26] *Historical Statistics of the United States*, p. 62, Series 134; Simon, *The Economic Consequences of Immigration*, pp. 22–34.

[27] Alisa Klaus, "De-Population and Race Suicide: Maternalism and Pronatalist Ideologies in France and the United States", in Seth Koven and Sonya Michel, *Mothers of a New World. Maternalist Politics and the Origins of Welfare States* (New York, 1993), pp. 188–190. The boost to population growth caused by immigration was further consolidated by relatively satisfactory birth-rates (*Historical Statistics of the United States*, p. 23, Series B 19).

[28] Muncy, *Creating a Female Dominion*, pp. 93–157.

[29] Berkowitz, *America's Welfare State*, pp. 96–97; Gordon, *Pitied But Not Entitled*, pp. 37–64; Kessler-Harris, "The Paradox of Motherhood", p. 337; Koven and Michel, "Womanly Duties", pp. 1085–1107; and Sonya Michel, "The Limits of Maternalism: Policies Towards American Wage-Earning Mothers during the Progressive Era", in Koven and Michel, *Mothers of a New World*, pp. 277–320.

When the Social Security Act of 1935 was passed, a new era of American social policy began. In a period of economic and demographic crisis, the need for more direct support for American breadwinners was recognized, and benefits such as unemployment insurance and old age insurance, tied to labour market attachment, were developed. As regards state attitudes to the male breadwinning system, however, little changed. The gendered, "two-channel" American welfare state took shape, built on earlier national experience. While men were increasingly covered by social insurance, most women got their benefits either as dependent wives to insured men or as recipients of public assistance. Mothers' pension programmes were followed by the more extensive Aid to Dependent Children (ADC).[30] When we now turn to our second case, Sweden, we will discover a very different welfare state history.

SWEDEN: THE HISTORICAL ROOTS OF A WEAK MALE BREADWINNER STATE

In the early twentieth century, Sweden differed from the United States in two crucial respects. First, per capita income in Sweden was only half the American figure. Capacity for reproductive investments was low.[31] Second, Sweden experienced great reproductive challenges, emigration and falling fertility, in the period up to the 1930s.[32] The combination of poverty and reproductive challenges contributed to shaping a distinctive Swedish blend of social policies, marked by public intervention and comparatively gender-neutral solutions to problems of social provision. The outlines of an interventionist, weak male breadwinner welfare state were discernible at an early date.

Early twentieth-century Sweden has been characterized as poor and egalitarian. For all except a remarkably limited upper and middle class, living conditions were trying and economic distress was widespread even among small entrepreneurs and farmers. The majority of the population made their living as labourers or small farmers in the countryside. Industrialization was largely rural and still at an initial stage. In 1910, 70 per cent of the population resided outside towns and boroughs, and close to 50 per cent made their living from agriculture.[33]

---

[30] Berkowitz, *America's Welfare State*, pp. 1–38 and 96–97; Gordon, *Pitied But Not Entitled*, pp. 145–285; Barbara J. Nelson, "The Origins of the Two-Channel Welfare State: Workmen's Compensation and Mothers' Aid", in Gordon, *Women, the State and Welfare*, pp. 123–151; and Sainsbury, *Gender, Equality*, pp. 58–63, 81–84, 89–90 and 113–116.

[31] Maddison, *Dynamic Forces*, pp. 6–7, table 1.1. The estimations refer to 1913.

[32] *Historical Statistics of Sweden*, vol. I (Stockholm, 1955), pp. 45–46, 68, tables B 2 and B 21.

[33] Gøsta Esping-Andersen, "Jämlikhet, effektivitet och makt. Socialdemokratisk välfärdspolitik", in Klaus Misgeld *et al.* (eds), *Socialdemokratins samhälle* (Stockholm, 1988), p. 224; Lennart Jörberg, "Structural Change and Economic Growth: Sweden in the 19th Century", in P.K. Brien (ed.), *The Industrial Revolution in Europe*, vol. 5 of *The Industrial*

The low capacity for reproductive investments was particularly evident in the countryside. Around the turn of the twentieth century, average incomes in rural districts were generally too modest to permit any exclusively private solutions to problems of poverty, sickness, childbirth or old age.[34] Instead, responsibilities of employers or household heads were complemented by state-directed intervention along traditional lines. Poor relief, long the most important type of social provision, was organized and financed by local authorities but regulated by national law. Medical care was organized partly by the state through a tax-financed scheme of district physicians, and partly by regional county councils with tax-raising powers, which were responsible for in-patient hospital services. In addition, state-educated midwives employed by local authorities played a crucial role in offering maternal and medical services in rural districts.[35] Only in more populated areas did strategies of self-reliance for some time develop more widely. Here, better-off entrepreneurs and employees could turn to the market by utilizing insurance companies and doctors in private practice, while workers organized their own sickness insurance funds.[36]

In contrast to the United States, Swedish society was heavily dependent on female labour, married and unmarried. There is ample historical evidence of the crucial role played by women in Swedish production, in particular within agriculture, and the difference between women's lot in Sweden and the United States is a recurrent theme in the emigration literature. By the turn of the twentieth century, important areas of production, most notably milking and dairying, were led almost exclusively by

Revolutions series (Oxford, 1994), pp. 411–454; Sven E. Olsson, *Social Policy and Welfare State in Sweden* (Lund, 1990), pp. 112–113; and Tom Söderberg, *Två sekel svensk medeklass* (Stockholm, 1972), p. 243, table 11. For income distribution, see Stein Kuhnle, "The Beginnings of the Nordic Welfare States: Similarities and Differences", Supplement, Special Congress Issue: The Nordic Welfare States, *Acta Sociologica*, 21 (1978), pp. 17–20; and *Ålderdomsförsäkringskommittén*, vol. I (Stockholm, 1912), pp. 66–68. Figures on urbanization and industrialization in *Historical Statistics of Sweden*, p. 21, table A 14; p. 29, table A 21.

[34] Joakim Persson, "Convergence in Per Capita Income and Migration across the Swedish Counties 1906–1990 *European Economic Review* (forthcoming); and *Ålderdomsförsäkringskommittén*, vol. IV (Stockholm, 1912), pp. 332–333, table 11.

[35] Åke Elmér, *Från fattigsverige till välfärdsstaten* (Stockholm, 1969), pp. 46–49; Torkel Jansson, "The Age of Associations. Principles and Forms of Organization Between Corporations and Mass Organizations. A Comparative Nordic Survey from a Swedish Viewpoint", *Scandinavan Journal of History*, 13, 4 (1988), pp. 326–327 and 334–339; Olsson, *Social Policy*, pp. 108–109; Sverker Oredsson, "Samhällelig eller enskild fattigvård?", *Scandia*, 37 (1971), pp. 175–215; Roger Qvarsell, "Mellan familj, arbetsgivare och stat", in Erik Amnå (ed.), *Medmänsklighet att hyra?* (Stockholm, 1995), pp. 19–22; and Christina Romlid, "Swedish Midwives and Their Instruments in the Eighteenth and Nineteenth Centuries", in Hilary Marland and Anne Marie Rafferty (eds), *Midwives, Society and Childbirth: Debates and Controversies in the Early Modern Period* (London, 1997), pp. 38–43.

[36] Rafael Lindqvist, *Från folkrörelse till välfärdsbyråkrati* (Lund, 1990), pp. 39–55; Kajsa Ohrlander, *I barnens och nationens intresse* (Stockholm, 1992), pp. 148–152; SOS, *Allmän hälso- och sjukvård år 1912* (Stockholm, 1914), pp. 84–89, table I.

women. Agrarian women normally combined domestic duties with all types of physically demanding outdoor work – such as piling hay, picking potatoes, and even ploughing. Their status was tied to working capacity and physical strength, rather than to motherhood or domestic virtues.[37]

Outside agriculture, the role of married women in production was less conspicuous. However, norms of male breadwinning were most strictly followed within the small middle class. As in the United States, married working-class women typically contributed to the family economy through unregistered part-time jobs, such as industrial home work, cleaning and laundry work. They also complemented wage incomes with home production of consumption goods such as textiles, clothes, vegetables and potatoes. Considering the low income levels in Sweden, it is reasonable to believe that these female contributions were of greater importance to family survival in Sweden than in the United States.[38]

The extensive workload of Swedish women is reflected in the comparatively limited scope of female philanthropy. Although many Swedes early on engaged in voluntary associations such as temperance and missions, most regions lacked larger numbers of middle-class women prepared to invest time or money in extensive philanthropic projects. Only in towns and cities, where income levels were higher and the middle class more numerous, did Swedish female philanthropy develop into a more significant social force. Given that few people yet resided in urban areas, however, the overall impact of this early female activity long remained limited. It is telling that the most flourishing philanthropic movement eventually developed in Stockholm, where average incomes around the turn of the twentieth century were higher than anywhere else in Sweden at the time.[39]

[37] Mats Hellspong and Orvar Löfgren, *Land och stad* (Stockholm, 1974), pp. 243–247; Sommestad and McMurry, "Farm Daughters and Industrialization"; Ann-Sofie Kälvemark (Ohlander), "Utvandring och självständighet", *Historisk tidskrift*, 2 (1983), pp. 154–173; Lars Olsson, "Den vita piskan", in Alf O. Johansson *et al.* (eds), *Dagsverken. 13 essäer i arbetets historia* (Lund, 1995), pp. 49–66.

[38] Lynn Karlsson, *Mothers as Breadwinners. Myth or Reality in Early Swedish Industry?*, Uppsala Papers in Economic History no. 39 (Uppsala, 1995), pp. 5–48; Lynn Karlsson and Ulla Wikander, "Om teknik, arbetsdelning och teknologi som formare av kvinnors – och mäns – arbetsvillkor", and Inger Jonsson, " 'Arbetssökande kvinnor göre sig icke besvär' ", both in *Historisk tidskrift*, 1 (1987), pp. 59–64 and 96–113; and Anita Nyberg, *Tekniken – kvinnornas befriare?* (Linköping, 1989), pp. 147–152.

[39] Birgitta Jordansson, " 'Goda människor från Göteborg'. Fattigvård och välgörenhet under 1800-talet", and Kerstin Thörn, "Föreningen för Välgörenhetens ordnande och bostadsfrågan", both in Marja Taussi Sjöberg and Tinne Vammen (eds), *På tröskeln till välfärden. Välgörenhetsformer och arenor i Norden 1800–1930* (Stockholm, 1995), pp. 84–103 and 129–151; and Ingrid Åberg, "Revivalism, Philanthropy and Emancipation. Women's Liberation and Organization in the Early Nineteenth Century", *Scandinavian Journal of History*, 13 (1988), pp. 399–420. Among all persons assessed for taxes in 1908, including tax on real estate, the average income in Stockholm was almost three times as high as in the countryside (*Ålderdomsförsäkringskommittén*, IV, pp. 314–315, table 10, and pp. 332-333, table 11).

Table 1. *Rates of gainful employment among women in Sweden and the United States, 1920*

	Sweden*		The United States
	Farm wives included	Farm wives excluded	European American women
All adult women	54.2	(36.2)	19.5
Married women	43.1	(3.9)	6.5

Sources: Amott and Matthaei, *Race, Gender and Work*, pp. 303, 305 (Tables 9–3, 9–4); *SOS, Folkräkning 1920: V*, pp. 10 (Table A), 61 and 68.
* For the inclusion/exclusion of farm wives, see the discussion of Swedish census data below.

Women's rates of gainful employment in Sweden and the United States in 1920 are compared in Table 1. Although it is difficult to make direct comparisons on the basis of the available statistics, the difference between the two countries is clear. In 1920, 36.3 per cent of Swedish adult women were registered as gainfully employed in the census, as compared to 19.5 per cent of all adult European American women. This official Swedish census figure underestimates the difference between the two countries, however, since the Swedish census, in contrast to the American one, did not distinguish between farm wives employed or not employed in outdoor farm work. All Swedish farm wives were formally registered as "wives".[40] As observed by Anita Nyberg, this exclusion of farm wives conceals the historically extensive female participation in Swedish agriculture and is at variance with current census practice in rural, developing countries. Including all farm wives in the labour force produces a more accurate understanding of rates of gainful employment in Sweden.[41] If this practice is followed, an even higher proportion – 54.2 per cent – of Swedish women can be regarded as gainfully employed in 1920. However, the inclusion of farm wives in the Swedish labour force has an even greater effect on married women's employment rates. If farm wives are included, 43.1 per cent of Swedish wives were gainfully employed in 1920, as compared to 6.5 per cent of European American wives. By contrast, if the census figures are taken at face value, the Swedish employment rate for married women is even lower than the corresponding American figure.[42]

Mass emigration from Sweden served further to reduce the national capacity for reproductive investments. In the period between 1851 and

---

[40] *SOS, Folkräkning 1920*, p. 11; *Thirteenth Census of the United States taken in 1910. Volume IV*, pp. 26–28.
[41] Anita Nyberg, "Vad är förvärvsarbete?", *Kvinnovetenskaplig tidskrift*, 1 (1987), pp. 54–65.
[42] It should be noted, however, that unregistered working wives of forestry and agricultural labourers are still not included (Nyberg, *Tekniken – kvinnornas befriare?*, pp. 147–151 and 154–155).

1930, roughly 1.4 million people emigrated, most of them to the United States. Net emigration peaked in the 1880s, but up to 1910 emigration was still extensive and it was not until the 1930s that emigration was replaced by modest immigration. The national loss of human resources caused by emigration was substantial, considering that the total Swedish population in 1900 amounted to only 5.1 million.[43] The most problematic economic aspect of emigration was not the total loss of people, however, but the fact that most emigrants were young adults. During the 1861–1915 period, 65 per cent of emigrants were aged between 15 and 29. The effect of this was to reduce the number of economically active citizens in Sweden shouldering the burden of large cohorts of children and – in particular – the elderly. In 1910, 8 per cent of the Swedish population was 65 years of age and over, as compared to only 4 per cent in the United States.[44]

In addition, mass emigration influenced women's scope for reproductive activities by increasing a long-standing surplus of women in the Swedish population. During the 1851–1915 period, men constituted 55 per cent of emigrants, and in 1910 there were 105 women to every 100 men in Sweden, as compared to 94 women to every 100 men in the United States.[45] A growing proportion of Swedish women remained unmarried, and the share of children born out of wedlock increased.[46] In 1910, only 46 per cent of the Swedish adult female population was married, as compared to 60 per cent in the United States.[47] Among Swedish women born in the years 1885–1889, more than 50 per cent never married.[48]

Emigration had a profound impact on Swedish gender and class relations. Most importantly, the continued heavy dependence on female labour served to nurture an ambivalent, but largely permissive, attitude towards women's gainful work. Although assumptions of *separate spheres* were strongly advocated by some internationally well-connected opinion-makers, most notably the author Ellen Key, Swedish notions of femininity had in practice to be reconciled with the widespread necessity of lifelong

---

[43] *Historical Statistics of Sweden*, p. 63, table B 16, pp. 64–65, table B 17, and p. 68, table B 21.

[44] Per Gunnar Edebalk, "Fattigvårdsfolket och pensionsstriden 1912/13", *Socialvetenskaplig tidskrift*, 3 (1995), pp. 266, and 269; *Historical Statistics of Sweden*, p. 71, table B 4, and p. 22, table A 16; and *Historical Statistics of the United States*, p. 8, Series A 20 and p. 10, Series A 84.

[45] *Historical Statistics of Sweden*, p. 5, table A 4, and p. 72, table B 25; *Historical Statistics of the United States*, p. 8, Series A 22-24.

[46] Gunnar Qvist, *Konsten att blifva en god flicka* (Stockholm, 1978), p. 102.

[47] *Historical Statistics of Sweden*, p. 28, table A 20, and *Historical Statistics of the United States*, p. 15, Series A 225.

[48] Robert Schoen and William L. Urton, *Marital Status Life Tables for Sweden* (Stockholm, 1979), pp. 16–17.

female providing.[49] Similarly, married women's crucial role in providing for their families shaped notions of housewifery as a breadwinning activity. According to the 1920 Marriage Act, both spouses were equally obliged to take care of home and children and to provide for the family. If the wife was not engaged in any gainful occupation, her domestic work was equated with male cash income as a contribution to family maintenance.[50]

More broadly, emigration contributed to a progressive national spirit of reflection and consensus. From the turn of the twentieth century, emigration was increasingly interpreted as a threat to the country, "draining it of its best and most valuable population".[51] Political debates were skewed towards economic and social reform. Quite naturally, the flourishing and liberal United States – preferred by so many Swedish emigrants – was often referred to as a model for the future but, in practice, aspirations to stop emigration and catch up economically actually strengthened the Swedish interventionist tradition. Labour gained strength, and conservative and liberal opinion-makers launched visions of the nation as a "home", marked by social solidarity and security and vitalized by the combined effort made by the entire population to achieve modernization. Such visions anticipated the later well-known metaphor of "the people's home", coined in the 1920s as a catchword for the social-democratic welfare state project.[52]

How, then, were Swedish state attitudes to the male breadwinning system shaped by the low capacity for reproductive investments and the challenge of emigration? Most importantly, traditional strategies of state intervention were encouraged. In the absence of a strong male breadwinning system, most people perceived public interventions in the sphere of human reproduction as necessary. Initially, the need for state support was judged most pressing in the countryside, but from the late nineteenth century, the challenge of emigration, an intensified process of industrialization and the rise of the labour movement conduced to strengthen interventionist tendencies in urban areas as well. From 1891, workers' sickness insurance funds were subsidized by the state, and in the following decades the parlia-

---

[49] Christina Carlsson, *Kvinnosyn och kvinnopolitik* (Lund, 1986), pp. 249–277; Beata Losman, *Kamp för ett nytt kvinnoliv* (Stockholm, 1980); and Ulla Wikander et al., *Det evigt kvinnliga* (Stockholm, 1994).

[50] Karin Widerberg, *Kvinnor, klasser och lagar* (Stockholm, 1989), p. 71.

[51] Ann-Sofie Kälvemark (Ohlander), "Swedish Emigration Policy in an International Perspective, 1840–1925", in Harald Runblom and Hans Norman (eds), *From Sweden to America. A History of the Migration* (Minneapolis, 1976), pp. 106–112 (quotation on p. 106).

[52] Walter Korpi, "Den svenska arbetarrörelsens förutsättningar och strategier", in Per Thullberg and Kjell Östberg (eds), *Den svenska modellen* (Lund, 1994), pp. 16–19; Kälvemark (Ohlander), "Swedish Emigration Policy", pp. 106–112; Bo Stråth, "Industriborgerskapets roll i den svenska samhällsomvandlingen", in Knut Kjeldstadli et al. (eds), *Formeringen av industrisamfunnet i Norden fram til 1920*, TMV skriftserie, 5 (Oslo, 1994), pp. 29–46.

ment passed several laws of national significance: the Factory Inspection Act (1889), the Old Age and Invalidity Pension Act (1913), the Occupational Injury Insurance Act (1916), the new Poor Relief Act (1918), the Eight-hour Law (1920), the Child Welfare Act (1924), and legislation establishing a state-subsidized Unemployment Insurance (1935).[53]

Second, the national reproductive experience encouraged a comparatively gender-neutral approach to problems of labour protection and family maintenance. This gender neutrality was first reflected in labour legislation. In contrast to the situation in the United States, Swedish men and women were normally covered by the same protective labour laws. Public protection was not specifically associated with femininity. The 1909 Night Work Prohibition for women, inspired by foreign examples, was the only major exception.[54] More importantly, Sweden also pioneered citizen-based entitlements which included women and men within the same structures of social provision and, in line with this gender-neutral approach, the role of mothers and married women as breadwinners was clearly emphasized.

The first decisive step towards a gender-neutral model of social citizenship in Sweden was taken with the passage of the 1913 Old Age Act. This Act, shaped by farmers' demand for a "people's insurance", introduced into Swedish social policy the principle of universal entitlements. It gave only small pension benefits, but all Swedish citizens – including married women – were covered by the same combined contributory and tax-financed scheme.[55] Women received lower benefits in relation to their contributions than men, but the principle of universalism nevertheless indicated that the unpaid work of married women was in principle deemed to be of comparable value to the national economy as the wage work of unmarried women.[56] Three years later, in 1916, the citizen-based approach of the Old Age Act was confirmed by a similarly broad ambition in the progressive and innovative Occupational Injury Insurance Act. In contrast to Workmen's Compensation in the United States, the Swedish occupa-

---

[53] Per-Gunnar Edebalk, "1916 års olycksfallsförsäkring", *Scandia*, 59, 1 (1993), pp. 116–119; and by the same author, "Fattigvårdsfolket", pp. 266–267, 269; Lindqvist, *Från folkrörelse till välfärdsbyråkrati*, pp. 51–53; Ohrlander, *I barnens och nationens intresse*, pp. 148–152; Olsson, *Social Policy*, p. 109; and *SOS 1971: 42, Försäkring och annat kontant stöd vid arbetslöshet* (Stockholm, 1971), pp. 70–72.

[54] This law was passed in the wake of widespread female opposition, see Carlsson, *Kvinnosyn och kvinnopolitik*, pp. 170–175; and Lynn Karlsson, "The Beginning of a 'Masculine Renaissance': The Debate on the 1909 Prohibition against Women's Night Work in Sweden", in Ulla Wikander et al., *Protecting Women*, pp. 252–253.

[55] Anders Berge, "Socialpolitik och normgivning i Sverige 1871–1913", *Arkiv*, 63–64 (1995), pp. 76–89; Olsson, *Social Policy*, pp. 83–89, 93–97; and Edebalk, "Fattigvårdsfolket", pp. 266–275.

[56] The lower benefits awarded to women were widely questioned at the time – also in parliament – but to no avail. See Kerstin Abukhanfusa, *Piskan och moroten* (Stockholm, 1987), pp. 28–45; *Ålderdomsförsäkringskommittén*, pp. 65–66 and 79–81.

tional insurance covered a major part of the labour market, including female sectors such as domestic service.[57]

Another crucial step towards a gender-neutral model of citizenship was the passage of the 1918 supplement to the Old Age Act. This supplement stated that poor, single mothers were to be entitled to child supplements from the public pension system, but only if they were permanently unable to work. The Swedish state thus explicitly demanded that single mothers give priority to breadwinning over motherhood. In line with the gender-neutral stance towards breadwinning duties, moreover, child supplements were not designed as a benefit confined to mothers, but as a form of support for parents of both sexes. Low-income couples and widowers incapable of working were also entitled to support. A similarly gender-neutral attitude marked the 1916 occupational injury insurance, which gave life annuities to widowers as well as to widows.[58]

As in the United States, middle-class women in Sweden were active in shaping early social policies. Their attitudes and strategies were somewhat different, however. Without backing from extensive female grass-roots organizations of the type prevalent in the United States, leading Swedish female reformers chose instead to cooperate with male opinion-makers, politicians and administrators. Their vision of a better future was related less closely to an expanding female sphere than to a future society in which male rationality and female empathy were to be fused and combined.[59] It is telling that Swedish female reformers did not follow the example of their American sisters in their intense lobbying for special labour legislation for women. Although Swedish middle-class reformers were profoundly influenced by the strong international movement calling for special protection of working women, and in principle supported its basic ideas, they did not work actively for any restrictive measures to regulate women's factory work. As shown by Lynn Karlsson, they chose instead to concentrate on other labour market problems, primarily the sweated conditions in home industry, and in this endeavour they did not explicitly use gender in arguing for regulations. In spite of the fact that women predominated in home industry, women's special need of protection was overshadowed by concern for workers of both sexes.[60]

It is clear that the gender-neutral stance of early Swedish social policies long reflected poverty and exploitation rather than emancipatory ambitions. In particular, women were given little help to combine wage work

---

[57] Edebalk, "1916 års olycksfallsförsäkring", p. 117.

[58] Ibid., p. 117; Åke Elmér, Folkpensioneringen i Sverige (Malmö, 1960), pp. 49–54; SFS 1918: 449, §6 and §33.

[59] The leading, gender-integrated Swedish social reform organization was Centralförbundet för Socialt arbete (CSA), see Centralförbundet för socialt arbete 1903–1928 (Stockholm, 1928), pp. 13–43; Kajsa Ohrlander, "Moderniserande kvinnlighet – gammal manlighet", Arkiv, 63–64 (1995), pp. 45–67; and Olsson, Social Policy, pp. 64–67.

[60] Karlsson, "The Beginning of a 'Masculine Renaissance' ", pp. 245–246.

and motherhood. Maternity leave, for example, was compulsory in industry from 1901, but it was not until 1931 that mothers on leave received any financial support.[61] As for childcare, crèches or day-care centres were rare before World War II, even in urban areas, and public support for childcare developed only slowly. If single mothers could not arrange daily care for their children, they had to send them away to relatives, often in the countryside, or were forced to board them out as foster children. It was not until the mid-1950s that children in day-care centres outnumbered foster children in Sweden.[62]

It is interesting to note, however, that the Swedish state chose at an early date to intervene in the private family sphere in ways that to some extent challenged patriarchal family power. This challenging state attitude was nurtured in particular by the threat of emigration, and it anticipated later population and equality policies. Many early reformers viewed the misery of Swedish children as a key obstacle to economic advance and national greatness. Male insobriety, brutality and neglect of home and family were seen as severe threats to national progress, and the need to protect women and children from the destructive effects of irresponsible masculinity came to motivate several legislative measures. From 1917, for example, the state backed the claims of mothers for economic support from the fathers of their children, and youth officers were appointed to look after the interests of single mothers and their children. Later programmes of maternity grants, advanced maintenance allowances, maternal care, universal family allowances, and universal maternity insurance enacted in the 1930s, 1940s and 1950s would focus on mothers and children in similar ways. Benefits were provided directly to the mothers.[63]

The 1930s mark the transition to a new era. In this period, Sweden could well have moved towards a male breadwinner model in social provision. Average incomes were rising, and the ideological tide turned towards domesticity. Instead, a sharp decline in birth-rates helped to confirm the gender-neutral approach to social citizenship. Birth-rates in Sweden declined from 24 in 1920 to 15 in 1930, reaching an international low of only 14 in 1934.[64]

---

[61] Ann-Sofie Ohlander, "The Invisible Child? The Struggle For a Social Democratic Family Policy in Sweden, 1900–1960s", in Bock and Thane, *Maternity and Gender Policies*, p. 60.

[62] Anita Nyberg, "Barnomsorgen. Ett kvinligt nollsummespel eller?", in Amnå, *Medmänsklighet att hyra?*, pp. 47–82.

[63] Teresa Kulawik, "Moderskapspolitik i Sverige och Tyskland i början på 1900-talet (1900–1930) – en skiss", in *Är Habermas intressant för forskning om kvinnor och den offentliga sektorn?* (Stockholm, 1991), pp. 34–37; Sainsbury, *Gender, Equality*, pp. 101–103 and 190–194; Ohlander, "The Invisible Child?", pp. 60–72; Ohlander, *I barnens och nationens intresse*, pp. 62–91; idem, "Moderniserande kvinnlighet", pp. 50–67; and Gena Weiner, *De räddade barnen* (Falkenberg, 1995), pp. 12–25 and 123–261.

[64] Allan Carlsson, *The Swedish Experiment in Family Politics. The Myrdals and the Interwar Population Crisis* (New Brunswick, NJ, 1990), pp. 6–26; Ann-Katrin Hatje, *Befolkningsfrågan och välfärden* (Stockholm, 1974), pp. 7–8; *Historical Statistics of Sweden*, I,

As in other European countries experiencing falling birth-rates, Sweden responded by enacting maternalist social policy measures such as maternity grants, marriage loans, free natal care and free deliveries (1937). The most distinctive feature of Swedish population policy, however, was the clear recognition of women's rights. With their influential book *Crisis in the Population Question*, Gunnar and Alva Myrdal succeeded in raising the population question as a starting-point for radical social reform policies aimed at influencing population growth in terms of both quantity and quality. They also argued, however, that higher birth-rates must be accompanied by freedom of choice for women (access to contraceptives), and that population policies must acknowledge employed mothers as a "social fact". Reforms should not support a male breadwinning system but give mothers – single or married – direct support for the costs associated with motherhood and caring and allow them to combine work and family without penalties.[65]

Gunnar and Alva Myrdal's standpoint on women's rights certainly sprang from Alva's feminist perspective, but it also mirrored the long-standing tradition of female breadwinning in Sweden. Although Alva Myrdal was more radical than most of her contemporaries, there was broad support for women's right to work in Swedish society at the time. This support was clearly revealed in the debates following proposals made by individual MPs in parliament in the wake of the Depression, suggesting that married women should be banned from working. In contrast to the situation in the United States, where women's organizations were split on this issue and most unions defended the family wage, all major women's organizations in Sweden united in their opposition to the proposal. The trade union movement eventually joined them. In 1939, a law was finally passed making it illegal to fire women by reason of marriage, pregnancy or childbearing if they had worked two years or more in a job. This piece of legislation marked the close of the early welfare state era and, seen in a long-term perspective, served as a bridge to the later rise of more explicit equality policies initiated in the late 1960s.[66]

What happened, then, in the intermediate period up to the 1960s? All in all, these decades of persistent economic growth and increased social spending reveal more ambivalent Swedish state attitudes to the male breadwinning system. On the one hand, the basically gender-neutral, citizen-based approach of the pre-war era was clearly confirmed and

pp. 45 and 46, table B 2; and Maddison, *Dynamic Forces*, p. 190, table A.2, and p. 234, table B.3.

[65] Carlsson, *The Swedish Experiment*, pp. 89 and 172–174; Hatje, *Befolkningsfrågan och välfärden*, pp. 32–37 and 237–245; Gunnar Myrdal, *Population. A Problem for Democracy* (Cambridge, MA, 1940), pp. 3–225; Sainsbury, *Gender, Equality*, p. 101.

[66] Barbara Hobson, "Feminist Strategies and Gendered Discourses in Welfare States: Married Women's Right to Work in the United States and Sweden", in Koven and Michel, *Mothers of a New World*, pp. 396–429.

developed, for example in the introduction of universal flat-rate pensions (1946) and in the passage of a citizen-based sickness and maternity insurance (1955). On the other hand, some policies in support of a male breadwinning system also emerged. Wife supplements, for example, were added to the unemployment insurance during the 1941–1964 period (along with child supplements, 1941–1973). Similarly, when the old age pension arrangements were reformed in 1946, wife supplements and means-tested pensions for widows aged 55 and over were introduced. The recognition of women's rights as wives reached its height in the early 1960s, when widows became entitled to pensions without means-testing at the age of only 36.[67] All in all, however, these post-war elements of a male-breadwinner model in Swedish social provision were limited in scope and, from the 1970s onwards, they were gradually eliminated.

CONCLUSION

Both in the United States and in Sweden modern welfare state formation commenced around the turn of the twentieth century. Swedish as well as American reformers were part of an internationally wide-ranging movement for social reform. At the national level, however, debates and institutional choices were shaped by strikingly different reproductive conditions. The residual American male breadwinner state has its historical roots in a society marked by economic prosperity and immigration. An abundance of wealth and labour was the basis for a strong confidence in the male breadwinning system. The Swedish weak male breadwinner state, by contrast, grew historically out of shared experiences of poverty and national backwardness, combined with dramatic reproductive challenges: in particular emigration, and later declining fertility. Strained reproductive conditions encouraged the belief that extensive state interventions were needed in the sphere of reproduction, and social policies recognized women's duties as both breadwinners and mothers.

Compared to those in the United States, Swedish state attitudes to the male breadwinning system were already distinctive in the early period of welfare state institutionalization, prior to the 1930s. First, the Swedish state was more strongly inclined to intervene in the sphere of reproduction. This interventionist attitude, which reflects the idea that human reproduction is a national concern, was an important prerequisite for the later adoption of a dual breadwinner model.

Second, Sweden early developed a citizen-based, universal approach to problems of social provision. With regard to labour protection and programmes of maintenance, this universal approach was largely gender-

---

[67] Edebalk, *Arbetslöshetsförsäkringen*, p. 21; Elmér, *Folkpensioneringen*, pp. 80–81; Sainsbury, *Gender, Equality*, pp. 63–67 and 190–194; *SOS 1971: 42*, pp. 73 and 208–210; Widerberg, *Kvinnor, klasser och lagar*, pp. 123–125.

neutral. Men as well as women were covered by protective labour legislation, and the introduction of citizen-based entitlements served to underline the basic similarity between married and unmarried women, and between women and men. With regard to maternal and child welfare, the citizen-based approach resulted in benefits targeted at children and mothers, either supplied in kind or paid to the mothers. Increasingly, these benefits were designed as universal entitlements. All in all, the citizen-based structure of social provision served to weaken the position of the male breadwinner.

Finally, early Swedish state attitudes towards single mothers and married women were marked by the primacy of breadwinning. The Swedish state recognized female breadwinning as a duty, and eventually also as a right. This emphasis on female breadwinning points to the modern Swedish welfare state, in which women's participation in the labour force is strongly encouraged.

According to Bo Rothstein, there are formative moments in political history when the enactment of new policies has a particularly strong impact on subsequent policy-making. Such formative moments are marked by challenging new economic and social conditions which extend freedom of action.[68]

I would suggest that the decades up to World War II constituted such a formative moment in Swedish welfare state history. During this period, Swedish politicians responded in innovative ways to dramatic economic and demographic challenges, and went a long way towards institutionalizing a comparatively gender-neutral model of citizenship. This development contrasted not only with the gender-divided approach prevalent in the contemporary United States, but also with the developing gender-divided structures of citizenship in neighbouring European welfare states, such as Britain, Germany and the Netherlands.

Further surveys and case studies are needed in order to explore the merits and limitations of an economic and demographic approach to welfare state formation. The most urgent task would be to compare the American and Swedish cases with strong male breadwinner states in Europe, such as Britain and the Netherlands, and with other modified or weak male breadwinner states, such as France. Britain stands out as a particularly interesting case. In the early twentieth century, per capita income in Britain was the highest in Europe, but – in contrast to the United States – Britain was experiencing lagging economic growth and reproductive challenges such as emigration, falling fertility and ageing. Similarly, the Netherlands and France have combined divergent levels of national income with strikingly varied reproductive experiences.

---

[68] Bo Rothstein, *Den korporativa staten* (Stockholm, 1992), pp. 17–20. Compare Skocpol, *Protecting Soldiers and Mothers*, pp. 57–60.

Comparing the Post-War Germanies: Breadwinner Ideology and Women's Employment in the Divided Nation, 1948–1970[*]

CHRISTINE VON OERTZEN AND ALMUT RIETZSCHEL

In 1989, when Germany became reunified after forty years of separation, no one could overlook the fact that East and West Germany differed greatly with regard to the position of women. The most striking difference of all seemed to lie in the rates of female employment: 91 per cent of all East German women under the age of 60 were counted as being employed, compared to only 55 per cent in West Germany.[1]

These figures give the impression that the male breadwinner system, a solid pillar of the traditional gender hierarchy, had been demolished in the East, whereas in the West it was at best crumbling round the edges. This interpretation also fits neatly into the standard accounts, which stress the differences between the two Germanies. While East German literature celebrated the new gender order by dwelling on women's successful emancipation, West German literature emphasized the view that reinforcing the traditional gendered division of labour was a key element in the reconstruction of society.[2]

Without denying the obvious dissimilarities, we would like to suggest a change of perspective. Shifting the main focus to the question of similarities, we shall trace the history of the male breadwinning experience in East and West Germany, starting in the turmoil of the post-war years. This approach seems to be particularly promising in relation to the 1950s and 1960s, when the common heritage still shaped life in both halves of

[*] This article is the product of a comparative project on the gender history of post-war Germany. The two authors are both due to finish their theses in 1997. Both studies are on part-time work, Christine von Oertzen's about its history in West Germany and Almut Rietzschel's about its development in East Germany.

[1] For West Germany (1989) see Friederike Maier, "Zwischen Arbeitsmarkt und Familie; Frauenarbeit in den alten Bundesländern", in Hildegard-Maria Nickel and Gisela Helwig (eds), *Frauen in Deutschland, 1945–1992* (Bonn, 1993), pp. 257–279; please note that the East German figure of 91 per cent includes female students and apprentices, see Gunnar Winkler (ed.), *Frauenreport '90* (Berlin, 1990), p. 63. Virginia Penrose presents data that are more closely comparable with the West German figures and calculates on this basis that 80 per cent of East German women were employed in 1987: see Penrose, "Vierzig Jahre SED-Frauenpolitik: Ziele, Strategien und Ergebnisse", *Frauenforschung: Informationsdienst des Forschungsinstituts Frau und Gesellschaft*, 8, 4 (1990), pp. 60–77, esp. p. 66.

[2] For West Germany: Annette Kuhn, "Power and Powerlessness: Women after 1945, or the Continuity of the Ideology of Feminity", *German History*, 7 (1989), pp. 35–46; for East Germany: Herta Kuhrig and Wulfram Speigner (eds), *Zur gesellscraflichen Stellung der Frau in der DDR* (Leipzig, 1978).

nternational Review of Social History* 42 (1997), Supplement, pp. 175–196

Germany. This included the powerful ideology of the male breadwinner family where "the husband was expected to be the main, preferably the sole, breadwinner and his wife was to assume responsibility for running the household, preferably on a full-time basis".[3] It is true that the East German state deliberately broke with the past by creating a new female role model of women as lifelong, full-time workers. But this does not necessarily mean that the ideology of the male breadwinner was eliminated in East Germany. We assume that it was ostensibly demolished but lived on beneath the surface. Our comparative approach therefore leads to the key issue of this paper: to what extent is the history of the male breadwinning experience really dissimilar or similar in East and West Germany?

Current research on the male breadwinner system has so far concentrated on the nineteenth century. It illustrates how the system was implemented in labour legislation, and how its ideology shaped and gendered class formation in Western Europe and in the US. Its origins and the explanatory factors involved in its rise are still hotly debated.[4] By concentrating on the twentieth century, when the male breadwinner system was already firmly established, our paper will contribute to the debate by posing other questions: how – and to what extent – did the breadwinner system endure on each side of the German border? And how can we explain its enormous capacity to adapt to changing political, social and economic conditions?[5]

The first two sections of our article analyse how the notion of the male breadwinner continued to shape the perception of women's employment in both halves of Germany. In the late 1940s, these debates centred on how to provide for war widows (part I). The breadwinner ideology remained influential in the 1950s and 1960s, when the debates on women's work focused on married women (part II). Part III examines the legal institutionalization of the breadwinner ideology, which helped to reproduce a gender system with a strong bias in favour of men. In the case of West Germany, the tax system will be a particular focus of attention, and in the case of East Germany the wage system. During the period of the 1950s and 1960s, the divergent paths adopted by the two German states in the 1940s became clearly apparent. While the breadwinner ideology was deliberately written into West German legislation, it is more difficult to

---

[3] Colin Creighton, "The Rise of the Male Breadwinner Family: A Reappraisal", *Comparative Studies in Society and History*, 38 (1996), pp. 311–337.

[4] A comprehensive overview of the nineteenth-century debate is given by Creighton, in *ibid.* For German case studies, see Sabine Schmitt, *Der Arbeiterinnenschutz im Deutschen Kaiserreich. Zur Konstruktion der schutzbedürftigen Arbeiterin* (Stuttgart, 1995); Kathleen Canning, *Languages of Labour and Gender. Female Factory Work in Germany, 1840–1914* (Ithaca, 1996).

[5] See Karin Hausen, "Frauenerwebstätigigkeit und erwerbstätige Frauen. Anmerkungen zur historischen Fonchung", in Gunilla Budde (ed.), *Frauen arbeiten. Uteibliche Erwerbstätigkeit in Ost- und West-deutschland nach 1945* (Göttingen, 1997), pp. 19–45.

detect in East Germany, since the state aimed to eradicate it. The issues we have selected – though differing in the two states – are those which can demonstrate most effectively the mechanisms responsible for the adaptability and persistence of the male breadwinner system.

I

After World War II, the German authorities of all four occupation zones had to cope with the problem of how to provide for war widows. The widows had lost not only their husbands but also the comfortable pensions instituted by the Nazi authorities. These were abolished by the Allied Control Council in 1945.[6] Although this did not result in a complete cessation of all public support for widows, the four military governments made it clear that widows under 60 were expected to earn their own living, even if they had children. In the turmoil of the initial post-war years, when everyone was preoccupied with the hardships of daily life, the impact of this policy did not immediately become fully apparent. This changed in the summer of 1948, when the two currency reforms were enacted, first in the West and then in the East. The dual currency reform can be identified as the starting-point of the two diverging paths followed by the authorities in East and West Germany in providing for war widows. Faced with the same problems, the East and West German administrations pursued measures which at first glance appear to be similar, but in fact reflect quite different ideas on how to replace the missing breadwinners.

The dual currency reform had a dramatic impact on the female labour market in both the East and the West. For the first time since 1946, unemployment offices were confronted with growing numbers of women for whom they could not find jobs. While many firms were dismissing workers, the currency reforms also created a new demand for jobs as "money" regained its lost importance and superseded strategies of survival which depended on barter and the black market. Since savings had been devaluated or exhausted, many women who had previously done their best to avoid joining the workforce now registered at the unemployment offices. Others were attracted to paid work because of the renewed availability of goods in the shops.[7]

In East Germany, war widows with dependent children suffered particularly from the increasing competition in the female labour market. Three years after the end of World War II, high-ranking officials left no doubt

---

[6] A detailed account in a broader context will be given in the forthcoming publication by Elizabeth D. Heineman: *Standing Alone: Single Women from the "Third Reich" to the Post-war Germanies*. For a general account of women in the post-war years, see her article: "The Hour of the Women: Memories of Germany's 'Crisis Years' and West German National Identity", *American Historical Review*, 101 (1996), pp. 354–395.

[7] For a detailed account see: Katherine Pence, "Labours of Consumption: Gendered Consumers in Post-War East and West German Reconstruction", in Lynn Abrams and Elizabeth Harvey (eds), *Gender Relations in German History: Power, Agency and Experience from the 16th to the 20th Century* (London, 1996), pp. 211–238.

that the East German state expected the war widows to replace the male breadwinner by seeking full-time employment. By restricting welfare payments as well as pensions to widows under the age of 60, the East German government tried to "force" the widows into the labour market.[8] These measures transmitted the clear message that was relentlessly preached to the widows: "We have no obligations toward the Nazi state".[9] In times of high unemployment, even those widows who had adjusted to the new political system and accepted the role of provider found it difficult to fulfil the expectations (and many did not, resolutely claiming that the state was obliged to take care of them because the death of their husbands was no fault of their own).

In 1948/1949, skilled female workers still had some chance of finding work, but many war widows were qualified only for untrained work for which there was no great demand. In addition, many of them had children to care for and could not work eight hours a day in a factory. What made things worse was the decline of the market for domestic production, in which many widows had previously found work. Most of them were dismissed when domestic industry broke down in 1948 due to wage increases, declining sales, scarcity of raw materials and production prohibitions.[10] In trying to cope with the problem of rising unemployment amongst welfare-dependent women with children, the East German labour administration fell back on the traditional idea of creating part-time jobs, which had been developed during the unemployment crisis of the 1930s. This idea of spreading the limited work available over as many women as possible was clearly a solution inspired by necessity rather than by choice. Widows were only to work part-time so long as there were not enough full-time jobs and not enough childcare facilities. The idea failed completely, partly because of the unwillingness of firms to create part-time jobs and partly because women on welfare were not interested in part-time work paying wages that were even lower than welfare support.

Facing truly bleak prospects in their search for full-time work, East German war widows waged a bitter war against married women in the workforce, whom they denounced as "double income earners". In their

[8] Daniela Weber, "Zwischen Fürsorge und Erwetbsarbeit. Alleinstehende Leipzigerinnem nach dem Zweiten Weltkrieg", in Susanne Schötz (ed.), *Frauenalltag in Leipzig. Weibliche Lebenszusammenhänge im 19. und 20. Jahrundert* (Weimar, 1997), pp. 295–318. For the restrictions, see "Anordnung zur Durchführung der Verordnung über Sozialfürsorge und des SMAD-Befehls Nr. 92/1946", which became law on 1 October 1948, published in *Zentralverordnungsblatt* 1948, pp. 469-473 and "Verordnung über die Zahlung von Renten an Kriegsinvaliden und Kriegshinterbliebene vom 21.7.1948", *ibid.* pp. 363-365. It went into operation on 1 November 1948.

[9] "Wir haben keine Verpflichtung gegenüber dem Nazistaat", said the high-ranking Saxon Oberregierungsrat Hausdorf during a lecture to local social welfare commissions in July 1949, in Bundesarchiv, Abteilung Potsdam (hereafter BAP), DQ-2 3730.

[10] A detailed picture of the decline of domestic industry is given in Sächsisches Hauptstaatsarchiv Dresden (hereafter SächsHStA), LRS, MfAuS, No. 318.

struggle to compete with other better-trained women, the war widows used the only weapon they had: the provider argument. In December 1949, when the prospect of finding work was particularly gloomy – there were only five vacancies for every hundred unemployed women – the Saxon Ministry of Labour registered a real "storm of protest against 'double income earners'". Day after day the staff of the labour offices were confronted with angry cries of "Get the 'double income earners' out of the factories! I need work. I need money to survive. The 'double income earners' just squander it at the free shops" (newly-opened state-run shops offering highly-priced unrationed goods, later known as HO-shops).[11]

Male workers sided with the war widows in their desire to banish married women from the labour market. They were ready to grant the widows provider status on condition that they did not compete with men. In 1947, a representative of a factory council suggested in a letter to the local Dresden branch of the Socialist Unity Party (SED) that married women with husbands to support them should be dismissed and their jobs given to welfare-supported war widows. This would mean that his factory could offer 10 to 15 jobs to war widows. The local party unit did not dare to answer this letter, but passed it on to the Saxon government, where it provoked widespread discussion. A high-ranking female official at the Labour Ministry declared that there was "something to be said for it" on condition that married women resigned of their own free will.[12] In 1948, employment offices in Saxony were advised to adopt this guideline, which seemed to resolve the conflict between social needs and ideological commitment: it acknowledged the war widows' claims without infringing married women's right to work. This policy did seem to make sense in 1947 and 1948, when large numbers of men were returning from the prisoner-of-war camps. The employment offices soon noted that their return often coincided with their wives' decision to give up employment. By 1949, however, it was clear that the Saxon policy was doomed to failure, since those married women who were still in employment showed no inclination to resign. Furthermore, Saxony's cautious admission that the marital status of women might play some role could be read as an implicit agreement that in times of high unemployment war widows should be preferred by the employment offices to married women. For this reason, it provoked a sharp response by the central administration in Berlin, which insisted that jobs should be assigned strictly on the basis of women's qualifications. Women's right to work regardless of their marital status became constitutional law in 1949. It was undoubtedly a noble cause, but it was not the

---

[11] The widows cried: "Sorgen Sie dafür, daß die Doppelverdiener aus den Betrieben verschwinden. Ich brauche eine Arbeit. Ich brauche das Geld zum Lebensunterhalt. Die 'Doppelverdiener' geben es im freien Kaufhaus aus!", in SächsHStA, LRS, MfAuS, No. 453, p. 31.
[12] The course of events is documented in SächsHStA, LRS, MfAuS, No. 453, pp. 38, 40 and 41.

policy followed in practice by the local employment offices, which continued to give clear priority to the war widows.[13] This was in line not only with the task of reducing welfare expenditure but also with the established practice of employment offices to favour those clients who could claim to be the family breadwinner.

In West Germany, a different solution/policy was pursued. The claim for women's "right to work" could also be heard in the immediate post-war years, but lost its emancipatory meaning and experienced a specific metamorphosis with the beginning of the Cold War.[14] Women were to have the right to work, but only if they "needed" to do so for economic reasons. Referring to the "naturalness" of the gender system, it was to be women's primary task as well as their primary "right" to care for the family while being supported by a male breadwinner.

Nothing illustrates this policy change between 1948 and 1950 more clearly than the attitudes and policies towards war widows with children. Pressurized by organizations of war-disabled men and POWs, trade unions, the labour ministries[15] and the communal public welfare organizations,[16] the labour administrations[17] began to seek employment for war widows. Nobody denied the difficulty of integrating widows and women

[13] See BAP, D Q-2, 2072. This file contains many documents on the campaign against "double income earners" and the efforts to crush it. The future Minister of Justice, Hilde Benjamin, initiated a review of policy in local unemployment offices when she was told that they refused to give jobs to married women. The Saxon policy was criticized in a letter sent on 17 January 1949 by the employment and welfare department of the central administration to the Saxon Minister of Labour.

[14] See Robert G. Moeller, *Protecting Motherhood. Women and the Family in the Politics of Post-war West Germany* (Berkeley, Los Angeles and Oxford, 1993), esp. p. 319f.

[15] Up to 1950, there was no central ministry of labour in West Germany. In so far as the allied military governments left anything for them to decide, it was the labour ministries of the "Bundesländer" that governed all policies concerning the labour market. Especially in the British Occupation Zone, important decisions were taken by the "Manpower Division" of the military government. Within this, the British instituted a "Zentralamt für Arbeit" (Central Labour Administration), a German authority exercising the executive powers of the manpower division for the whole zone. In the American and French zones, there were no comparable authorities, because labour policies were left much more to the Germans themselves. The labour ministries in all of the "Bundesländer" represented the official authorities. Beside these, the labour administrations on the country (Landesarbeitsämter) and local (Arbeitsämter) level were responsible for finding jobs (Arbeitsvermittlung) and for bearing the costs of unemployment insurance (Arbeitslosenversicherung). The labour administrations were part of the autonomous German labour administration (Arbeitsverwaltung). Destroyed by the Nazis, the central institution of the labour administration (Bundesanstalt für Arbeitsvermittlung und Arbeitslosenversicherung, BAVAV) was not restored until 1952. Until then, the labour administrations of the Bundesländer (Landesarbeitsämter) represented the highest authorities with regard to job finding and unemployment insurance.

[16] Public welfare (öffentliche Wohlfahrt) was organized at local level and widely financed by the municipal authorities. The cities and counties had to provide for the public welfare organizations (Wohlfahrtsverbände) which bore the costs of the public welfare system.

[17] See footnote 15.

"with family responsibilities" (*häuslich gebundene Frauen*) into the "normal" and "free" labour market, which were quite similar to the East German case. However, the financial "burden" that these women imposed on the communal welfare system meant that a solution needed to be found. Furthermore, and even more importantly, the aim of "providing" widows with work had an important conceptual background: part-time work would enhance the social integration of war widows and women refugees with children. It would reinforce women's self-confidence and their feeling of being "useful". This interpretation of the meaning of "work" was far from being emancipatory; rather it was clearly shaped by ideas of an adapted male "breadwinner model": going out to work would not only meet an economic need, but would also help to restore the individual power and dignity of the widows and "provide" them with self-achieved economic independence from public support.[18]

In this sense, part-time work was perceived as a less-than-ideal solution, but in a very different way from in East Germany. The war had prevented widows from living their lives in accordance with the social norm of the housewife. Under these conditions, part-time work was the most suitable way for them to function in their new role of provider. West Germans insisted that widows with children could not be expected to cope with a normal full-time job. In some of the larger cities, the labour administrations tried to introduce needlework centres with flexible working hours for mothers who "needed" work (*erwerbsbedürftige Mütter*). As in East Germany, however, none of these measures lasted long. The introduction of part-time work in industry came nowhere near to realization. Close inspection reveals that attempts to achieve it were blocked at a number of levels. "Radical" women trade unionists, for example, demanded a legal quota to institutionalize part-time work for widows in factories and offices: under regulations for war-disabled men, employers would be fined if they did not make a fixed percentage of part-time jobs available to war widows. However, this demand was turned down in 1949. In favour of the efforts to institute the quota system for the war-disabled male breadwinners, high-ranking male trade unionists rejected the proposal.

The most important change in the meaning of employment for widows was promoted by the labour administration and in the legal debate concerning the right to unemployment support. In 1948, in an attempt to integrate widows and women with dependent children into the labour market, the British allies had introduced a new system of state support which was meant to replace the abolished war pensions.[19] Under the new system, unemployment benefits did not depend on a previous record of

---

[18] Decree of the Hesse Ministry of Labour to the Hesse labour administration, 10 October 1948, Hessisches Hauptstaatsarchiv Wiesbaden (hereafter HStAH), Dep. 940, No. 109.
[19] Kurt Draeger, "Die neue Arbeitslosenfürsarge", in *Arbeitsblatt für die Britische zone 2* (1948), pp. 41–48.

employment. This regulation meant that widows who were fit to work (*"arbeitsfähige"*) could apply for unemployment benefits, even if they had never been part of the workforce. As a result, the official employment agencies were responsible for their support, and should therefore be eager to find jobs for them in order to reduce the total costs of the benefits system. But instead of encouraging this effort to provide clients with work meeting their unusual needs, the law actually promoted the opposite. Male workers were still given privileged access to the few jobs available on the grounds of their responsibilities as breadwinners. By contrast, widows, married women and single mothers with "family responsibilities" were labelled as "bogus unemployed" who were "not available" for the labour market because they could not work the whole day. They were therefore excluded from unemployment support and left to the public welfare system. This was worse than unemployment support not only because it often meant lower benefits (which had to be paid back in better times) and no extra health insurance, but also because it was regarded as support for the poor and disabled. Receiving welfare payments meant exclusion from society.

To justify this practice, labour administration officials claimed in 1951 that war widows and refugee women with children did not need work but money. They would be best taken care of by way of satisfactory state pensions. This argument was consistent with another topic that was dominating the political agenda and attracting great interest at the time: from 1945 on, the West German authorities had aimed to change allied policies on widows and war-disabled men, which were perceived as degrading.[20] In 1950, a new law restored the abolished state support for the "victims of the war". This milestone in West German reconstruction sanctioned a clearly gendered concept of state provision. Whereas it explicitly provided for a combination of "work" and "support" for disabled men, it reinforced the ideal of widows as housewives and mothers, which included "work" only in a very subordinate way. What widows with children "needed" in the first instance was full financial support in the form of state pensions. Defined in this way, they were excluded from the "right to work". The legal quota system provided "work" primarily for disabled male victims of the war – it was only to be given to widows if no war-disabled man was available.[21]

When the "double income" campaign emerged in West Germany at the beginning of the 1950s, it had a very different connotation from the one in East Germany. The Western campaign built upon a clearly gendered

[20] Up to 1949, however, West Germans had no legal sovereignty and thus had to cope with the problems of disabled breadwinners, who could hardly be integrated into the workforce, as well as with widows for whom it was impossible to "provide".

[21] Bundesversorgungsgesetz of 12 December 1950, Bundesgesetzblatt I 1950, pp. 791f.

hierarchy: it insisted that no married women should be employed so long as any *male* worker was in need of a job to fulfil his duty as a breadwinner. The "need" for jobs for widows and women without male support was not completely ignored in this chorus of discrimination against the employment of married women, but it had no lobby comparable to that in East Germany. Improving the situation of West German widows meant calling for higher pensions. Despite the fact that most widows were unable even to survive on this support and therefore had to seek full-time or part-time employment, they were still regarded as being "provided for" in a reconstructed breadwinner system.

II

As the years passed, all East German war widows were integrated into the workforce. As a result, the proportion of women in employment almost equalled that of men. In 1950, 40 per cent of the workforce was female, and ten years later 45 per cent. Even more impressively, the percentage of women in the 15 to 60 year age group who were in employment rose from 44 per cent in 1950 to 62 per cent in 1960. Judging by these figures, the new model of lifelong employment for women seemed to have taken secure root. But this picture does not reveal the whole truth. The rising numbers of women in employment were partly due to a significant shift in the age structure of East Germany's population. Because the number of women of employable age was declining, the percentage of women in employment rose rapidly without any significant rise in the actual numbers in work. To put it the other way round: a considerable proportion of married women remained outside the workforce.[22] To some extent this was to be expected. People needed time to adapt to the new system. First, older couples who had grown up with the breadwinner/housewife ideology and organized their lives accordingly were unlikely to change their lifestyle just because the East German government tried to institute a new ideology. Though the state did not encourage married women to stay at home, it did not attempt to force them into the labour market either. So long as husband and wife agreed between themselves on the traditional division of labour, the state did not interfere. Second, although young women might adapt more easily to the new role model, many left the workforce after giving birth to children if the husband's wages were enough to support the family

---

[22] Since East German statistics did not count married women as a separate category, this conclusion has to be reached by deduction. In 1955, 3,395,600 women were in employment, equivalent to 55 per cent of all women of employable age. Although five years later only 60,800 more women had joined the workforce, the proportion of women in employment soared to 62 per cent. All figures presented in this paragraph are taken from Penrose, "Vierzig Jahre SED-Frauenpolitik", p. 66.

because they still believed that a small child needed its mother and should not be placed in institutional care.[23]

On the other hand, some mothers who would have preferred to return to work after their maternity leave were forced to stay at home because they could not get a place in a crèche (for the under-threes) or later in a kindergarten (for the three to six year olds). This problem cannot be explained away simply as a difficulty of the transitional period. It is true that a dense network of childcare facilities could not be constructed overnight, but the slowness of the process was due partly to the fact that the male breadwinner system remained deeply ingrained in East German policies towards women, despite efforts to abolish it. For example, married women who tried to obtain a childcare place were asked whether they owned a TV or a fridge: if so, they did not need to work and therefore did not need a place in a crèche.[24] Even high-ranking male politicians did not really want mothers to join the workforce. They gave due public support to the official goal of all women entering full-time employment in order to achieve true emancipation, but some of them were only paying lip-service to the official communist doctrine. This became evident in 1961, when the chronic labour shortage led to renewed efforts to attract housewives into the labour force. Former Minister of Labour Fritz Macher was not the only one who admitted privately that mothers of small children would be better off staying at home because "these workers cost us more than they produce".[25] This calculation could only be based on the assumption that it was women's natural duty to take care of their children. Only within the logic of the breadwinner ideology did it make sense to weigh the expenditures for building and maintaining childcare facilities against women's productivity.

Nevertheless, high-ranking male officials did make this calculation and therefore favoured part-time, rather than full-time, work for mothers because they assumed it was "cheaper". In late 1960, when Clara Zetkin's son, the professor of medicine Maxim Zetkin, proposed incorporating a right for mothers to work part-time into the new statute of industrial law, his chances of success were not very high. Many SED and trade union officials feared (correctly) that women currently working full-time would be encouraged to reduce their working hours. Zetkin's proposal was, however, strongly supported by the state council, the collective body headed

---

[23] In 1960, the question of "who is the better mother?", those staying at home or those going out to work, was fiercely debated in the SED newspaper *Neues Deutschland*: see Gesine Obertreis, *Familienpolitik in der DDR 1945–1980* (Opladen, 1986), pp. 157f.

[24] See the lecture on problems of socialist education given at the meeting of the women's committee of the FDGB executive on 31 May 1961 in Stiftung Archiv der Parteien und Massenorganisationen der DDR im Bundesarchiv (hereafter BA-SAPMO), DY 34/4238.

[25] The off-hand remark "daß diese Arbeitskräfte uns mehr kosten als sie bringen" was made to a female union colleague during a conference of the FDGB executive: see memo written by Fridl Lewin on 7 April 1961, in BA-SAPMO, DY 34/2146.

by Walter Ulbricht. Its members were fascinated by the concept of part-time work because it made women's work outside the home more "profit-able". Scientific research was enthusiastically cited to "prove" that mothers who worked part-time organized the day care of their children privately and did not need expensive state-run childcare facilities to com-bine the roles of mother and paid employee. This was not the only advan-tage of part-time work in the eyes of party and state officials. They also calculated that staff not required for childminding in state facilities could instead be diverted into "productive" branches of the economy.[26] The intervention of the state council doubtless smoothed the way for the even-tual grant of the right to work part-time to women whose "family duties" temporarily prevented them from working full-time.[27]

The discussions on the "profitability" of women's work indicate that the breadwinner ideology was still shaping the debates on married women's employment. The strength of its influence becomes even more obvious when the framework of policy towards women is examined closely. Policy towards women, as defined by the SED, still assumed that women remained responsible for running the household and caring for the children, even when they had joined the workforce. This unquestioned assumption was what lay behind the concept of relieving mothers in full-time employment of as many household tasks as possible. Even female politicians like former Social Democrat Käthe Kern, who fought hard to establish equality between the sexes in the workplace, failed to recognize that the ambitious plan to help women combine the roles of mother and worker helped to confirm the traditional gender division within the family. The manifold measures they initiated to ease women's "double burden" (e.g. building childcare facilities, laundries and factory canteens) certainly satisfied women's needs, but at the same time they reinforced the notion that bringing up children and doing the housework were women's work. How deeply this notion was embedded in East German policies towards women is indicated by the language employed by party and trade union officials – of both sexes – to define the goals of these policies. They constantly spoke of women's duties as mothers, wives and housewives, as if this were the most natural thing in the world. Only on very rare occa-sions was this language ever closely scrutinized. The following anony-mous author, who attempted to evaluate the state of policies towards women in the mid-1960s, was one of the few who grasped the significance of language in this respect. The often-cited term "women's duties as wives and mothers", this author pointed out, "is not used in such a way that it

---

[26] Letter of 6 January 1961 from the state council to the executive of the FDGB, in BA-SAPMO, DY 34/217/281/6389.

[27] Section 3 (4) of the *Gesetzbuch der Arbeit* stated: "Die Betriebsleiter sollen die Möglich-keiten schaffen, daß auch die Frauen, die durch familiäre Pflichten vorübergehend verhin-dert sind, ganztägig zu arbeiten, durch Teilbeschäftigung ihr Recht auf Arbeit wahrnehmen können", in *Gesetzblatt* 1961, Part I, p. 29.

can be assumed that women *regard* this work as their duty, but that it *is* their duty".[28]

The constant reference to the special duties of women supported the traditional division of labour within the family. This system of ascribing all unpaid housework to women had a clear impact on the way in which the East German population thought about women's work, as is shown by two opinion polls on the role of women in the family and in society which were conducted in 1968 and 1970. Admittedly, both surveys document the radical change in attitudes towards women's employment. In contrast to West German attitudes, an overwhelming majority in the East now approved of the employment of married women outside the home. But only 25 per cent of those surveyed were prepared to agree with the official role model of women's lifelong full-time employment, whereas more than 50 per cent accepted the idea of part-time work after marriage. Worse still, male industrial workers – whom the Marxist-Leninist ideology regarded as the avant-garde – were particularly tenacious in their preference for the housewife model. Around 30 per cent of the male factory workers surveyed thought that married women should not work at all, or should at any rate give up work once the necessary household items had been bought.[29]

In West Germany, the debate on the employment of women shifted its focus to married women once the economic situation improved during the 1950s. It was almost unanimously agreed that the best help for a married woman – unless she was highly qualified – was a good job for her husband. Even female union officials fighting for equal rights and pay for women in the labour market did so on this premise: married women were to be protected as workers only so long as the breadwinner system lacked efficiency and failed to support a family on a single income.

Despite these notions, the female workforce rose steadily once the peak of unemployment had been overcome in 1952. Moreover, the percentage of married women workers shot up and married women became increasingly visible in the labour market. At the end of 1954, when the government and industrial federations were predicting full employment and a future economic need for even more female married

---

[28] "Der Begriff Pflicht [werde] nicht so verwendet, daß man annehmen könne, die Frauen würden diese Arbeiten als ihre Pflicht *betrachten*, sondern als *seien* es ihre Pflichten": (undated) analysis of the state of scientific work on "The woman in the socialist society", in BA-SAPMO, DY 34/4293.

[29] Both surveys are documented in BA-SAPMO, DY 30/IV 2/2.042/2. Included in the 30 per cent of male factory workers are those who preferred not to answer this question. Although the opinion polls were conducted by an institute supervised and controlled by the SED (Institut für Meinungsforschung beim ZK der SED), they can be regarded as providing a true picture. The participants had to fill out a written questionnaire which could not be traced back to the individual participant.

workers, the question of part-time work once again came up for debate. Once more, discussions centred around the meaning of "work" for women. The debates on part-time work during the 1950s were devoid of any idea of sexual equality with regard to the duties of paid work and family work. In fact, they centred explicitly on the "double burden" borne by married women workers and women's associations – and even the women's branch of the trade unions (DGB) – only accepted concepts of married women's work that relieved women of the burden of full-time gainful employment in order to preserve their energies for their domestic duties.[30]

So long as married women's work could be justified on the basis of "economic need", it did not threaten traditional beliefs concerning gender relations. Yet the ever-growing percentage of married women in the workforce demanded new ways of coping with the "biggest social revolution of our times", as a national newspaper put it in 1956.[31] Official figures seemed to confirm this perception: between 1950 and 1961 the percentage of married women in the female workforce rose from 19 to 35, and by 1970 as many as 50 per cent of all women workers were married.[32] It is obvious that this trend did not decline with the dawn of economic prosperity in the late 1950s, although those years marked the peak of the breadwinner ideology and practice. For the first time, increased male wages made it possible for families actually to live solely on the income of the male breadwinner. Ironically, however, employers and the government were at this very time encouraging married "housewives" to enter employment in order to alleviate the constant labour shortage.

Under these circumstances, attitudes towards married women's employment began to change. Their participation in the labour force could no longer be explained away or excused as a failure of the male breadwinner system. In the early 1960s, the economic and social shift from deprivation to prosperity undermined these justifications.[33] The argument that the

---

[30] For the women's associations see: Halbtagsarbeit – Teilzeitarbeit – für Frauen. Report of a nation-wide conference hosted by the "Arbeitsgemeinschaft der Wählerinnen" in Munich, 27 to 29 October 1955, Manuscript, Deutsches Zentralarchiv für soziale Fragen, ZI 13349; Olga Amann, "Halbtagsarbeit für Frauen", in Ruth Bergholtz (ed.), *Die Wirtschaft braucht die Frau* (Darmstadt, 1966), pp. 222–237; for the trade unions: "Da haben wir uns alle schrecklich geirrt [...]", German trade unions (DGB) (ed.), *Die Geschichte der gewerkschaftlichen Frauenarbeit im Deutschen Gewerkschaftsbund von 1945–1960* (Pfaffenweiler, 1993).
[31] *Westdeutsche Allgemeine Zeitung*, 11 January 1956.
[32] For these figures, see Angelika Willms, "Grundzüge der Entwicklung der Frauenarbeit von 1880–1980", in W. Müller, H. Willms and J. Hanell, *Strukturwandel der Frauenarbeit 1880–1980* (Frankfurt/M., 1983), p. 35.
[33] Claudia Born and Helga Krueger (eds), *Erwerbsverläufe von Ehepartnern und die Modernisierung weiblicher Lebensläufe* (Weinheim, 1993); Michael Wildt, *Am Beginn der Konsumgesellschaft. Mangelerfahrung, Lebenshaltung, Wohlstandhoffnung in Westdeutschland in den fünfziger Jahren* (Hamburg, 1994).

employment of married women was a reflection of economic "need" became an insult to every male breadwinner's capacity to provide for his family and threatened his social prestige. It was only tolerable for "housewives" to go out to work if they did *not* do it for economic reasons, but rather to satisfy a personal "need" or to achieve a "better life" in a modern consumer society. Detached from mere economic need, "work" for married women became more openly a matter of their own decision and desire. This option created a new image of the married woman worker. Alongside the exploited victim of hostile economic conditions, there now appeared on the scene the self-confident and active wife who sought employment in order to earn some extra income and for the sake of a pleasant change from the everyday routine of house and family work.

This image did in fact match the reality of the new clientele being addressed by the intense efforts to recruit women into the labour market.[34] The high level of breadwinners' incomes now gave "housewives" a stronger position from which to claim improved working conditions, such as special arrangements for working hours or transport to the workplace. The increasing percentage of married women in employment was partly due to the growth in part-time work. Between 1958 and 1970, the proportion of part-time workers in the female workforce rose from about 4 to over 19 per cent. Most women working part-time were married and had children; in 1970, every second married mother in the workforce had a part-time job.[35]

"The working housewife has become a hit", the well-known journalist Rosemarie Winter noted in October 1960 in a radio magazine programme on part-time employment.[36] She hastened to add that she would not deny that many families still had an urgent need for women's additional income. Nevertheless, compared to the 1950s, something in the meaning of work had definitely changed: "Whether or not married women are working for economic reasons, people think it is good for them: a vivid experience, a change from domestic routine, something to talk about, and even a matter of prestige."[37] Even men, she continued, would talk about their working

---

[34] See, for example, the page one banner headline of a famous daily yellow press newspaper, "Damit lockt die Industrie die Hausfrauen": *Bild-Zeitung*, 16 September 1961.

[35] In 1970, the proportion of married women workers in part-time jobs who had no children was 41 per cent. For all figures (except those referring to 1958) see: "Frauen mit Teilzeitarbeit. Ergebnisse des Mikrozensus", *Wirtschaft und Statistik* (1971), pp. 416–418; "Die Erwerbstätigkeit der Mütter und die Betreuung der Kinder. Ergebnis der Mikrozensus-Befragung 1969", *ibid.*, pp. 68–88. For 1958 see: *Gewerkschaftliche Beiträge zur Frauenarbeit, Heft 3: Ergebnisse einer Befragung über die Belastung der erwerbstätigen Frauen durch Beruf, Haushalt und Familie* (Düsseldorf, 1961), p. 25.

[36] "Sie sucht Zuverdienst". Script for a radio magazine programme broadcast on 10 October 1960 by Rosemarie Winter, HStAH, Abt. 2050, No. 36.

[37] "[. . .] ganz allgemein und überall [sieht man] in der Berufsarbeit der Hausfrau, ob sie nun eine Existenzgrundlage oder Zusatzverdienst bildet, eine Erfahrungsbereicherung, eine

wives with pride – so long as they benefited from the higher family income without having to sacrifice valued privileges. The debates on the tax system discussed below show that one key "privilege" which was to be upheld was their *status* as breadwinners, which was linked to substantial benefits, both inside and outside the home.

By the mid-1960s, part-time work was becoming an established part of the new and widely accepted idea of married women's lives. It was seen as representing a specific compromise between women's personal or economic needs and their distinct social role in both the family *and* the workforce, without weakening the male breadwinner ideology. All political parties and even the churches gave part-time work a key position in their ideas for a "family policy" taking account of the changing social and economic conditions in West Germany. Social-democratic women became the first to promote part-time work in this way. They included emancipatory intentions and deduced the "right" to work (part-time) from a new and "Western" female lifestyle; with more or less hesitation, the conservative "c"-parties[38] and both the Protestant and the Catholic church subsequently approved part-time work, because it allayed deep-rooted fears that integrating married women into the labour market would destabilize gender hierarchies both within the family and in society as a whole.

III

Images and meanings of "work" for men and women which are written into norms and regulations shape gender hierarchies and vice versa. The analysis of the treatment of married women's income in the West German tax system provides a prime example of these complex interdependencies. Starting in 1950, the debates on "spouse taxation" (*Ehegattenbesteuerung*) mirror the changing view of women's work in relation to the breadwinner's income and status. At the beginning of the 1950s, married women in gainful employment paid their own taxes. These regulations were still formally based on legislation introduced by the Nazis. Immediately after coming to power in 1933, the Nazi authorities had repealed the Weimar taxation rules so as to make married women's income once again subject in general to a "household taxation", as it had been until 1922. This measure was clearly meant to discourage and discriminate against the employment of married women. But in 1942, in order to recruit women into the war industry, the tax system was changed again: as under the Weimar laws, married women's income was now taxed separately so long as it resulted from gainful employment.

Abwechlsung und Ergänzung des eintönigen Einerlei, einen Gesprächsstoff, der Anlaß zum Mitreden gibt, ja sogar einen Geltungsfaktor [. . .]", *ibid.*, p. 1.
[38] The Christian Democratic Union (CDU) and the Bavarian Christian Social Union (CSU).

The first attack by the Ministry of Finance on married women's taxation coincided with the height of the "double income campaign" in 1950. As mentioned above, this campaign marked a significant change in attitudes towards widows and towards married women's "right" to work. In this context, however, it is obvious that the West German authorities could not easily dispute married women's place in the workforce. Given the determined resistance by the social-democratic opposition in parliament and the vigorous protests by women all over the country, the plan was doomed to failure. However, the conservative government parties succeeded in gaining cross-party agreement that a serious review of spouse taxation was required. The main conflict in the West German parliamentary debates centred on the question of whether a wife's earnings should again be subjected to a general household taxation or be taxed as her own separate income. The former system would clearly produce a higher level of taxation on the whole "family" income than the latter; on the other hand, it recognized the dominant status of the male breadwinner as "head" of the household and was meant to discourage married women from working and restore the "natural order of the sexes".[39]

The debate continued until 1958. Finally the Supreme Court rejected the idea of household taxation. Based on its suggestions, the new tax law introduced separate taxation and equal rights for men and women: if both husband and wife were employed, their earnings were to be taxed in the same way and be given the same fiscal status. Consequently, husbands would lose their tax status as sole breadwinners in their families and would have to share with their working wives all the benefits of that status, including general tax rebates, flat rates on professional outlay, and deductions for children.[40]

When the law came into force in September 1958, married male workers reacted with pure indignation. Many of them would not allow their wives to continue working. This was especially awkward for employers in "female" branches of industry with a heavy demand for seasonal and part-time work. Innumerable women resigned from one day to the next, complaining that their jobs were no longer "worthwhile".[41] The economic situation in the late 1950s favoured this attitude: it was easier now for families to do without the extra income from women's "insignificant" work (*geringfügige, d.h. versicherungsfreie Beschäftigung*). As a result, however, employers faced severe labour shortages. Politicians and the administration had to react instantly.

---

[39] See Ministry of Finance memorandum on the taxation of spouses, 18 November 1955, Bundesarchiv Koblenz (hereafter BAK), B 126/6296, o.P.

[40] Tax law (*Steueränderungsgesetz*), 18 July 1957, BGBl. I, p. 473.

[41] Numerous petitions give vivid impressions of the situation in different branches of manufacturing and other industry, as well as in the newspaper world and the dairy industry. An impressive summary can be found in Petition of the German Federation of Industry and Commerce, Frankfurt, to the Ministry of Finance, 28 October 1958, BAK, B 126/19006.

Petitions to the Ministry of Finance urging the government to change the law reveal why it provoked so much resistance.[42] In the first place, it turned out that legislation had simply "overlooked" the high percentage (25 per cent) of married women with an "insignificant" (*geringfügiges, steuerfreies*) income. For all these couples, "equal taxation" meant losing half of all tax deductions, because the wife's income was tax-free anyway. The wife could not use the tax deductions, but nor could they be transferred to her husband's income.

The Ministry of Finance reacted quickly to this complaint. In order to rescue the harvest for the canning industry ("*Konservenkampagne*") in the autumn of 1958, the law was changed within a month to allow the wife's tax deductions to be transferred to the husband's tax return where the wife's income was below the tax threshold. The result of this amendment was to reinstate the tax privileges enjoyed by the breadwinner prior to the tax reform. It went even further: the new tax regime could actually save the family money if the wife's income was lower than 1,200 DM a year.

However, the new regulations did not stop the vigorous complaints. They made taxation subject to an extremely complicated procedure. If the wife went out to work, she still needed a detailed pay slip (*Lohnsteuerkarte*), even if her modest earnings were not subject to tax. Furthermore, the husband had to ask his employer to issue him with a detailed pay slip, showing tax deducted, and get the taxation bracket (*Lohnsteuerklasse*) changed from "III" to "IV" at the local tax office (*Finanzamt*). Not only villages, but even towns like Wolfsburg did not have their own official office, so that it could take a whole day to get the slips changed. If a wife participated in several types of seasonal work spread over the year, the whole performance had to be repeated at the beginning and end of each period of work. The sources show that many people – husbands – just did not see the point of this "waste" of time and energy.

Even more important in provoking lasting resistance was yet another change that had accompanied the original tax reform: the technique of taxation made public what spouses could hitherto keep secret. Women disapproved of the system and stayed at home in order to maintain the male breadwinners' (and their own) respectability. The reason was that to obtain the tax form, they now had to apply for it from the local authority. In small municipalities they would be personally known to officials and the official application would amount to swearing an oath of disclosure: it would look as if they "needed" the work and the money.

Men complained that they feared loss of standing in the workplace if it became known that their wives worked. This seemed to be particularly embarrassing for high-ranking and skilled workers, as well as for

---

[42] All petitions quoted can be found in BAK, B 126/19006.

employees in white-collar branches. Although this argument attracted much sympathy, further investigation reveals much greater ambivalence. Married male workers were not afraid of being looked at askance by their colleagues because their wives earned a little money on the side. As could be shown above, wives' "working on the side" (*Mitarbeit/Zuverdienst*) was widely accepted, provided that these "extra earnings" did not affect the men's status as breadwinners. However, it was completely unacceptable – and therefore best concealed – when husbands lost the privileges of their former tax bracket (III). As the change in tax bracket only had a negative impact on the "family income" as a whole if the wife's earnings were almost as high as the husband's, other than merely financial reasons must have provoked the men's resistance. The change in taxation status seemed not only to threaten men's privileges, but also their identity as sole breadwinners.

In the face of the vigorous complaints, the Ministry of Finance took action to undermine the hard-won principle of equal taxation. Since an immediate response seemed to be required, the Ministry officials decided to introduce a separate new tax form for women (*Lohnsteuerkarte F*) which would eliminate the related tax status of the spouses. By defining the family income as "an entity", the new form treated the women's "extra" earnings as a "second income" of the breadwinner. Consequently, if their earnings exceeded the tax threshold, they were charged tax at a high rate and lost all rebates and child deductions. Thus, married women who wanted to work were no longer dependent on their husbands' consent. On the other hand, men no longer needed to reject their wives' wishes, because their taxation status as breadwinners was not challenged.[43]

This solution swiftly took the heat out of the situation. It eased the situation in the labour market, but did much more than that: the new tax form for married women with low earnings provided a highly effective instrument to deal with the general trend of increasing numbers of married women joining the workforce. Hastily introduced for those below the tax threshold in 1961, the gendered taxation of spouses became an integral component of the West German tax system in 1965. The new tax law offered two tax options to all wage earning married couples. If the male breadwinner was unwilling to share his privileged status with his wife, her income would be taxed at a high rate without any deductions. In West Germany, it was only under these terms that the idea of the married woman worker could gain acceptance.

In East Germany, the traditional wage system based on the principle that men were entitled to higher wages than women was strongly defended by male workers. How strongly becomes evident when analysing the history of the famous Order No. 253, by which the Soviet Military Govern-

---

[43] Advice to local councils concerning the new tax form (*Lohnsteuerkarte F*), 12 December 1960, BAK, B 126/19006, pp. 161–166.

ment (SMAD) is usually credited with implementing the principle of equal pay for equal work in August 1946.[44] This was true only in a very strict sense, since the law did not cover typically female occupations like those in the textile industry. An explanatory letter from the SMAD made it very clear that Order No. 253, which required "equal pay for equal work regardless of age and sex", referred only to women performing men's work.[45] Any work which did not require exactly the same degree of physical strength was not rated as equal and could therefore be less well paid. There is no doubt that leading female politicians did their best to combat the systematic undervaluation of female work. Their efforts were supported by the East German trade union, the Free German Federation of Unions (FDGB), whose leaders at least recognized the need to increase women's wages. The union made the best of Order No. 253 by drawing the conclusion that it meant that skilled female workers should not be paid less than their male *unskilled* colleagues.[46] Even though this plan did not openly challenge the traditional wage hierarchy, since the male pay-lead was only to be reduced, not eliminated, it still met with strong resistance.

Though most employers and trustees were unwilling to increase women's wages, they were not the main obstacle, as leading female SED and FDGB officials discovered on their study tours. They observed that it was factory councils (*Betriebsräte*) which most fiercely opposed the idea of paying women at least the minimum male wage.[47] In our opinion, it was not the wage increase that the workers' representatives resisted most bitterly, but rather the whole idea of *comparing* men's and women's wages. Comparing skilled female work with unskilled male labour was just one step away from comparing skilled work by both sexes, and that would have put an end to the systematic undervaluation of female work. Because the comparison threatened to undermine a gender order that guaranteed high breadwinner wages for men, factory councils did their best to prevent the proposed wage increase from being implemented. Close

---

[44] Order No. 253 was published together with explanatory notes in *Jahrbuch für Arbeit und Sozialfürsorge, Bd. 1* (Berlin, 1947), pp. 317–319. For a celebratory account written by East German historians, see Marlies Eilenstein and Ernst Schotte, "Die Durchsetzung des Prinzips 'gleicher Lohn für gleiche Arbeit' für Frauen in der damaligen Sowjetischen Besatzungzone", *Jahrbuch für Wirtschaftsgeschichte*, 3 (1975), pp. 43–52; the critical analysis given in the present paper is based on Christine von Oertzen and Almut Rietzschel, "Neuer Wein in alten Schläuchen: Geschlechterpolitik und Frauenerwerbsarbeit im besetzten Deutschland zwischen Kriegsende und Währungsreform", *Ariadne: Almanach des Archivs der deutschen Frauenbewegung*, 27 (1975), pp. 28–35.

[45] The SMAD's interpretation was published as a commentary on the Order in the *Jahrbuch für Arbeit und Sozialfürsorge*, see footnote 44.

[46] Internal letter from Friedel Malter to the trade union's executive on 28 October 1946, enclosing an account written by a committee set up by the women's section of the ZK of the SED after a study tour of Saxony, in BA-SAPMO DY 34/A 281.

[47] Account concerning the implementation of Order No. 253, written after a study tour of Thuringia in November 1946, in BA-SAPMO DY 34/A 281.

scrutiny of their arguments reveals how deeply the systematic wage discrimination against women was ingrained in society. Women earned less than men not just because they did not have the same qualifications, but in fact because their work was stripped of any qualifications at all. A workers' representative in a confectionery factory vehemently refused to compare the work of a skilled female worker who received 0.56 Reichsmark per hour with that of a male unskilled labourer loading and unloading goods. His work, he argued, required more physical strength and ought, therefore, to be paid better. When this traditional explanation was challenged by pointing out that female workers also performed packing work, this workers' representative argued that women's packing work differed greatly "because it does not require any skill at all".[48] This strategy of classifying female work as unskilled and requiring no special knowledge or training was widespread. Male workers preferred to believe that aptitude and dexterity were simply innate qualities of the female sex. Because they were assumed to be part of "women's nature" and refused the label of "acquired skill", such abilities did not need to be reflected in pay scales.

East German male workers and their representatives could not prevent the abolition of separate wage and salary classifications for men and women (which was upheld by the courts in West Germany[49]). Though they lost this battle, they did not face complete failure. The introduction of six (1948/1949) and later eight (1953) wage scales classifying workers regardless of sex but in accordance with their qualifications did not mean the end of privileged breadwinner wages. Beneath the veneer of equality, the idea lived on that a "woman's wage" was a second income and not meant to support a family.[50] In 1988, after four decades of serious efforts to raise women's qualifications, most female production workers (*Produktionsarbeiterinnen*) still found themselves on the lower wage scales, whereas their male colleagues dominated the higher ones. Fifty-six per cent of female production workers received wages on scales 4 and 5, compared with 21 per cent of male production workers. The latter fared better in the prestigious wage scales 7 and 8, occupied by 43 per cent of male production workers but only 13 per cent of their female colleagues.[51] This pay gap may have been due in part to real differences in qualifications, but was certainly also "achieved" by putting men on to higher wage

---

[48] In German "weil sie keine besonderen Fähigkeiten erfordern": for the complete reference see footnote 45.

[49] Petra Drohsel, *Die Lohndiskriminierung der Frauen. Eine Studie über Lohn und Lohndiskriminierung von erwerbstätigen Frauen in der Bundesrepublik Deutschland, 1945–1984* (Marburg, 1986).

[50] See Rosemarie Eichfeld, "Frauenerwerbstätigkeit, Qualifikation und Entlohnung in fünf Betrieben des Kreises Freiberg/Sachsen in den Jahren 1945 bis 1980", in Karin Hausen and Gertraude Krell (eds), *Frauenerwerbsarbeit: Forschungen zu Geschichte und Gegenwart* (Munich, 1993), pp. 167–185, esp. pp. 176–179 and 181–185.

[51] Winkler, *Frauenreport '90*, p. 91.

scales than they could claim on the basis of their qualifications.[52] This procedure allowed breadwinner wages to be introduced through the back door. The tacit assertion of men's privileged position overcame all efforts to close the pay gap. The SED struggled in vain to do so by abolishing the two lowest wage scales for unskilled work. When this was achieved in 1980, it meant pay increases for the women concerned but not the end of the systematic undervaluation of female work.

CONCLUSIONS

Summing up the evidence and trying to evaluate the similarities and differences in the male breadwinner experience in East and West Germany, we would like to suggest three conclusions. First, although the East German experience differed fundamentally from that in the West, the evidence shows that the standard account of East German women's history needs to be revised to take account of the fact that the breadwinning ideology was much more influential than previously thought. Second, the gap between the two states, which had been narrow in the 1940s, widened in the 1950s and 1960s. The greatest similarities are to be found in the immediate post-war years, when part-time work was seen as a possible solution to the problem of providing for the war widows. Even at this stage, however, there were considerable differences. In West Germany the problem was eventually to be solved by pension schemes based on the idea that mothers should not be in employment but should stay at home. In East Germany, by contrast, war widows were expected to work full-time. The differences became much stronger in the 1950s when the two halves of Germany tried to implement/encourage diametrically opposed female role models. Taken at face value, the ideologies could not have been more dissimilar. Examined more closely, however, the differences appear smaller. In East Germany, the persistent reservations about the employment of mothers reveal that the breadwinner ideology survived beneath the official norm of the lifelong, full-time working mother. That the dissimilarities should not be overstated is also supported by the West German experience of the 1960s. Here, the breadwinner ideology remained strong indeed, although economic prosperity brought growing opportunities for married women to work and prompted the change from the "housewife" norm to the new role model of the "working housewife". Third, the East German experience suggests a new model of the male breadwinning system. It differs fundamentally from the established one in that women – regardless of their marital status – were given the same "right to work" as men. However, the new model still deserves to be labelled as a breadwinner system because it suffered from one severe flaw: the policy of equality between the sexes did not include any reform of the deeply gen-

---

[52] Eichfeld, "Frauenerwerbstätigkeit", p. 177.

dered system of labour division within the family. From the beginning, women were ascribed "special" duties as wives and mothers. How deeply this line of thought remained ingrained in East German policies is revealed by the debate on mothers' "profitability" as workers.

Finally, we would like to comment on another key aspect of the male breadwinner system: its enormous capacity to adapt to very different political frameworks seems to be the secret of its persistence. Tracing its development at the legal level reveals the mechanisms of its propagation. The process of writing the male breadwinner system into law was the result of tangible processes of negotiation. These are not only detectable at the institutional level: our analysis of the East German wage system and the West German tax system illustrates that individual men and women took an active part in the process of propagation.

As the West German case shows, the battles to defend and claim breadwinner's privileges were fought in a very private sphere: they were decided within families, between the spouses. When husbands complained and insisted on their tax privileges as breadwinners, wives gave in. Women had two main reasons consciously to surrender the principle of equal taxation: first, they recognized a shared interest in upholding the respectability of the family. Second, they gave up the power struggle for the sake of domestic harmony. In the short run, this strategy brought married women increased personal freedom (*Handlungsspielräume*) and greater financial independence, even if they did not participate in tax benefits. Furthermore, they were ready to accept tax discrimination because they themselves saw their earnings as "extra" income. Thus, by actually challenging the practice of breadwinning, they unconsciously helped to reinforce its ideological framework, even though – in the long run – they did not profit by it.

Copying

Guidelines for contributors

Manuscripts are considered for publication on the understanding that they are not currently under consideration elsewhere and that the material – in substance as well as form – has not been previously published.

Two copies of the manuscript should be submitted.

Each article should be accompanied by a summary, not exceeding 100 words, outlining the principal conclusions and methods in the context of currently accepted views on the subject.

All material – including quotations and notes – must be double-spaced with generous margins. Use of dot-matrix printers is discouraged.

Notes should be numbered consecutively and placed at the end of the text.

Spelling should be consistent throughout (e.g. Labour and Labor are both acceptable, but only one of these forms should be used in an article).

Turns of phrase using masculine forms as universals are not acceptable.

Sample Citation Forms

Book: E. P. Thompson, *The Making of the English Working Class* (London, 1963), pp. 320–322.

Journal: Walter Galenson, "The Unionization of the American Steel Industry", *International Review of Social History*, 1 (1956), pp. 8–40.

Detailed guidelines are available from the editor on request.

Twenty-five free offprints of each article are provided, and authors may purchase additional copies provided these are ordered at proof stage.

Printed in the United States
By Bookmasters